THE BEAT GOES ON

The Beat Goes On

The Rock File Reader

Edited by

Charlie Gillett *and* Simon Frith

Pluto  Press

LONDON • EAST HAVEN, CT

First published 1996 by Pluto Press
345 Archway Road, London N6 5AA
and 140 Commerce Street, East Haven
Connecticut 06512, USA

British Library Cataloguing in Publication Data
A catalogue record for this book is available from the British Library

ISBN 0 7453 1079 6 **hbk**

Library of Congress Cataloguing in Publication Data
applied for

Designed and produced for Pluto Press by
Chase Production Services, Chipping Norton, OX7 5QR
Typeset from disk by Stanford DTP Services, Milton Keynes
Printed in the EC by the Cromwell Press, Broughton Gifford

Contents

Lists of Photographs
and Tables

Preface

This is a shock, for the editors and contributors alike. None of us would have guessed that pieces which had been written 'off the cuff' for *Rock File* as contemporary commentary on the state of pop in the 1970s could have been considered by a publisher for reissue 20 years on. Is this how a singer feels when a member of the audience at a gig shouts out the name of a song from years ago? What – you remember that one?

The genesis for *Rock File* came from reactions to my history of rock 'n' roll, *The Sound of the City*, first published in 1970. In that volume I tried to provide a conceptual framework to show the links between the best records of the previous 20 years. But from readers' responses, it became clear that many of them couldn't care less about the links I had agonised over – they just used the book as a reference for settling arguments about which year certain songs had been released, and who sung them. If *that* was what they wanted, it would be more efficient simply to list the 'facts' – the names of the singers and songs, dates of chart entry, highest chart position, etc. – in a format similar to the one Joel Whitburn had designed for his then recently-published compendium of American hit singles, *Record Research*.

An unadorned list of hits seemed a little 'dry', so I modified the concept in an attempt to emulate *Wisden's Cricketers' Almanac*. Each year, cricket fans can buy a new *Wisden* to pore over accounts of every ball bowled, every run scored, in every first-class match around the world, backed up by scrupulously-compiled lists of all-time bests. At the front of each edition is a collection of 'think pieces' on the state of the game, outstanding cricketers of the just-finished season, etc. So, inspired by *Wisden*, the format of *Rock File* was to be a similar split between 'fact' and 'opinion': a log of hit singles at the back of the book, to be updated each year, accompanied by reflective pieces on pop and rock from writers who might welcome a rare chance to write an article not directly connected to a newly-released album.

The *Rock File* concept became a reality in 1972 when Pete Fowler, an occasional contributor to the magazine *Cream* who made his living teaching social studies to art students in the north of England, volunteered (with Annie Fowler) to collate the UK chart hit singles for the first volume. Pete also agreed to put down on paper some of his observations about the tastes and opinions of his students. The resulting piece, 'Skins Rule', contradicted much of the wishful thinking that passed for sociology and social anthropology at the time and has subsequently been anthologised at least twice before *The Beat Goes On.**

Reaction to the first volume of *Rock File* was encouraging but hardly life-changing, and when the original publisher lost interest, another offered to carry on the series. Simon Frith became joint-editor and Steve Nugent expanded the Fowlers' chart logs by researching songwriters, producers, albums and US hits. The 'think pieces' on various aspects of contemporary pop production and consumption were also continued. Most of them were commissioned from the pool of freelance journalists who wrote for two monthly magazines which surfaced during the early 1970s, *Cream* and *Let It Rock*. *Cream* was conceived, published and edited by a maverick sports journalist at the *Observer*, Bob Houston, who soon attracted a bunch of keen young writers, many of whom had recently left university and were flattered and delighted to contribute more-or-less untouched copy to a professionally-printed publication with a four-colour cover. While we grumbled about low rates of pay and what seemed to be compromised decisions about which artists should be featured on the cover each month, few of us understood the nature of Bob's battles to cajole advertisements out of dubious record company marketing departments, as he valiantly tried to cover his costs of production.

When *Cream* stumbled and fell in the early 1970s, some of its writers persuaded another publisher to pick up the concept and carry it on as *Let It Rock*, under the stewardship of editor John Pidgeon. Contributors were again paid below union scale rates, but the economics still didn't work, and the venture folded after four years. Amazingly, it took another ten years before marketing professionals could be persuaded of the potential behind a 'serious' approach to pop, and advertisers began to recognise that buyers of rock albums were a conveniently-visible tip of a huge market to which they could pitch their campaigns for cars, beer, clothes and cosmetics. Now newsagents' shelves sag under a weight of music magazines fighting for attention and there is a small army of British-based freelances who make a living from writing about pop and rock.

Between 1973 and 1978, four further volumes of *Rock File* were published, each edition selling out its 20,000 print run. The publisher,

---

* In Hanif Kureishi and Jon Savage (eds), *The Faber Book of Pop* (Faber, 1994) and Clinton Heylin (ed.), *The Penguin Book of Rock and Roll Writing* (Penguin, 1993).

however, was not convinced the market could be much bigger and the series ended with *Rock File 5*, leaving the way clear for Guinness to pick up the chart log concept and re-package it as *The Guinness Book of British Hit Singles*, with each edition outselling *Rock File* more than ten times over.

And that seemed to be that, until Pluto Press suggested that the time was right to reexamine some of the contributions to *Rock File*. The first step in preparation for this anthology was to look at the pieces again and agree that maybe they did have some value. Just what that value is, is considered by Simon Frith in his Introduction. The second step was to reestablish contact with the contributors, obtain their permission and invite any second thoughts. Everyone was enthusiastic and Pete Fowler's ruminations even grew into an afterword to the volume, 'The Shadow of Our Night'.

It has been fascinating to discover and collate the activities of the contributors in the years since *Rock File* ceased. That so many went on to write books is gratifying, if hardly surprising. It was less predictable that two would become professors, or that two others, former co-workers at *Black Music* magazine, would later edit very different religious publications. Pete Wingfield's production credits make the rest of us proud by association!

Charlie Gillett

Introduction:
Backward and Forward

Simon Frith

On the day I started to write this introduction I read that Charlie Rich had died. I hadn't noticed this news or seen an obituary anywhere, but the story was picked up by a writer on *Scotland on Sunday* who thought, rightly, that Rich's musical life mattered more than as just a footnote to a list of country hit makers. Charlie Rich, to put this another way, is important less as a name to be indexed in the *Guinness Hits of the 70s* than as a person through whom a certain sort of music history was lived. In the 1950s he was one of Sam Phillips' stable of young rock 'n' roll stars, and perhaps the one in whom the fusion of black and white, secular and religious Southern American music was most deeply embedded. When he became a big star, briefly in the 1970s, it was with another version of the same musical mixture, as an easy-on-the-ear lounge singer who drew inextricably on blues and hillbilly and Tin Pan Alley principles of American ballad singing – it was Charlie Rich, making a bridge between Hoagy Carmichael and Roy Orbison, who mapped out the space that Willie Nelson was soon to occupy. And Rich was equally important as a site – a life – on which a certain sort of musical history was based. In part this was an American history: Rich gave writers like Greil Marcus and Dave Marsh a way of making sense of the racial, regional and cultural roots of rock music; in part a personal history: Peter Guralnick's essay on Rich, 'Feel Like Going Home', remains the classic of rock critic romanticism, the artist as restless hero. (In 1992, putting his money where his tastes were, Guralnick brought Rich back from the twilight circuit of a has-been to re-record 'Feel Like Going Home', on his last album, *Pictures and Paintings*.)

To think again about Rich's career as a musician, as a name, was, I realised, to be back with the questions that lay behind *Rock File*, the book series we edited at around the same time that Charlie Rich was a commercial star. We too were trying to make sense of a musical world whose roots, we took for granted, lay in 1950s American rock 'n' roll,

1

in the coming together of urban and rural sensibilities, black and white style. We were, in fact, witnessing without always realising it (although Pete Fowler's 'Skins Rule' still seems singularly prescient) the fragmentation of pop taste along the lines of class and race and market. The heroes of rock 'n' roll history – heroes, like Charlie Rich, for touching all musical bases – were about to slip through the holes in radio formats and between niche markets.

Reading Alistair MacKay's celebration of Charlie Rich in *Scotland on Sunday* I wondered how many of his readers had ever heard of Rich, how many owned a Rich record. Reading this selection of articles from *Rock File* I wonder how familiar the 1970s will seem to readers, and how strange.

Pop music has an odd relationship with time. The best pop works as news; it is immediate, momentary, disposable. It matters as soon as you hear it; it is forgotten when it is gone. Unlike art, pop doesn't claim lasting value; it is part of the everyday. And *Rock File* was originally conceived in news terms, as a year book, an almanac, a record of what happened in a pop year as it happened, before history got to work on its meaning. (And in the 1970s *Rock File* was therefore about keeping true to the belief in pop-as-news as critics began to develop the new ideology of rock-as-art.)

The essence of the resulting assembly of facts and figures (*Rock File* pioneered the chart logs that were turned into a highly successful publishing venture by Guinness) was gloriously random, an account of pop history which had as much to with commercial accident as cultural impact. As Greil Marcus once remarked, to read American musical history through Joel Whitburn's *Record Research* is to enter an alternative universe (the universe of Golden radio) in which the Bee Gees are far more important than Bob Dylan, the Stones a novelty act, and *Frampton Live* the phenomenon of the 1970s[*]. And there's no reason why this shouldn't be pop's real history; the critics' elaborate tracing of influences and originality a self-deluding fiction.

But our celebration of pop immediacy and disposability was tempered by another kind of argument. The chart logs were accompanied by sociological essays. Pop, we wanted to make clear, was also a *sign* of the times. The most lightweight hit reveals something about its moment. (This is an argument taken up effectively by the BBC TV series, *The Rock 'n' Roll Years*, in which newsreel footage is accompanied by contemporaneous hits, an exercise in mutual illumination.) The question was, what does pop reveal? The *Rock File* answers were social and political rather than

---

[*] See Greil Marcus' review of *The Billboard Book of Number One Hits* in *Popular Music* 6(1) 1987, pp. 110–11.

musical or literary. What was revealing were not sounds or lyrics as such, but their popularity. What mattered about a record or act were its sales figures, its place in our lists. In Pete Fowler's chapter on skinheads, in my piece on youth cults, in Andrew Weiner's account of Black Sabbath, in Stephen Barnard's description of David Cassidy, the concern is audiences, fans, markets. This in turn meant that *Rock File* paid more attention to the marketeers – the A&R people and DJs, Charlie Gillett's 'professionals' – than to musicians; and took more interest in marketing decisions than in musical judgements. In this context, Bob Edmands' disillusion with 1960s rock stars and Dave Laing's exploration of 'progressive Englishness' seem oddly old-fashioned (which tells us something about how critical assumptions have changed since the 1970s).

What was less obvious in the 1970s than it is now was pop's other relationship to time, as nostalgia. This is partly an aspect of pop's time-boundness: music, more than any other medium, fixes a mood or event in history and in memory. Music 'takes us back', whether to private or public moments. That said, some music is more obviously nostalgic than others. It's not just that time-bound pop is, paradoxically, more evocative than timeless classical music, but that even within pop some kinds of music seem more evocative than others. Nostalgia describes a mood – a way of thinking about the past – and not just a recollection. Nostalgia is a longing for the past, a regret for the present, a mixture of pleasure and loss, an indulgence in the wish that things were different. To be nostalgic, music doesn't just have to be old – to have associations – it must articulate those associations in the right way. The right kind of music (most Beatles' tracks, for example) is 'nostalgic' even on first hearing, and while most pop music can become nostalgic (even the Sex Pistols' 'Anarchy in the UK') some records are more obviously 'naturally' nostalgic than others – Simon Bates' 'Our Tune' slot on BBC Radio One was a useful guide to the nostalgic music of the 1970s.

How times change – how music changes – have their effects on what we are nostalgic for as well, of course. It is the essence of nostalgia to remember – or fantasise – a time of innocence, a time when we didn't know what would happen to us, a time before disappointment. What comes after determines how we think about before; our sense of innocence is defined by our later knowingness. If nostalgic pop is always innocent pop, unknowing and unselfconscious, then this judgement itself is determined by what the music later became. A nostalgic judgement is a historical judgement, whether personally, in terms of our own regrets, or socially (so that nostalgia for the 1970s is shaped by the Thatcherite 1980s). In terms of pop history this means constant shifts in how we hear the past. Who would have thought that 1990s nostalgia for glam rock would focus not on Marc Bolan or Slade or Sweet but on Gary Glitter!

Slade

I'm not sure that *Rock File* itself has this kind of nostalgic appeal. The series was of its moment but it wasn't unknowing; it was about pop as news but it was also trying to establish a historical record, to make sense of pop movements, to look forward as well as back. Some things we got surprisingly right; some things quite wrong (and it is our mistakes for which I am now, of course, nostalgic).

There are three ways of writing the history of popular music: as progress, as cycle or as hidden. All three approaches were taken in *Rock File*.

The Whig approach (as the belief in built-in progress is termed by academic historians) – past sounds unfolding in logical order to the present – comes ready made, as it were. The industry sells us a new act as a replacement for previous acts – either building on and learning from the past or making it redundant: who wants last year's releases when they can listen to this year's? Musicians claim each new album as better than their previous ones – as their musical skills develop, as they master technology, as they throw off commercial shackles. As consumers, our tastes develop and our knowledge grows. But even as I write this my doubts are obvious. It seems equally clear that in pop (unlike jazz or classical music) more skill doesn't necessarily mean better music. Groups' first records are often their best (hence the recurring problem of the 'difficult second album'); commercial constraints actually get tighter as companies (and musicians) learn how to position themselves; most pop fans over a certain age (25 or so) believe that their old records are better than their new ones.

These arguments were clear by the early 1970s when the very notion of 'progressive' rock (as discussed in Dave Laing's piece) struck an increasing number of critics (like Pete Fowler) as regressive. The suggestion here (familiar in Britain from jazz arguments in the early 1950s) is that popular music history is always a matter of decline, not progress. Music that bursts through from 'the people' inevitably loses its power and sweetness as it becomes self-conscious and ambitious, more 'knowing' both commercially and artistically (this is the folk view of the pop story). If the value of a pop genre lies in novelty or shock value then its value goes as it becomes familiar and routine; if the appeal of a musician is to give us a fresh take on love and living then that appeal must grow stale. This critical line (the first sign of 1970s disillusion with the 1960s) has become as familiar as the belief in musical progress. It is taken for granted by most people now, I'd guess (not just by the critics), that a new Rolling Stones album will never match their old ones; that a 'comeback', whether by Al Green or Al Stewart, by Sweet or Santana, is a gesture at past glories rather than a promise of new ones.

Except for people who think that pop music has degenerated systematically since Stephen Foster (or Scott Joplin or Bing Crosby or Elvis Presley), the alternative line to pop progress is not a linear fall from grace but, rather, a cultural cycle. This is explained in both musical and marketing terms. Musically, pop history is seen as the rise and fall of stars, as the endless emergence of new trends from the musical margins and their 'mainstreaming'. Such musical life cycles can be mapped across demographic markets, as each new generation listens to its own teenybop stars, its own subcultural icons, its own dance floor groove. From this cyclical perspective the 'always new' of pop is the 'never anything new'; the new Dylan, the next Beatles, the punk revival are just that, reruns of history, old tinctures in new bottles.

Pop history thus becomes a matter of tracing parallels, drawing out familiar patterns. We read *Rock File* now, not for a reminder of what was unfamiliar about the 1970s, but to recognise what was being established as routine: the teenybop TV stardom of David Cassidy is interesting for the way it prefigures the Bay City Rollers, Bros and Take That; the self-regarding rock politics skewered in Bob Edmands' 'Have Pity for the Rich' is fascinating as an early example of the cynicism we were later to feel for Sting or the Clash; Carl Gayle's account of 1970s rude reggae obviously anticipates debates about Jamaican dance-hall music to come. Such essays feed into the 1990s concept of retro, the sense that all pop music is a matter now of recalling the past. We distinguish between such current British acts as Pulp and Blur, Oasis and Suede, Elastica and Supergrass by tracing the past pop sounds and figures to whom they variously refer.

Spot the references – this describes a third sort of pop history: tracing the unexpected connections (an approach to music history celebrated in the TV version of Pete Frame's *Rock Family Trees*). It was this approach to history that really lay at the heart of *Rock File* which was, if nothing else, a book for and by collectors (all our contributors were, I fear, boys of the sort anatomised in Nick Hornby's novel *High Fidelity*).

The pleasure here is to point out what no one else realised – the person who *really* invented disco; the track that is actually the first punk record; the unexpected line from reggae to Chicago soul (Johnny Copasetic's piece here is a classic of this genre). And I suspect that the greatest pleasure of this volume for readers will precisely be the discoveries on offer, the concealed insights, the throwaway names, the links we didn't then make: Bob Edmands' casual reference to Sweet's 'punk image'; Andrew Weiner's condensation of 20-years-of-heavy-metal-to-come in an evening of Black Sabbath; the early appearance of Pete Waterman as both provincial DJ and indie record man.

From a collector's point of view the 1970s are fascinating not for nostalgic reasons, nor because they were, in themselves, particularly exciting musically. (Though I believe now that the early 1970s were the best ever time for dance music, I didn't know that then.) Rather, the 1970s matter as the transition point between two different musical eras. I would now explain this in two ways. First, the period from the mid-1950s to the mid-1970s (from rock 'n' roll to punk) is the same time period as that from the mid-1970s to the present. If, back then, we were trying to make sense of popular music post-rock, now we read the same articles, examine the same sounds for clues to the why and what of punk. (Think of it this way: what sense would a collection of articles written on the pop scene in 1955 have made when read in 1975?) Second, 1978 was the key year in the history of the record industry, the moment when (for a variety of reasons) postwar sales growth stopped and there was a major rethink of corporate sales strategy. In short, we edited *Rock File* before we knew anything about the impact of either punk or the recession (both of which had their own disruptive effect on the reading of rock history). The clues were here alright: indie ideology; youth subcultures; the class opposition of rock and pop; teenybop and TV and disco; the unexpected global entanglements of the African musical diaspora; the problems of rock riches. The clues were here, but we didn't yet know the puzzle we had to solve.

For me, the *Rock File* volumes, like old music magazines, are most interesting for the way they reveal what we didn't know. The problem of pop's power as news and nostalgia is that it makes it impossible to remember what the music first sounded like: how we heard it before we knew what it would become, what it would stand for. The distorting effect of memory is obvious in the case of group names, which invariably seem silly (the Beatles!) until they take on the resonance of what they name: successful groups' names always feel right; unsuccessful group names remain silly.

It seems impossible to recollect the first hearing of any sound. What did I think of 'Love Me Do' when I first heard it on the radio, before I knew who the Beatles were, before I knew what the Beatles would become? The film *Backbeat* was an interesting attempt to reconstruct the group before they were the Beatles but it couldn't escape the banal effects of the Hollywood biopic, the recurring 'ironies': 'One day you'll be superstars!' What I wanted to see was a film about the Beatles who wouldn't one day be superstars, who couldn't even have had a concept of such superstardom, who were just another British provincial group.

The most successful attempt I've seen to reconstruct what a key pop moment meant, at the time, is the most obscure: the pilot show for an aborted Granada series, *Teenage*, written and presented by Jon Savage and Peter York. In the episode that focused on the Teddy Boy there's a scene in which an 'ordinary' 1950s family (ordinary à la John Waters; exaggeratedly ordinary) is watching on television a succession of cheery bands and crooners and, suddenly, Bill Haley and the Comets. Quite unexpectedly the track, 'Rock Around the Clock', which has long sounded like old-fashioned good time music (how could *this* ever have been heard as revolutionary?), hit me as a truly strange and threatening record. Rock 'n' roll before anyone knew what rock 'n' roll would be; rock 'n' roll before the pop historians and collectors had got to work on where it came from.

One value of *The Beat Goes On*, then, is as a historical document in itself, as the record of a sensibility that it is impossible otherwise to reconstruct. How did we listen to the sounds of the seventies in the 1970s? All the writers here make certain assumptions: rock music is youth music; rock music is mass mediated; rock music is mechanically reproduced; rock music has roots. Rock is thus the site for a certain sort of politics (social truths voiced in entertainment) and a certain sort of aesthetics (most obvious in Pete Wingfield's chapter: technique at the service of emotion).

This is what I would call now a romanticised folk sensibility: good music is taken to show (and shape) everyday life, everyday dreams. There's a suspicion of the grand artistic claim, the grand emotive gesture;

business acumen is valued above expressive pretension. Missing here are what later came to be the most obvious pop aspects of the 1970s: art school sensibility, the romanticised rock cynicism of a David Bowie or Roxy Music (which was to feed into punk); and funk sensibility, the politicised soul cynicism of a George Clinton or Last Poets (which was to feed into hiphop and rap).

What most surprises me reading these contributions again, in fact, is how uncynical the writers seem. We were, in a sense, learning how to write about rock seriously, and we obviously drew on the sociological approach of pioneering pop culture critics like Colin MacInnes and George Melly. The *Rock File* style was a little detached; we were well aware of the age effect (and the sense of writers watching other people have fun has been a feature of rock writing ever since (jazz was never written about this way). But the basic tone was admiration – for the producers, for the musicians, for the audience. We were fans, but as collectors not club members, our love of music tied up with a delight in arcane knowledge about the who and what rather than the why and how of sounds and styles.

Most strikingly of all, *Rock File* was not written as a consumer guide (how to spend your money) nor were *Rock File* writers exclusive, drawing taste boundaries, pitching genres against each other. The dominant feeling here is a sense of musical fascination. If these essays now seem naive (the nostalgia effect) they still have the impact of all good music writing: they make me want to listen. And to remember a time when the rock world was open to all sorts of interpretation.

PART ONE: THE MUSIC

1

Roll Over Lonnie (Tell George Formby the News)

Dave Laing

In the 1950s and early 1960s, entertainment in Britain was show business, a particularly archaic sector of a fairly decrepit economy. Showbiz ensured the survival, in a faded way, of the only national popular tradition that had been more than half-alive earlier in the century – the music-hall. The music-hall singers and comedians had something like a two-way relationship with their audiences. Songs and jokes came out of common cultural references: political events, local geography ('I Knocked 'Em In The Old Kent Road'), cockney dialect terms ('My Old Dutch'). Singers and audience were all Londoners or British, and part of the 'common folk'. The lingering strength of the tradition in the 1950s came through less in particular forms but in a certain style, a sense of good-humour in comedians and pub-singing, even though the halls themselves had long since been replaced by institutions dominated by American modes: cinemas, big bands, crooners, musicals.

Artistically, then, this tradition was just about played out, but it could still be relied on to invoke a nostalgia for a British past which could seem much more attractive than a present where America, Russia and African nationalism were each doing their bit to consign the Empire to the dustbin of history. And while the main developments in British music over the last 20 years have come from musicians with ideas borrowed from across the Atlantic (skiffle, Trad, Merseybeat, London R&B), most of them had to take account of the British 'heritage' as they reached for a wider audience.

Trad jazz got straightforwardly embroiled in this tradition because it already was *traditional*. It only took an enterprising bandleader to chuck in 'Hello Dolly' or 'If You Were The Only Girl In The World', and he was in on the folk-memory. Some went a lot further. Acker Bilk worked on an image of cider and haystacks plus a bit of country-bumpkin comedy, which is still being exploited by Benny Hill and Adge Cutler

11

and the Wurzels, who this year followed up earlier records about drinking cider with a version of the Diamonds' 'Little Darling', featuring a spoken passage in best Somerset idiot dialect: 'Moi darlin', oi luvs ee …'. Terrible.

Not much better were the Temperance Seven, who were heavier on deadpan humour of the P.G. Wodehouse English eccentric kind. It was claimed by their publicists that their debut was in 1902 at the Pasadena Cocoa Rooms, Balls Pond Road, and the band featured a 1920s-style vocalist, 'Whispering' Paul McDowell, with megaphone and impeccable upperclass manner. In their wake came other comic trad bands, notably the Bonzo Dog Doo-Dah Band, who later were to graduate from trad and silliness to rock and lunacy.

The mixture of new and old in skiffle and the first homegrown rock 'n' roll was more striking. In Donegan's and Tommy Steele's records, the personality and the music quickly became dissociated until the latter was ditched altogether in favour of songs which merely emphasised what likeable guys they were. 'Rock Island Line' and 'Singing The Blues' had a naive excitement. 'My Old Man's A Dustman' and 'Nairobi' were just novelty songs with a stronger beat than usual.

English showbiz took nearly all the new music in its stride, and nowhere more blatantly than in much of the coverage of rock 'n' roll, trad and skiffle by television and films. In his book *Trad Mad* (1962), Brian Matthew describes the approach of the architect of *Top Of The Pops*, Johnny Stewart, to a new trad TV series: 'Jazz is still jazz', he said, 'whether it is played on Salisbury Plain or the lounge of a luxury liner. But it is not enhanced by dingy surroundings and old hangers-on. I want to prove to its detractors that it is a most entertaining form of music, which does not have to be presented in dirt and discomfort! …'. The show was called *Trad Fad*.

The rock 'n' roll films of the pre-Beatles era seemed equally designed to make the new music safe for the status quo. The first two Tommy Steele movies had classically conservative story-lines: *The Tommy Steele Story* was rags to riches in a contemporary 'coffee bar to Royal Variety Performance' form (implication: what's all this nonsense about class barriers? Any working-class lad with talent can get to the top without an old school tie.). *The Duke Wore Jeans* presented another version of the same idea: these aristocrats dig rock just like us. Underneath the accents and the money, they're just ordinary people. *The Golden Disc* and *It's Trad Dad* had similar emphases. The book of the film of the latter ends like this:

Helen (Shapiro) and Craig (Douglas) then went into a twist number – RING-A-DING. This was the cue for everyone to join in, and in a moment the Town Centre was filled with people dancing the twist.

Even the Mayor and the Police Chief were grabbed by partners. And so everything came happily to

THE LIVING END.

Greil Marcus has written that The Band are able to confront the American heritage in their music because they are outsiders, Canadians. The same can be said of the way the Beatles combined various rock and soul styles in 1962–63 and brought it all back home to change the face of music in the US as well as Britain. But if the origins of the Mersey sound were American, people in the US at least felt that there was something indelibly English about the Fab Four and the others that came after. Something other than their accents, that is. 'The English Invasion' is a term still nostalgically tossed around by some American rock writers to describe all the bands who made it in the States in the mid-1960s, from the Stones to Peter and Gordon.

The Englishness of the music (as opposed to the personnel) of these bands had at least three separate forms. Apart from the involvement of the Kinks in the music-hall tradition I've been describing, there were the beginnings of a British folk-rock in Donovan and songs like the Stones' 'Lady Jane', and also aggressive social-realist songs like 'My Generation' and 'Nineteenth Nervous Breakdown'. In these terms, the Beatles had less of Britain in their sound than most, because they relied on neither English musical tradition nor experience for the effect and meaning of their songs. Like The Band, they created music that was sometimes more American than the work of many contemporary US musicians.

While the Beatles enjoyed mass popularity in the United States, the Kinks' following, though large, was always a cult one. This is directly related to the centrality of a particular version of England, mediated via the music-hall stance, in virtually all Ray Davies' songs after the early punk rock phase of 'You Really Got Me'. To an American ear, this kind of thing, with its appropriate syncopated rhythm and muted brass-band style backing, must have the same kind of cross-cultural appeal that 'Wichita Lineman' or 'Route 66' holds for us:

I like my football on a Saturday
Roast beef on Sunday's alright
I go to Blackpool for my holidays
Sit in the autumn sunlight.
        Ray Davies (for The Kinks),
        'Autumn Almanac' (1967)

In the English context, the Kinks' achievement also seemed considerable. These were the first post-rock 'n' roll songs to concern themselves with the details of English life without treating them purely comically. The father of the narrator of 'Dead End Street' or 'Autumn Almanac' might well have been a dustman, but he could never have been presented as the implicitly absurd figure of Donegan's song.

Yet, there's a certain ambiguity in Davies' attitude towards the lifestyle he sings about, which wasn't there in George Formby, perhaps the greatest of pre-war comic singers in the music-hall mode. Formby could take for granted that the way of life his songs were comic variations on was that of his audience. But one certain thing about the Kinks' rock audience is that they have never known or have rejected the lifestyle of the traditional working class in its resistance to change and its insularity ('This is my street and I'm never gonna leave it'). Very few Kinks fans would be happy about going to Blackpool for their holidays.

In his attitude to his material, Davies thus has to undertake a delicate balancing act between nostalgia and mockery, in singing and playing as well as in the lyrics. My own feeling is that in the songs directly concerned with traditional working-class or upperclass ('Sunny Afternoon') lifestyles, the Kinks are so much within the music-hall approach that they fail to distance themselves from their material, and that nostalgia dominates. And even in an explicitly satirical piece like 'Dedicated Follower of Fashion' or 'Well Respected Man' the trendies and commuters don't seem to be criticised from any counter-cultural anti-capitalist position, but from the much more conventional and suspect 'common sense' vantage-point that *Private Eye* tends to adopt, which is just as likely to be reactionary as progressive.

The problem, which has become more acute in the Kinks' later work, is that the music-hall tradition, embedded as it is in only the more archaic aspects of British life, is incapable of providing the basis for any more far-reaching music. The same might seem to be even more true of British folk song, especially as it has always been the preserve of fanatical purists, yet it has spawned some of the best rock music produced here in the past five years.

The emergence of the English Underground in 1967–68 was not simply a matter of duplicating Haight-Ashbury in Notting Hill and importing a few Aussies to produce outrageous magazines. The English 'progressive' music which coalesced at that time brought together several separate developments that had been burrowing away in the cultural background during the Beatlemania years. The names of Syd Barrett, Pete Brown, Arthur Brown, Donovan, the Moody Blues, the Incredible String Band and Fairport Convention suggest the range of activity involved. What was happening could be very crudely classified into avant-garde composition, anarchic/subversive humour in the Goon Show tradition, and the first successful liberation of folk music from its embalmed traditional state.

To begin with, the most striking music was produced by the first two of these, which Barrett and Pink Floyd combined brilliantly in songs like 'Arnold Layne', the tale of a kleptomaniac with sexual problems, and instrumental pieces like 'Set The Controls For The Heart Of The Sun', the psychedelic answer to 'Telstar'.

In a very different way, Cream, the most successful British band of the time, also combined instrumental experimentation with surreal lyrics. Their writer, Pete Brown, had been involved since the late 1950s in attempts to combine poetry and jazz and in the loose anti-establishment group of poets which included members of later groups like the Scaffold and the Liverpool Scene. Brown's collaboration with Jack Bruce on the latter's two post-Cream solo albums is probably his finest work so far.

Apart from Bruce's *Songs For A Tailor* and *Harmony Row*, musicians working in this area have produced little major music in the last few years. Family began strongly with songs like 'The Weaver's Answer' and 'How High The Lie', but later albums have been disappointing, while Jethro Tull's thin vein of ideas soon ran out. In contrast, English folk-rock has developed steadily and unspectacularly since the breakthrough signalled by the Incredibles' *Layers Of The Onion* and the first Fairport album, until the last year has seen the emergence of the first top ten hits in the style (from Lindisfarne) since Donovan was a frequent visitor to *Top Of The Pops*.

The first attempts to drag traditional music into the twentieth century failed because the musicians involved (Ewan MacColl, Sydney Carter, Ian Campbell, etc.) wanted to preserve the tradition while giving it different subject-matter like factory life or anti-H Bomb sentiments. But to be at all meaningful, folk music had to come to terms not only with modern life but with modern music. The first musician to realise this was, of course, Bob Dylan, and his influence on the genesis of British folk-rock was all-pervasive. His 'I'll Keep It With Mine' and 'Percy's Song' were models for much of the early Fairport Convention repertoire, the Incredible String Band acknowledged his importance in 'Back In The 1960s' and Lindisfarne's 'Meet Me On The Corner' sounds like a re-working of 'Mr Tambourine Man'.

Dylan also pointed the way in his earliest work for contemporary singer-songwriters, of whom Ralph McTell and John Martyn have come out with notable albums in the last year. This isn't folk-rock though, since the weight is still on the music as composition rather than perfor-

Lindisfarne

mance, on the words rather than the whole sound. Part of the originality of Lindisfarne lies in the fact that they can take songs full of the detail that is essential for singer-songwriters and make them into rock music. It's as if McTell wrote songs you could dance to.

What's also striking about the *Fog On The Tyne* album is that Lindisfarne have created a whole set of songs that take the measure of a specific British situation – the young unemployed in a provincial city making what they can of a situation full of dead ends – without being merely local or anecdotal in their references. Looked at this way, the key song is the title track, with its account, both ironical and joyful, of the satisfactions available when you've too much time and not enough money to spend. That general theme and its implications are worked out in several of the other songs: 'Uncle Sam', where 'someone's joined the army'; 'Together Forever': 'sitting on a bench watching the day go by' and 'City Song': 'someday soon I'm going miles and miles away'.

Musically, the group have a good-time jug-band type of lineup. But they make more imaginative use of it than Mungo Jerry with their serried ranks of strumming skiffle-style guitars. Lindisfarne's rhythm is carried on up-tempo songs like 'Meet Me On The Corner' by a chugging harmonica, and piano is featured just as much as guitar. It's a sound in which you can hear the contribution of each player, which swings rather than drives along, and puts me in mind of that line from 'Down The Road Apiece': 'just an old piano and a knocked-out bass'.

By now Lindisfarne are miles and miles away from the experiences which underlie *Fog On The Tyne*. They're a Top Ten touring band, and the records they will make are going to be different, just as the Who were when they became everybody's band instead of just the mods', and the Stones when they were no longer just the property of R&B freaks.

For rock, by definition, is a rootless music, unlike the various folk and semi-folk traditions it is made out of. The great rock musicians take what they need from anywhere they can, and the criterion is not whether a riff or a phrase has been used before, but whether it works in its new context, whether nothing else would have done instead. Not the least impressive thing about Lindisfarne is that their music shows that they know this, and they're unlikely to get trapped in a fruitless search for roots to cling to, as some of the traditionally-oriented folk-rock bands have done. And as the Kinks did, only to find themselves making major music in a very minor mode.

Lindisfarne, and some of the ex-Fairport Convention people, notably Ian Matthews and Richard Thompson, have created the possibility for themselves of fully liberating the energies of traditional music from its outworn forms. If they succeed they will have produced a music that is British without being insular or nostalgic, and that could be a major musical event of the 1970s.

(1972)

AFTERWORD

As a prediction, I suppose that last sentence wasn't so bad. The folk-rock genre did spawn some minor masterpieces in the 1970s, such as Richard and Linda Thompson's *I Want To See The Bright Lights Tonight*, Steeleye Span's *All Around My Hat* and *Third Light* by the underrated Decameron. But it wasn't the biggest event in British rock during the decade – that honour went to Johnny Rotten, Ian Dury, Paul Weller and the pub rock/punk/new wave nexus.

More generally, what happened to my hopes for music that is 'British without being insular or nostalgic'? One thing that's clear is that what I identified as the showbiz/music-hall stream has not dried up in the last 20-odd years. Here's Suggs of Madness, talking to Q magazine in the mid-1980s : 'We wanted to be entertainers, for want of a better word, like a fairground attraction or like music hall performers.' It could be

Formby or Donegan speaking. The best songs of Madness exemplify the strengths of that older British approach to music making but for every Madness, there's been a Morrissey with his insularity verging on racism and half-a-dozen Chas and Daves with their beer-commercial 'jolly cockney' cocktail of sentimental nostalgia and exaggerated bonhomie.

While the article usefully identified certain hardy trends in pop produced in Britain, it failed to see that to speak of a 'British' music in the singular was to overlook the fact that there are competing cultural, national, political and ethnic ideas and images of identity within the British Isles and within the music created there.

In particular, there is now a large body of music which, implicitly or otherwise, contests the accepted mainstream portrayal of Britishness (which usually equates to Englishness) and is determinedly anti-nostalgic. Very little of this other British music owes anything to the strands described in 'Roll Over Lonnie'. While there are some admirable things happening within the English folk music world, many of them are limited by an unquestioning acceptance of a 'traditional' way of singing and playing that was constructed by the folk song profession-als of the 1950s.

Instead, almost all the most important commentaries on what it feels like to live in the various parts of Britain have come from musicians working outside the white English pop mainstream. In folk itself, the contribution of Irish music, from Planxty and Moving Hearts in the 1970s to Christy Moore and the Saw Doctors in the 1980s and 1990s, adds up to a considerable national music that both celebrates and criticises the Irish way of life. In England, the musics brought by other immigrant communities has been transformed by younger generations into Anglo-Caribbean and Anglo-Asian sounds. The roll-call of singers and bands would include Steel Pulse, Matumbi, the Specials, UB40, Jazzie B, Smiley Culture, Apache Indian, Bally Sagoo, Sheila Chandra and dozens more. If anyone wanted to seek out music that's 'British without being insular or nostalgic' today they'd have to start from here rather than Lindisfarne's foggy Tyne.

2

Doom Patrol: Black Sabbath at the Rainbow

Andrew Weiner

A BLITZKRIEG IN THE TEENAGE WASTELAND

For the last six months, I've been living about a half-mile from the Rainbow Theatre. I pass it nearly every day. It's part of the scenery: a very large, very ugly and more than usually rundown old cinema, in the most rundown part of Seven Sisters Road. A strange choice of name and an even stranger choice of venue for what was once promoted as England's answer to the Fillmores.

When the Rainbow first opened, the relevant entrepreneurs made all the appropriate noises about establishing contact with the immediate community. The immediate community is mostly Greek Cypriot, small shopkeepers and restaurant owners. Give or take a few Donny Osmond posters, they still don't appear to be too impressed with the Rainbow. But then, it isn't that impressive. It's just a rundown old cinema that someone decided to turn into a rock theatre.

Most Fridays and Saturdays the freaks appear. And they're part of the scenery too, as predictable as the Arsenal crowds on alternate Saturdays. Now and again, though, a particular crowd will stand out as unusual. The kids who queued up all night in midwinter for Eric Clapton tickets; they must have been unusually devoted. Or the Osmonds' crowd, that was unusually spectacular, mounted policemen and screaming boppers halfway to Holloway Road. That was the best crowd I've seen yet, much better than *Tommy*. For *Tommy* they had a mobile generator with 20th Century Fox spotlights, very low camp.

As it happened, there was nothing so very unusual about the Black Sabbath audience. Or at least, they didn't live up to their outlandish mass media billing. I'd half-expected to see swarms of kids decked out with silver crucifixes, completely dressed in black, chanting spells or totally downed out on mandrax and cheap alcohol. But they were, for the most part, ordinary kids. Younger than you'd see at an Eric Clapton revival meeting; harder than you'd see for, say, Joni Mitchell or Colin Blunstone. A few of them did wear crucifixes. A few of them did look a little wasted. But none of them had horns, or pointed tails.

Still, I thought there had to be something special about a Black Sabbath audience. There had to be. To identify with and gain pleasure from the mostly bone-rattling and doomladen tracts of despair which fill up their four albums to date, they had to be something special.

CHILDREN OF THE GRAVE

Despite the blitzkrieg nature of their sound, Black Sabbath are moralists. Like Bob Dylan, like William Burroughs, like most artists trying to deal with a serious present situation in an honest way ... They are a band with a conscience who have looked around them and taken it upon themselves to reflect the chaos in ways that they see as positive.

Lester Bangs, *Creem*, June 1972

Black Sabbath are perhaps the only band in existence who have got the non-art of their music right down to a fine art. Each song is a pastiche of the previous one and a guide of things yet to come ... With glazed eyes fixed on the stage, the seat holders rise up as one, then with arms well over their head rock backwards and forwards in slow motion like seaweed.

Roy Carr, *NME*, 24 March 1973

Black Sabbath could very well claim to be one of England's last remaining truly *underground* bands. Any third-rate support act has a better chance of getting an album track played on *Sounds of the Seventies*, or a gig on the *Old Grey Whistle Test*, or even a moderately sympathetic write-up in the music weeklies. In a cultural atmosphere in which 'heavy' means Argent and 'progressive' means Focus, Black Sabbath simply do not fit.

So they're underground. But they're also very overground, in the sense that they're also tremendously successful. They hit the Top Ten with their very first album back in 1970. That success, which caught the self-styled English counter-cultural vanguard completely unawares, was decidedly not based upon good reviews and big radio coverage. It was based upon the reputation Sabbath had quietly built up around the country as a live band. Well, not quietly. But *invisibly*. People saw Sabbath and liked them and went back and saw them again and told their friends. And finally, a lot of people bought their album, to the barely muted disgust of that counter-cultural vanguard.

Sabbath went on from there, to the point where they could sell out every gig they announced, where they could hit the album charts again and again with the most minimal outside support. They went on to find success in America on a scale inviting comparison with Grand Funk Railroad, so mysterious a phenomenon did it appear to the American critical establishment. A 'phenomenon', by my own tentative definition, is something which its supporters don't need to understand and its opponents don't want to understand.

And they've even had a Top Three single. 'Paranoid'. Maybe you remember it?

Finished with my woman
'cos she couldn't help me
with my mind ...

A riff like a pneumatic drill on speed. A vocal more cracked and feeble than Keith Relf, walled in by that thunderous noise, calling out for help. Perhaps the bleakest hit single in living memory. Bleaker than any death song, because insanity is always bleaker than death. Insanity is living death.

I need someone to show me
the things in life that I can find
I can't see the things that make
true happiness
I must be blind.

Sabbath never followed up 'Paranoid'. They got too sick of all the teeny-boppers invading their gigs screaming 'play "Paranoid"!'. Still, they'd closed a strange connection, whether or not they were prepared to face up to its full consequences.

If Black Sabbath had followed 'Paranoid', they could well have established themselves as the biggest singles band since the Stones. They could perhaps have pre-empted Bolan, Bowie, Slade. Think of that. Sabbath on *Top Of The Pops*, month after month, churning out their Awful Warnings:

everywhere is misery and woe
pollution kills the air, the land, the sea
man prepares to meet his destiny.
                    'Paranoid' (1970)

How could Gary Glitter hope to follow that? How could anyone follow that?

It's only Teenage Wasteland

Don't cry / don't raise your eye / it's only teenage wasteland.
Pete Townsend, 'Baba O'Reilly' (1971)

Now there's no reason to believe that the members of Black Sabbath are necessarily, in their private lives, quite as doomladen as their music appears to suggest. No more than Slade are likely to be quite as happy and raving in their private lives as they are in their own music. The question is irrelevant. We're not dealing with people, we're dealing with the public personas they choose to project, and the response to those personas.

I liked 'Paranoid', personally, but I never could get to like their albums. On every level, they seemed too much of the same. The same heavy metal sub-Cream riffs, the same cracked vocals, the same persistently doomy lyrics. And those lyrics, in print – as Sabbath presented them on their first three albums – looked too clumsy and crabbed to be taken seriously.

And then, there was more than a hint of contrivance, of mere gimmickry. Plus the more appalling implications of their apparent involvement with black magic. Once upon a time there was a band called Earth who were successful in Birmingham but nowhere else. Everyone thought they had a neat guitarist in Tony Iommi, but they weren't getting any place. It got to the point where Iommi almost joined Jethro Tull. But that didn't work out at all, so Iommi went back to Earth. Earth became Black Sabbath. And Black Sabbath, quite suddenly, took off.

Earth became Black Sabbath at the tail-end of a fairly spectacular boom in the black magic business. Polanski's *Rosemary's Baby*, itself based upon a best-selling creapocreapo novel. Exposés in the *News of the World*, full frontal nudie witches in the television night. Thrills for a jaded nation. This month: Black Magic. Next month: Was God An Astronaut? Coming Soon: The End Of The World.

Now black magic has around three major selling points. First of all, it offers 'knowledge' as to the meaning of life/secrets of the cosmos. Second, it offers 'power' over your fellow human beings; power you couldn't otherwise achieve or in any way deserve, power without any responsibility. And finally, mythically at least, it offers easy sex.

So black magic promises knowledge and power to the ignorant and impotent. Most of all, power. Lester Bangs: 'What black magic is about is absolute control.' Black magic appeals most to people who believe themselves to have nothing at all, no possessions, no future, nothing. It appealed a great deal, for example, to Charles Manson. And superficially at least, it ought to have appealed to the burnt out post-psychedel-ic casualties strewn across the teenage wasteland.

Now Black Sabbath, like Grand Funk Railroad, stand out as one of the ultimate teenage-wasteland bands (e.g. bands supported vehemently by kids too wrecked to believe what they read in *Melody Maker* and *Rolling Stone*, if they read them at all). So it looked like a clear connection. Black Sabbath equals black magic equals fodder for feeble minds. And so the overwhelming volume, the simplistic lyrics.

But that's all wrong. First of all, Sabbath are English. And the English teenage wasteland is a lot different to the American variety. England always was a teenage wasteland, particularly in places like Birmingham and points north, and acid didn't make much difference to it one way or another. Well sure, you can see the damage here and there, permanently wrecked minds, junkies and Krishna fiends and scientologists. But it was limited, it never really permeated all the way through. In America, though, acid and the War together managed to lay waste to what was by any standard a relative teenage paradise, with Charles Manson and the rest of the mindwarp kids as a partial fall-out from the Fall.

Black Sabbath don't relate to any of that, except by implication (and the later contamination of American touring). They relate to the English experience. They relate to casual street-fighting and mind-numbing boredom and schools that are day internment camps and above all that the prospect of dead-end factory jobs. They relate to the entire depressing, English working-class experience.

Now Sabbath are fighting against that background. They're fighting it, but they're not invoking black magic in their fight. In point of fact, they took a stand *against* black magic. Their songs warned against it. They used to wear those crucifixes to fend off evil spirits. And while a part of that was complete hype-bullshit, the gimmickry of 1970 as flower power was the gimmickry of 1967, as Mod was the gimmickry of 1965, a further part of it was very concurrent with their general world view.

TALKIN' WORLD WAR THREE BLUES

Day of judgement, God is calling
on their knees the war pigs crawling
begging mercy for their sins
Satan laughing spreads his wings.
                    'War Pigs' (1970)

Black Sabbath are also interested in World War Three. In fact, they're obsessed with it. Again and again their songs resolve into atomic war, death and destruction, Satan reaping. But for Black Sabbath the contest is simpler, Good v. Evil. And they're fighting their own share of the preliminary skirmishes, out on the neural battlefields.

Sometimes, in their songs, Final War is seen as inevitable, on the principle that everything bad that can possibly happen will happen. Sometimes it's held up as a strong possibility, unless people Change Their Ways. And sometimes it's positively welcomed. 'War Pigs', for example, sets up the bad guys ...

> politicians hide themselves away
> they only started the war
> why should they go out to fight?
> they leave that all to the poor ...

... and then gives them their just desserts. But though Black Sabbath appear to have a fairly shrewd idea of what's happening in the world right now, I can't claim that their solutions appeal to me. It may comfort them to think that the war pigs will burn in hell while we ascend to heaven, and so what if they do blow us all up. It may comfort them, but it doesn't comfort me.

So you have to take Sabbath's stuff metaphorically, or not take it at all. And on the level of metaphor, it's truly compelling stuff. See the generals gathered 'just like witches at Black Masses'. It's the people who seek and manipulate power who are the damned. It's Nixon who's Manson, not Sabbath.

WHITE NOISE AND AFFIRMATION

> Everybody is a star
> one big circle
> going round and round.
> > Sly Stone, 'Everybody is a Star' (1969)

Inside, the Rainbow is rococo enough Odeon Grand Opera. And very full, the fullest cinema I've been in since *The Godfather*. But of course, it isn't a cinema. The support band, Badger, play a fairly loud set to fairly polite applause. Lyrics about Jesus and such like. No one seems to want an encore. Badger depart. Or maybe it was Necromandus?

Interlude. The sound system plays records while people buy ice creams. A curious selection, culminating in Bowie's 'Space Oddity'.

And then, a moment's silence. Followed by uproar. From behind, from in front, from above, from every corner of the place, uproar. Footstomping, handclapping, chanting. 'SABBATH. SABBATH. SABBATH'. More like a Spurs gig than any rock concert I've ever seen, though I've never seen Slade. And it goes on and on. Kids shouting and screaming and flashing peace signs. It goes on and on. 'OZZY, OZZY'. Good humoured at first, but then a little impatient, a little ragged. All the more sinister in conjunction with those peace signs.

Peace signs. Usually, I despise people who flash peace signs. But these kids aren't playing Hippies And Straights, Woodstock Nation, they're playing some different game. Still, it seems weird, incongruous. And what will happen, I can't help wondering, when Sabbath actually appear? Can they live up to this? What will happen if they *don't* appear? A genuine rock 'n' roll riot? It's a good setting, anyway. And it'll make a lot of people very happy.

The lights go up and Sabbath come on and go straight into their first song. Iommi immediately hits his Number One Riff, totally drowning out singer Osbourne. You literally can't hear a word. I thought that this first song was perhaps 'Sweet Leaf', but it couldn't have been, because they announced 'Sweet Leaf' as the second song. It could be that they played it twice. It could even be that they played it five or six times throughout the evening. It could even be that Iommi thought they were playing 'Sweet Leaf' while Ozzy Osbourne was trying to sing, 'Electric Funeral'.

But the point is this: it doesn't matter. It doesn't matter which song they're playing. It doesn't matter that they seem to be cranking out the same one-and-a-half riffs nearly every time. In point of fact, that's one of the main virtues of their performance, the main roots of their appeal. And once you get used to the idea, you may find yourself liking it better and better.

Iommi is a strange guitarist. So motionless, at first I thought he was the bass player. And clearly very adept, as he proves later in his obligatory – and finally, tedious – ten-minute solo excursion. But the main point of his playing is not the virtuoso reconstruction of lost chords from forgotten universes. The point of it is volume and power. Iommi, more than anyone, has taken the rationale of electric amplification through to its fullest implications. Through and beyond, perhaps to the point of absurdity. But these kids in the audience they'd all like to play like Iommi. Not like Hendrix or Clapton or any other silver-fingered guitar God you could mention. They want to play like Iommi. WHAM. WHAM WHAM. And they could, too. Or at least, they *think* they could. And that, again, is one of the main virtues of Black Sabbath.

So Iommi is the power centre of the band, and perhaps in compensation he keeps very still indeed. Ozzy Osbourne is an unexpectedly mobile lead singer, considering the generally depressing and down nature of the lyrics he is called upon to deliver. He doesn't have many moves. I counted four: standing still and singing; hopping across the stage and inviting the audience to clap their hands; miming to Geezers bass riffs, Joe Cocker style: flashing peace signs with both hands high above his head. So he's no Jagger, and that's just as well. There's at least a suggestion of spontaneity about it, however well rehearsed it may be in actual fact. Spontaneity, and – weirdly enough – pure enjoyment.

You don't hear the bass, but you feel it hit you in the stomach. You don't hear the drums, except as general background noise. All you hear are those thunderous riffs and broken vocal fragments riding out through the storm. 'War Pigs' is most nearly *serious*, most nearly audible. 'Children of the Grave' is chaos again. Not downer-rock, as the title might suggest, but a hymn of affirmation. Affirmation and white noise.

> Revolution in their minds
> the children start to march
> against the world they have to live in
> oh ! the hate that's in their hearts
> they're tired of being pushed around
> and told just what to do
> they'll fight the world until they've won
> and loves comes flowing through.
>   'Children of the Grave' (1971)

Osbourne flashing his peace signs in time with the ascending chords. And maybe a thousand kids flashing them right back, call and response. I think of accounts of Sly Stone concerts, the clever clever analogies with Nuremberg. But it isn't that way at all.

What Black Sabbath are proposing here, more or less, is Peace and Love. The old Monterey and Woodstock Vision, the old bullshit myth. But there's a big difference. A difference that makes their message acceptable to this fairly-toughlooking audience. Makes it not just acceptable, but desirable. Because what Sabbath are dealing in here, whether they know it or not, is armed love. High-decibel heavy metal siren-screaming machine-gun-firing armed love. Armed love, because there's no other choice.

> show the world that love is still alive
> you must be brave
> or you children of today
> are children of the grave.

Black Sabbath's music unleashes tremendous power. And that's its main appeal. But it's not a case of Sabbath possessing that power and using it to batter their audience into submission. It's not even a case of Sabbath offering to share their power with us. It's not like that because the power is ours already, and Sabbath are part of us. And if that wasn't so, then they wouldn't have this crowd going crazy.

Send any four kids up from the floor, and they'll try and play like that. Send Black Sabbath back into the depths of the audience, and this is the music they'd go and see. That's the theory, anyway. The kids believe it, and Sabbath believe it, though they wouldn't necessarily express it in those terms. That's the theory, though in practice it can't be true. In practice, like it or not, Black Sabbath are superstars. And though they still wear it well, sooner or later it's going to have to take its toll.

Sooner or later, Sabbath are going to have to edge into lame virtuoso trips, unanswerable-mysteries-of-the-human-condition lyrics. In fact it's happening already. It's happening on their last album *Volume Four*, with its fey joke about cocaine on the sleeve and its dubious attempts at diversification. Their thoroughgoing *professionalism* is evident in the way they handle the demands for an encore:

'What do you want to hear?'

'PARANOID.'

'What do you want to hear?

'PARANOID.'

Complete identification with audience gives way to a simple understanding of their needs. Which may, in turn, give way to complete indifference to those needs. It may do, it may not. Black Sabbath remain, in present circumstances, designed to alienate the successful performer from his audience as quickly and cleanly as possible, the nearest thing to a people's band we have. And that's no unimportant thing.

(1973)

In 1973, when I wrote 'Doom Patrol', I was working on an MSc. in social psychology at the London School of Economics, and freelancing for *New Society*, *Cream* and *New Musical Express*. For *New Society* I wrote earnest, thumb-sucking pieces about the Real Meaning of various pop phenomena. For *Cream* and *New Musical Express* I wrote much the same thing in a somewhat livelier manner. I had no musical education, no special knowledge of rock history. But I was pretty good at doing Real Meaning.

I was interested in how rock stars reflected society, and how they shaped it; and in the function of rock music, the role it played in people's lives.

I didn't bring any particular theoretical apparatus to this project. Cultural studies hardly existed. My acquaintance with sociology was limited (although I was much impressed with Charlie Gillett's approach in his book *The Sound of the City*). I had read a little Adorno, absorbed a little Marx. My professors at the LSE had done major work on the impact of television on the child. But mostly I relied on instinct, and the example set by better writers (Greil Marcus, Lester Bangs, Simon Frith).

'Doom Patrol' was originally commissioned by Bob Houston, editor of *Cream* magazine, and appeared in the May 1973 issue. I'm not sure now whether it was my idea or Bob Houston's, although I suspect the latter – I was never big on fieldwork (and I avoided rock star interviews like the plague). Charlie Gillett picked up the piece, excised an ill-advised J.G. Ballard quote about fighting World War Three on the neural battlefields, and otherwise ran it as-is.

Cream, like its more tedious (although longer-lived) rival, *Let It Rock*, was a forerunner of today's glossy rock magazines like *Q* and *Mojo*. As such, it was very much ahead of its time. Bob Houston didn't know or care much about rock (he was a jazz fan), but he found writers who did: Charlie Gillett, Charles Shaar Murray, Ian MacDonald, Neil Spencer, Mick Farren, Clive James, Simon Frith, half the writers in this book ... . It was an appealing package, but hardly anyone read it.

'Doom Patrol' was neither the best nor the worst of my dozens of articles on rock: the best was probably a piece on the Real Meaning of the Beach Boys for *Cream*, hopelessly jumbled by the printer. The opening seems long-winded, the closing forced. But there is some decent stuff in between.

And while many have written about the Real Meaning of the Beach Boys, hardly anyone (other than the late, great Lester Bangs) attempted the same for Black Sabbath. So I'm pleased to see this piece back in print.

3

Are You Ready For Rude and Rough Reggae?
Carl Gayle

THE REAL THING

Chris Blackwell, the white Jamaican boss of Island Records, said recently that he would like to get rid of the name 'reggae'. It was alright at first but now everyone uses it, including people who neither care for nor understand the music but think that anything with a repetitive Jamaican rhythm is reggae.

'Reggae' was really the name of the dance that replaced 'rock steady', just as the latter had replaced 'ska' or 'bluebeat'. As a dance became popular Jamaican musicians capitalised on it by making records to suit the dance fans. Thus with 'reggae' came such records as 'Bangerang' and 'No More Heartaches', which were real reggae records. Sometimes, indeed, the lyrics of such songs simply contained the word reggae used over and over again, as in 'Do the Reggay' by the Maytals, a great favourite at the time. In the normal course of events, as a dance's popularity decreased, its name became less frequently used in records, and this is what should have happened to the term 'reggae'.

By this time, however, records such as 'Israelites', 'Return of Django', 'Liquidator' and 'Long Shot Kick the Bucket' were making the English national charts because they were also being bought by skinheads, who at that time identified with the music and with some of its musicians, people like Desmond Dekker and the Pioneers. Out of this trend another developed, whereby records such as 'Reggae in Your Jeggae', 'Moon Hop' and 'Skinhead Moon Stomp' were specially made for the skinheads who, in turn, found new favourites like Dandy and Derrick Morgan.

By then the name 'reggae' was hardly used by the real fans but it remained popular with the skinheads who continued to buy things like 'Elizabethan Reggae', even in early 1970. It was this type of skinhead music which eventually gained the greater exposure (via the charts, etc.)

as opposed to the music genuinely in the same vein as 'Long Shot Kick the Bucket' (such as 'Alidina' by the Maytals or 'Too Proud to Beg' by the Uniques) which was not made for skinheads but typified the music that the real reggae fans were enjoying. The two types of record were separable but were conveniently heaped together as 'reggae' by the people who were more interested in the financial rewards than the music itself. The result was that when the skinhead trend ended in 1970 so did reggae chart success.

The next trend was for the musicians to aim for a wider market by commercialising their sound. At first this was done by adding strings and background vocals, and by using a less ethnic approach in the singing (e.g. 'Wonderful World, Beautiful People' and 'You Can Get It If You Really Want It'); later on, 'reggae' versions of other wellknown songs appeared (e.g. 'Young Gifted and Black'). This commercial trend further widened the gap between what was widely known as 'reggae' and what the real fans were digging.

When someone is looking for a reggae party to go to on a Saturday night he might ask 'Where is the blues?' but he won't use the word reggae, not if he's a real fan. To him 'reggae' now refers to the stuff (like 'Suzanne Beware of the Devil') that gets into the charts and not to his music, which gets very little airplay and never makes the charts. Groups like Greyhound or the Pioneers are dismissed as 'commercial' (compare the latter's 'Long Shot Kick the Bucket' to their 'Let Your Yeah Be Yeah') and by using the term 'blues' the real fan is subconsciously affirming his music's affinity, in feel and intensity, with blues music.

Real reggae tunes must be danceable (witness 'Breakfast In Bed' by Lorna Bennett or 'Jimmy Brown' by Ken Parker), there must be a continuous, repetitive riff to provide the dance beat. In 'rock steady' the bass sound was even more important than now, you danced to it alone. People who criticise reggae music by saying that it all sounds the same are usually referring to the repetitive rhythm and fail to understand that repetition is inherent in the music's quality.

None the less, the lyrics are always equally important, even in the spoken comments over a background tune that are the trademark of someone like U Roy. If the words are incomprehensible they still form a vital part of the total effect or 'feel', as in the blues – they are never surreal as in much pop or progressive music.

The singing is very important, too. Again as in blues, the ethnic voice, its mannerisms, its tone and most important its Jamaican accent, contributes much to the final sound. Eric Donaldson, one of the most popular singers on the scene, is a good example. He has a falsetto voice which I disliked at first but which provides a very ethnic quality. This, more than any other factor, has been responsible for his quick success.

'Cherry Oh Baby', his first hit, won 1971's Jamaican Song Festival and 'Blue Boot' is even better.

When I hear DJs call Paul Simon's 'Mother and Child Reunion' a good reggae record I have to disagree. It can't be considered a reggae record just because the backing was done by reggae musicians, and, like many white blues copyists, Simon falls down because of his voice. Even things like 'Black and White' by Greyhound or 'Suzanne Beware of the Devil' by Dandy Livingstone, which are good pop songs, are not good reggae records. Such musicians no longer retain the 'feel' which was evident in their music at the outset.

The real enthusiasts are fed up with this type of commercial reggae which is popular and gets exposure on the radio. Hearing a few good tunes on Radio London's *Reggae Time* is not nearly enough to relieve the frustration of having to wait a week or of being disappointed by a group like Greyhound on *Top Of The Pops*. *Reggae Time*'s Steve Barnard is doing a good job and gaining much popularity and, granted, he can't satisfy all of the people all of the time, but many fans feel that the programme should deal with real reggae music only, they want to hear more heavy ethnic sounds. I agree! Soul fans couldn't complain – there are other programmes (Dave Simmonds' R&B show and, to a lesser extent, Charlie Gillett's *Honky Tonk*) which cater for them.

But television is really the most effective means of getting the real music across and getting it understood. I can remember when 'Return of Django' by the Upsetters was used in a TV commercial. Do they still use it? Even more effective and to the point was a play shown earlier this year on BBC1 featuring Louise Bennett, the Jamaican actress/comedienne. Reggae music was given a boost by being featured throughout and was apparently well received. Note also the interest paid to the film *The Harder They Come* by many rock music fans.

The interest taken in reggae by soul and progressive musicians will help to break down all types of barriers between music fans and to popularise the real stuff, but the imitators (like Paul Simon) should be ready to admit that they are imitators and that they can't achieve a true sound, or at least, not yet. They should be credited for taking the music to a new and wider audience but they should not pretend that they are originators. The new audience will inevitably discover the real stuff (people like Prince Buster, Laurel Aitken, the Maytals, etc.) and these artists should, in turn, receive the acclaim they deserve not only from their new audience but also from the musicians – just as Muddy Waters, B.B. King, etc., were acclaimed by their imitators. White musicians like Paul McCartney have already found new scope in Jamaican music but are, so far, wrongly attempting to duplicate it instead of using it to add something to their own type of music.

But before reggae music can become more acceptable in its ethnic form it must be promoted so that people outside the circles can gain a better understanding – you can't like something you don't understand. This is why the Sound Systems fans who completely dismiss commercial reggae are not helping the situation. Even if it is a commercial dilution at least some reggae does get into the charts and people like Jimmy Cliff can't be expected to limit their scope by sticking solely to ethnic reggae. It is only someone like Cliff who can take the music to another audience.

Meanwhile 'outsiders' should look into the Sound Systems, since they are where the best ethnic music is played. All the big systems (Sir Coxsone, Count Shelley, etc.) have a large following who expect (and get) the very latest sounds. If the people who understand the music and recognise the importance of the Sound Systems would communicate their knowledge in the press then rock fans would gain a much better understanding of reggae music. To whet your appetites these LPs are recommended (all on Trojan, except where noted):

Tighten Up, vol. 4 (TBL 163); *Reggae Chartbusters, vol. I* (TBL 105) or *vol. 2* (TBL 147); *Club Reggae, vol. 4* (TBL 188); *The Harder They Come* soundtrack, Island (ILPS9202); *Jimmy Cliff* (TRL S16); *Eric Donaldson* (JAG 5401); *Monkey Man* by the Maytals; *Trojan's Greatest Hits, vol. 2, Sixteen Dynamic Hits* (TBL 191). The LP by the Maytals and *Tighten Up, vol. 4* are particularly recommended.*

WATCH THIS SOUND

The biggest, most competitive Sound Systems (the forerunners of the present mobile discos) have been around since the early 1960s. They have always been able to provide the very latest sounds and a few 'specials' which they own exclusively (through arrangements with Jamaican producers and artists). In a 1971 Sound Systems contest between Sir Coxsone and Duke Reid, both produced their own specials, drawing wild cheers from their respective supporters.

An important trend among the DJs operating the Systems developed out of the 'ska' era, and influenced, or led to, later styles. The fast tempo ska records were especially popular with young dancers, who shuffled their feet fast but stylishly in time to the jerky bass riffs typical of records like 'Confucius' by Don Drummond, 'Al Capone' by Prince

---

* *Tighten Up, vol. 4* has been reissued with *Tighten Up, vol. 3* on CDTRL 307. Most of the *Reggae Chartbusters* and *Trojan's Greatest Hits* volumes are on *Celebration: Twenty Five Years of Trojan Records* (DCTRD 413). *Jimmy Cliff* is now on CDTRL 16 and *The Harder They Come* sound track album is Island RRCD22.

Buster or 'Broadway Jungle' by the Maytals. The DJs developed a habit of egging on the dancers, making scat noises and interjecting comments into their amplified microphones like those on the traditional ska number, 'Lawless Street'. There was a time when a Sound System's reputation was dependent on its DJ's ability on the mike, and though the styles and the music have changed, the practice is still widespread.

In 1967 the Ram Jam club in Brixton became the most popular among Jamaicans because the new 'rock steady' sounds, such as 'Ba Ba Boom' by the Jamaicans, 'Rock Steady' by Alton Ellis, 'Get Ready, Rock Steady' by the Soul Agents and 'Train to Skaville' by the Ethiopians were well featured. It was here that the English kids who came along were exposed to the Jamaican music, probably for the first time. Records like 'Everybody Rude Now' by Keith McCarthy, 'Tougher Than Tough' and 'Court Dismiss' by Derrick Morgan, 'Judge Dread' by Prince Buster (hence his successful tour that year) and '007' by Desmond Dekker, which reflected the 'rude boy' problem currently of prime concern in Jamaica, were very well received, particularly as they were such good dance records. English kids soon discovered that they could hear other goodies – like 'Sir Collin's Special' by Lester Sterling (one of the first DJ talkover tunes); 'Fatty Fatty' by the Heptones and 'Kill Me Dead' by Derrick Morgan (two suggestive records) and the Hamlins' 'Soul and Inspiration' (a very good sentimental record) – only on the Sound Systems.

By 1968, the resident London Systems, like Sir Coxsone at the Ram Jam in Brixton and the Go Go club at the Oval, Count Shelley at the 007 in Dalston, Sir Fanso at the Sunset in Islington, Neville at the Ska Bar, Woolwich, and, later, Duke Reid at the Blue Ribbon in Peckham, drew consistently large audiences. The majority of the records that they were playing were not released as singles for weeks, sometimes never at all. Nevertheless, records, such as 'Gimme Little Loving' by the Pioneers, or 'The Upsetter' and 'People Funny Boy' by Lee Perry, sold in good quantities at 'pre-release' prices. These records typified a new, harder sound and contrasted with and outsold old sounds like the rock steady styled 'Do the Beng Beng' (Derrick Morgan). The new, heavier, more intense sounds could especially be appreciated when listening to Neville's System. He had a style of playing records, with the treble control turned right up, that later became popular among other Systems. The effect of it was to produce a sharper, tighter sound, particularly noticeable in the rhythm guitar, which seemed to cut across the rest of the instruments. 'Seeing Is Knowing' by Stranger Cole and Gladys and 'Woman A Grumble' by Derrick Morgan (in his new style) were two favourites which amply demonstrated this.

A notable aspect of the young whites was that the majority preferred records like 'Fire In Your Wire' (Laurel Aitken), 'Bang Bang Lulu' (Lloyd

Terrell) and 'Rough Rider' (Prince Buster), because of their 'rude' content, to, say, '54–56, That's My Number' by the Maytals which was for me as good as Desmond Dekker's hit, 'Ah It Mek', but which was only a 'hit' among the ethnic fans.

The Sound Systems helped to create the boom that Jamaican music enjoyed in 1969. More English kids were being attracted by the sounds the Systems were playing uniquely, records such as 'Too Proud To Beg' by the Uniques and 'Decimal Money' by the Maytals, which were as acceptable to them as songs like the Pioneers' 'Long Shot Kick the Bucket' which they had, in turn, helped to reach the charts. They were also attracted by faster tempo records such as 'Work It' by the Viceroys and 'Mama Look Deh' by the Pioneers, records which led to the making of 'reggae' (a faster music than rock steady). Another very popular record, 'Tighten Up' by the Untouchables, also brought with it a new dance and (later on) an LP of the same name containing other similar sounding tunes, such as 'John Jones' by Rudy Mills and 'Watch This Sound' by the Uniques (a re-titled version of Steve Stills' 'For What It's Worth').

Meanwhile, Alton Ellis, who did a version of Tyrone Davis' 'Change My Mind' re-titled 'Change Of Plans', John Holt singing 'Tonight', Pat Kelly with 'How Long Will It Take' and Slim Smith with 'Everyone Needs Love' paved the way for the smoother, sentimental vocalists. Together with the good instrumentals that Clancy Eccles and the Dynamites and Lee Perry and the Upsetters were consistently making, these smoother sounds offered a relief from the heavier stuff that the Systems were playing.

Another development was the talkover. Just as King Stitt with 'Fire Corner', 'The Ugly One' and 'Vigorton Two' in 1968 and Sir Collins (in 1967) had successfully recorded in the ska-influenced DJ style, so (in late 1970) did U Roy, who was himself a Sound System operator. It brought him quick recognition just because the style was already so common-place among the Systems. U Roy's records, 'Wear You To the Ball', 'Wake The Town' and 'Rule the Nation', occupied the first three positions in the Jamaican charts for several weeks, created a new excitement and were well featured by all the other DJs. Everyone wanted to hear the latest U Roy tune, and his style was soon imitated by other recording artists.

The type of music that the Sound Systems are playing today has not changed much since 1969, though in 1971 there was a revival of a type of record which reflected life back home. When records like 'Johnny Too Bad' by the Slickers, 'Let the Power Fall' by Max Romeo or 'Rivers of Babylon' by the Melodians were played loud they evoked a real feeling of spiritual togetherness in the audience. But they never displaced happier tunes like 'One-eye Enos' (the Maytals) and 'Flashing My Whip' (U Roy) or sentimental ones like 'Stick By Me' (John Holt) and 'Stand

By Your Man' (Merlene Webber) and the Systems still offer a complete range of Jamaican music.

Even when some of their supporters were consistently causing trouble, the Sound Systems always found somewhere to play. And whether it was in a pub, bath hall or a cold basement there has always been an enthusiastic audience. If you go to the Roaring Twenties club in Carnaby Street, where Sir Coxsone is the resident DJ, you won't hear any commercial 'reggae' and you might be disappointed with the records that you do hear, but you will notice the complete involvement of the audience, which, encouraged by the Sound Systems and their records, is the market for the real ethnic music.

DUB WISE SKANK: TALKOVER

Jamaica's four biggest talkover artists (singers who talk and shout over a rhythm, or whose voices are dubbed on to an old recording) are Dennis Alcapone, Big Youth, I Roy and U Roy. Most others who have recorded in this style are once-only, 'have a go' opportunists, who would not have got into a studio, let alone made a record, but for U Roy who made the style popular and demanded 'Do not imitate, because I originate.' But a few of these opportunists have made very good records – Prince Jazzbo's 'Mr Harry Skank' (TE921), 'Vampire Rock' (GR3034) by Jah Fish – and I hope we'll be hearing more from them since the records are still party favourites.

The decline of U Roy, the emergence of Big Youth and I Roy, and the chart consistency of Dennis Alcapone, even when he has been a little overshadowed by the other two's arrival, are all good talking points on the Jamaican music scene. Most agree that U Roy's sharpest imitators have captured the feel for this type of music much better than the man himself who seems to have lost it for the moment.

U Roy's arrival late in 1970 was a time of rejuvenation and excitement on the scene. Not that the music was at a low ebb then; it wasn't. It was just that U Roy's sounds (which on close examination were definitely a rip off from King Stitt, 1969's DJ hero, and only a continuation of the ska DJ's style in the mould of the present music) were so different from everything else, and so immediately infectious. Maybe it was because whatever U Roy was doing, he always created the energy which only the best records have, making you happy or sad, making you want to dance and shout. Maybe he did create. King Stitt was never quite like this, he only hinted at it. U Roy was intense from start to finish, shouting, singing and screaming from a self-induced excitement which was only possible when he felt the rhythm. He was revealing his musical soul. It wouldn't have worked any other way, no one was gonna listen to a guy shouting on a microphone unless they were involved. He was one of us, he just cut discs directly for us to play.

So U Roy made the records and we always bought them because they were and are still the best sounds around, records like 'You'll Never Get Away' (DR2514), 'Tom Drunk' (DR2517), 'Flashing My Whip' (DR2519), 'Love I Tender' (DU105), etc. He made 'specials' expressly for the big Sound Systems, and when he came to England hundreds went, anxious and curious, to see and hear him, raved with him and came away very satisfied. And now these same people have put him down with the usual 'he's gone commercial'. Well maybe they're right. His records are just not as good as they used to be; there are too many and they are not as urgent or intense as they should be. Maybe the people who put him on *Reggae Time* have something to do with it all.

'Ripe Cherry' (DYN422), one of Dennis Alcapone's first hits, used the music to 'Cherry Oh Baby', Eric Donaldson's festival winner. Before they became so popular the annoying thing about these DJ recordings was that they spoiled the original song. Now that we're used to them they are accepted as records in their own right and we wonder why we ever used to quibble. Alcapone was the first imitator and although he was good I suspected that he was 'created' to cash in, like the Monkees. But Alcapone has his stern supporters, his phrases are unique, and he has made some very good records – 'Teacher Teacher', 'It Must Come', 'Master Key', 'Out Of This World', 'Musical Alphabet', etc. Even as I write he tops the charts with 'Cassius Clay' (JP808), a fine record (with the great catch phrase 'chi wa wa chi woo') that celebrates the master's win over Bugner. But his popularity or anyone else's for that matter has so far never matched U Roy's at its height.

The two most fashionable musical hosts of the moment are Big Youth and I Roy. Their styles are distinctive, although I Roy has the most easily recognisable voice; more piercing than King Stitt's, and usually accompanied by heavy echo effects. Big Youth's and I Roy's popularity might be because they are the latest imitators, but the more likely reason is that their voices integrate more readily with the currently prevalent 'skank' sounds. The other two, particularly U Roy, are falling behind because the backing music of their best records comes from the late rock steady and mid-reggae periods.

It's not easy to pin down just why Big Youth is the most popular right now, but his records do catch the attention quicker than most. His voice is heavy and outlandish and his phrases are usually more controlled and sensible than U Roy's or Alcapone's. Maybe it's because Big Youth was the one to come up with 'Ace 90 Skank' (DT492). The record introduced this dance to the floors of Jamaica, and since the term

Big Youth

'skank' had been used repeatedly in records since 1970 (when it was used in a record called 'El Paso') and the dance was popular, it's only natural that the name should stick and eventually come to describe the actual music which hasn't changed much apart from losing a little pace and leaning too much on bass and drums. Whether 'skank' replaces 'reggae' or not doesn't really matter; what is more important is that new musical styles and new dances do emerge almost every week.

Again, Big Youth's emergence might be connected with his two very ethnic recordings 'Foreman v Frazier' (GR3040) and 'George Foreman'.

These two records really captured the feel and excitement of what it meant to Jamaicans at the time of the fight. The event was a showdown and George Foreman was the people's hero because he beat Joe Frazier, so Big Youth became the people's hero because we could relive the excitement through his music.

I Roy has made the least records of the four, and much of his stuff is owned by Sound Systems and pre-release addicts only. On his latest record, 'Black Man Time' (DT503), his voice nails you, then the melodic bass line grabs you and makes you move to it. The vocal isn't as piercing as it can be on this but as the record builds, those nonsensical phrases rip out and suddenly at the chorus he almost sings (would you believe it!), and of course you catch the verse and almost sing too. And although what he is singing or shouting is made up on the spot and many of the words are not grammatically correct (they're sound effects really) it is effective, it is original and it's a respected skill.*

RUDE REGGAE

How do you make a hit without really trying? Simple. Just overdub some half-sung, half-spoken, suggestive nursery rhyme lyrics on to a reggae-backing track (preferably an old instrumental). Judge Dread's 'Big Six' (Big Shot B1608) was a poor effort by any standard, yet it has sold over 300,000 copies. 'Big Seven' (Big Shot B1613) was an even bigger seller, and the only change was a slightly better backing track.

Judge Dread (real name Alex Hughes) seems to like the Jamaican sound, which I can understand, but the one-time debt-collector, bouncer, DJ, etc. isn't helping the music's already misunderstood reputation (or his own) with these substandard rude reggae records. Maybe it's a good thing that the lyrics prevent radio exposure – outsiders would be misled even further. The Judge's records would certainly not have sold so well if it hadn't been for the 'suggestive' lyrics but surely he can do better than:

Mary had a little pig
She couldn't stop it grunting
She took it up the garden path
And kicked its little rump in

This kind of thing only comes across as pathetic to true reggae fans.

OK! So where's the real stuff then? Well, try this for a start: 'Pussy Price' (Nu Beat NB046), issued by Laurel Aitken in 1968. This is one of

---

* Most of the great talkover records have now been issued on CD: *Hit the Road Jack* by Big Youth (Trojan CDTRL 137) and *Your Ace from Space* by U Roy (CDTRL 359).

the most directly offensive rude records ever, more offensive even than his others – 'Fire In Your Wire' and 'The Rise and Fall of Laurel Aitken' – and as influential on rude reggae as Prince Buster's 1967 'Rough Rider'. Aitken's gruff voice is well suited to his subject, which is quickly made clear:

> What a way pussy price gone up
> One time you get it for thirty cent
> Now if you follow pussy
> You can't pay your rent

When I started to play this, to refresh my memory, the lady of the house (not my mother) complained: 'Don't play that record again! Whatever you do, don't play that record.' I didn't argue – it's not as if the lyrics are easily forgotten anyway. Aitken makes no attempt at subtlety, the music is as crude as the lyrics, hard, direct and apt. He sings: 'Pussy strike' (girls were hard to get), 'Cocky crash' (guy's frustrated, becoming desperate), 'Batty take over' (desperate enough to turn queer), and it's so effective that it used to make the 'grown ups' leave the room at parties. The youngsters just laughed, of course – if it was so offensive why did it sell so well?

Other records had the same effect. Lloyd Terrell's 'Birth Control' (Puma PM710), for instance:

> Meeow. Doris, the pussy dirty
> Meeow. Doris, the pussy dirty
> Doris, go right in that bathroom and wash the pussy right now come on ... Meeow

The meeows enhanced the record's catch and if the meaning was ever in doubt, all was later revealed: 'Gimme the birth control / me no want no pickney [kids]'.

Prince Buster's 'Big Five' (Buster label) was another. He took a reggae version of 'Rainy Night In Georgia' and changed the lyrics to produce the most influential rude reggae record yet:

> Heavy rain falling
> I can feel my ... getting stiff in hand
> Gonna be a wet wet night in big five
> Screamin screamin night in big five
> It will be pussy versus cocky tonight.

Prince Buster's records usually have a boastful quality, this one had an additional abrasiveness:

Today I smoked an ounce of weed
Tonight I'm gonna plant a seed
In her womb alright

and in 'Wreck a Pum Pum' (Pama – deleted) the singer revealed his frustration with similar aggression (to the tune of 'Little Drummer Boy'):

I want a girl to wreck her pum pum
[repeated]
And if she ugly I don't mind
I have a dick and I want a grind

Rude reggae can be outrageous and amusing simultaneously, as 'Trial of Pama Dice' (Sioux S1022) by Lloyd Dice and Mum, proved. Pama Dice comes up for trial on a rape charge (for which he subsequently gets 1000 years) before a Judge Dread-type magistrate (Prince Buster's character) who completely dominates the proceedings, being Judge, Prosecution and Jury. Pama Dice is denied the chance to speak and has to listen to his accuser's (Mum's) story, which might not be as innocent as it seems:

It was last Thursday night and I was going home and he came up to me and he said 'Hello', so I said 'Ello.' (When are we going to get to the point?). And he said 'Can I kiss you?' So I said 'No.' So he said 'Oh!' Then he pushed me and hit me and he started to, you know, wreck the pum pum.

'Fatty Fatty' (Studio One SO2014) is both flirty and dirty. It's a very melodic tune, sung in a typically laid back 'rock steady', almost hypnotic, style – the Heptones haven't had a record since. The bouncy, bubbling, guitar intro (is it a bass?) is the very same one that Jackie Mittoo used in his organ-based instrumental 'Ram Jam'. The call and response method, using a male chorus, works well: 'I need a fat a very very fat girl (fat girl tonight), I'm in the mood (I'm in the mood), I'm feeling rude, girl (I'm feeling rude)'. The bracketed words are sung by the chorus and create the atmosphere: 'I say now, when you feel it girl you're gonna say it is (so nice!)'. The bass and lead guitars duet in the same fashion, making the song as memorable as the experience, so nice!

Derrick Morgan's 'Kill Me Dead' (Pyramid – deleted) proved that you didn't have to be crude to be rude. A smooth horn warning gets it off – look out, here I come! Then the catch line is sung, achingly – 'Mind you kill me dead' – and repeated three more times to get it home. The whole thing just slides along till: 'I said the pressure is hot take your hands from me neck – hold me round me waist wind me wind me line – rub and squeeze now'. All this time a girl duet, sexy voices, reply to each line 'Old lady!' (or is it 'oh Lloydy!'?) or an occasional 'Rub it up, push it up!'. The lyrical climax is as good as any I've heard: 'The river comes down – old lady!'. The musical experience is as satisfying – who said repetition was boring?

The most successful rude reggae records were 'Bang Bang Lulu' by Lloyd Terrell (Pama PM710) and 'Wet Dream' by Max Romeo (Unity UN503), which both captured the attention of young white reggae listeners, using double-meaning (if obvious) lyrics and easily memorable tunes and choruses:

> Bang Bang Lulu's gone away
> Who is gonna bang bang when
> Lulu's gone away?

and

> Every night me go to sleep me have
> wet dream
> Lie down gal, make me push it up
> push it up, lie down.

In the former song the imagination didn't have to be stretched to discover the omitted word as the singer dramatically built the story behind the song:

> Lulu had a boyfriend
> His name was Tommy Tucker He
> took her down the alley To see if he
> could …

And you would have to be very naive to believe Max Romeo's claims that the words 'push it up' in 'Wet Dream' were misinterpreted, and really referred to his attempts to prop something up into his leaking ceiling when it rained. Besides, what about the second verse? 'Look how you big and fat, like a big big shot, give the crumpet to big foot Joe, give the fanny to me!'

More recently, one of the biggest-selling rude records among ethnic fans has been 'Big Seven' (also known as 'Punaani') by Charlie Ace and Fay (Pama PM853). The guy is in a hurry: 'Take it off no!' 'Wait no', comes the reply. 'Just because you know I can make eight eighty eighty.' (Work that one out!) The chick then phones up the 'sex station' DJ who proceeds to play his tune and provide an accompaniment for the couple 'doing their thing' (judging by the amount of oohs, aahs, moans and groans). 'Do it the same way', she moans, 'If I scream do it the same way.' An ingenious record.

Let me finish with one of the first rude records, by Justin Hines, 'Penny Reel O'. The record was extremely popular, maybe because it illustrated an ideal way of settling debts:

> Gal you owe me a little
> money – Penny reel O
> And you no have it back fi
> gimme – Penny reel O
> I beg you shub your cushu
> gimme – Penny reel O
> And let me rub out me
> money – Penny reel O

For those of you whose curiosity has been whetted, check out the following LPs. Prince Buster's *Big Five* (Melodisc MLP12-157) and Lloydie and the Lowbites' *Censored* (Lowbite 001) are the most offensive and the best musically, the latter containing very good cover versions of the most well-known rude reggae tunes, Prince Buster taking the rhythms of other popular reggae tunes and adding his own rude lyrics. Also good value are *Birth Control*, an anthology on Economy (SEC032) and Max Romeo's *A Dream* (Pama PMLPll). The former LP includes the title track plus 'Pussy Price' and 'Ben Wood Dick' by Laurel Aitken and others in the same vein from Max Romeo, the Ethiopians, etc. 'Wet Dream' is on *A Dream*, with tracks like 'The Horn', 'Wine Her Goosie', etc. The LP *Bang Bang Lulu* (Pama PMLPP4) contains non-rude items (e.g. by Derrick Morgan and Lynn Taitt and the Jets) as well as the title track, 'Wet Dream', again and other not so well-known rude material[*].

We all need humour, whatever our musical tastes, and it's fair to say that 'rude reggae' satisfies both the commercial and ethnic audiences, its common appeal being its sexual suggestiveness, which is so basic that it makes you laugh (or blush!). There's a lesson to be learned from this. Rock musicians, for instance, are too hung up on their 'image'. What little humour there is left in rock comes wrapped up in irony or cynicism, which doesn't help to make rock accessible to the fans of other music. I'm not complaining, just observing. The music from the people who've generated the most interest recently, Bolan, Bowie and Berry, has an abrasive sexual quality. What we need is music we can all identify with. Long live rude reggae!

(1974)

---

[*] Several of the tracks mentioned here are on *Adults Only, vol. 1* (Trojan CDTRL 305) and *vol. 2* (CDTRL 308).

4

Playing Records

Simon Frith and Tony Cummings

INTRODUCTION

In *Rock File 2* we surveyed a year of singles in Britain (from September 1972 to August 1973) and drew up a league table of record companies based on the findings. I've been keeping tabs again this year but with less focus on the final figures (the pattern of 1972–73 was continued) than in the processes which led to them. As much shit was flung as before, as little of it stuck. More and more I think of the pop marketplace as a battlefield – the record buyer struggling just quirkily enough to frustrate the record companies' attempts to control his tastes and their sales.

The outcome is less certain than it is in other consumer battles because the means of persuasion that record companies control most directly (advertising) is their least effective one. Telling people to listen to a record isn't the same as making them hear it and one complete spin on Radio One is worth any number of full-page ads in *NME*, or critical raves from a reviewer, or 30-second spots on Capital or ITV (K Tel sells records that everyone has already heard). Even weeny idols must be heard as well as seen; the increasingly beseeching pictures of Ricky Wilde in *Jackie* didn't compensate for the BBC's lukewarm shoulder, and the only other direct promotion a company can use is live performance, which increasingly means a gathering of an already mutual admiration society. Shows can confirm star status (which guarantees sales of the next record) but, at least in the singles market, they rarely cause it – sellout concerts follow sellout records and in 1973–74 only Cockney Rebel could have claimed otherwise.

To sell a single, record companies have got to get a sound to the public and they can only do this indirectly, through a middle man, the disc jockey. The DJ's position in the record sales struggle is ambiguous not because of the legal restraints (payola, in all its various forms, represents the record companies' attempt to win the battle unfairly, by controlling the DJ) but because of the nature of his job to please the public. He can't simply be on the record sellers' side (whether innocently or not) because if he doesn't play what his public want to hear, he'll be out of work himself (this was the defence made by several American DJs in the payola scandals of the 1950s). But neither can he simply be on the record buyers' side (not even John Peel) because, like it or not, his position is one of control (over what his public will hear) and his effect is on sales (a DJ who never moved anyone to buy anything would be a failure even by his own standards). Whose side is a disc jockey on? He sits and hopes that the records he plays will sell, not because that will benefit him directly but because if his taste is thus confirmed then his audience will continue to tune their trannies to hear him.

The DJ's role is important but ambiguous and it has been made more important (and more ambiguous) by the development since the 1960s of two stages on which to perform it – the discotheque as well as the radio. Clubs with records as their only means of entertainment came to Britain (from France, I suppose) in the early 1960s. Before then DJs and records had been used in ballrooms (such as Jimmy Saville's Teen and Twenty Club in Manchester), but not as alternatives to live music – imagine what would have happened to the Beatles had the Cavern been a disco and had its kids preferred original records to live covers. Initially discotheques served two sorts of in-crowd – rock aristocrats seeking exclusion, and soul freaks; but by the late 1960s, as live rock became increasingly undanceable, expensive and in the wrong places (colleges and concert halls), discos took on pop (rather than cult) significance, as places where a lot of record buyers were hearing a lot of records. Record companies were slow to realise the implications, but finally began to notice inexplicably high sales for records which they had inadvertently neglected to delete from their catalogues. Backtracking through their sales departments to the source of demand, they discovered: the Northern scene.

At least one man in the record business was already ahead of them: John Abbey. His magazine *Blues and Soul* was a fortnightly bible for the fans, with details of bestselling records here and in the United States, reviews of new releases, and biographical information on the 'stars' of this underworld. In addition, John supervised labels directed at the market, Action for B&C, then Mojo for Polydor, and currently Contempo for Pye. The sales of his and other records in this field convinced IPC (publisher of *Melody Maker*, *New Musical Express*, and *Disc*) that it was worth launching a magazine, *Black Music*, for the audience, and among several in-depth pieces featured in early issues was this report on the Northern Soul scene by Tony Cummings.

THE NORTHERN DISCOS

The Northern Soul scene is an inheritance from Britain's mod era of the early and mid-1960s. The mods were the first to discover soul (or R&B as it was still called) and soon the music of new-wave black artists like the Miracles, Marvelettes, and Impressions was blasting from the allnight discotheques which began to spring up all over London's Soho. It was a heady time, when short hair was hip, clothes and dances changed literally from week to week, and energy was sustained on pills and scotch-and-coke.

British bands began to copy the music, just as they had copied the rougher sounds of Chuck, Bo, Muddy and Wolf a few years earlier. Soon clubs all over Britain were playing soul. The music of Detroit and Memphis began to hit the charts. It was the dance music of the time. A golden age. It didn't last long. Too much success, too much exposure, was killing the soul goose. By 1968 the psychedelic era had arrived and with it, new tastes in clothes, drugs and music. Many kids – including many former mods – preferred the heavier, more daring sounds of rock to the 'Gotta-gotta' predictability which much of soul had fallen into.

Within months UK clubs which had featured a soul discotheque (boosted with the occasional visit of an Edwin Starr or a Geno Washington) had been swayed by the 'soul-is-idiot-dancing-music' bile which was streaming forth from the followers of the new music. Each month saw more clubs close or move over to a progressive rock policy. By 1968 London was a soul-less wilderness save for a few clubs playing James Brown or reggae for a black/white integrated audience. The bulk of the kids who went to the clubs in the south of England wanted head-blasting rock. To Southern disco dwellers soul was passe. Their Northern cousins didn't agree.

When the 'soul boom' got under way in Britain the kids from Manchester, Stoke, Leicester and other points North who wanted a blast of the sounds at first journeyed down to the 'Smoke'. But soon they were forming their own little clubs, the Oodly Boodly (later the Night Owl) in Leicester, the Mojo in Sheffield, the Dungeon in Nottingham, and the Twisted Wheel in Manchester. And it was the latter which became the place that legends are made of. It was the club, it played the best records, had the best DJs and attracted the biggest crowds.

By 1968 the decline in the South of England soul scene was complete. Nobody told the Wheelites. A kid who journeyed there from Crewe remembered:

> Yeah, the Wheel scene was fantastic. There was an atmosphere about the place
> that was really electric. The all nighters were packed. Girls and fellows came
> from all over the North. In the early days they played all the big Motown
> things but bit by bit it kind of changed. They started playing more and more
> rare sounds. Not only records that had only been released in the States but
> sounds that hadn't sold at all there either.

The change in the record play list was significant, though it's difficult
to identify the exact reasons for obscure discs (like Chuck Woods'
'Seven Days Too Long' or Larry Williams and Johnny Watson's 'A
Quitter Never Wins') becoming such popular sounds. One reason may
have been that it had become more and more apparent that the black
American music scene had splintered into several diverse schools. Areas
like psychedelic soul or hard James Brown style funk were selling more
and more, and the careering dance beats of the old-style Motown were
no longer the staple diet of the US soul charts. The lack of appropriately stomping hits necessitated the DJs digging deeper and deeper
into the morass of discs which never made it.

Another factor must have been the kind of kids who went to the
Northern clubs and the kind of dancing they did. A fan explained:

> A lot of the kids who used to go to soul discos in London and then went on
> to rock, heavy music like, were middle class, white-collar workers and such.
> But in the North it was, still is, very much a working-class scene. We didn't
> want anything to do with progressive music so we stayed with soul. And the
> kind of soul we wanted was fast dance things. We work hard, bloody hard,
> and we want to work hard on the dance floor. The faster the better.

Fast dancing wasn't the only kind of speed on the Northern scene. With
a proliferation of allnighters there was a parallel increase in the amount
of dope taken by the minority. Said a fan at Leeds: 'The scene has
always been a pill scene. It's all uppers to make things go that much
faster. It's all a part of the soul thing.' For some it undoubtedly was. Bit
by bit the police started clamping down and by 1970 drug raids produced
a considerable trove of black bombers and hapless victims. In 1970 the
Twisted Wheel, after a couple of busts, was forced to close. A fan who'd
been dedicated to the Northern club scene for a decade reminisced:

> Something changed when the Wheel closed. You know there was never
> quite the same everything-for-the-good-of-the-music scene. We used to go
> to clubs like the Mojo (Sheffield), The Lantern (Market Harborough), Up The
> Junction (Crewe), The Blue Orchid (Derby) but the police stopped the all
> nighters there too. The pill heads were making it tough for the kids who just

wanted to hear sounds. Then the Torch (Hanley, near Stoke) became the number one scene.

But times they were a changin'. As far back as 1969 DJs like Les Cockell and Tony Jebb were playing rarities to the exclusion of hits. A record had to contain a fast, percussive dance beat but it *had* to be totally unknown. DJ Ian Levine explained:

> Each area of the North and the Midlands has, or had, one club which kids would travel long distances to come to. A club couldn't be filled just by the kids in the immediate vicinity, there weren't that many soul fans. So the disc jockeys took to playing rare records, records nobody else had. If the kids wanted to hear them, they'd have to come to the club, that was the only way.

Unfortunately it wasn't. The scourge of the bootleggers was about to see to that. But certainly club disc jockeys were taking on the role of product-hunters (the first DJs relied on super hip record collectors to discover their obscurities but now several of the top disc jockeys find their own rarities) and promotion men (acting as the initial means of exposure for obscure records). In 1970 Tami Lynn's 'I'm Gonna Run Away From You' a years-old forgotten dancer from Atlantic's archives became *the* Northern record. Polydor's Mojo label picked up on it and the record made the Top Ten – the first of many such Northern revivals to break into the pop charts.

Meanwhile, up North the sound got rarer and rarer, and DJs had to pay for the obscurity. One told me: 'If I find a top sound which nobody else has got I'll pay £10 for it. There are a couple of DJs who'll pay up to £50 but usually that's so they can pass it on to the pressers.' With the disc jockeys becoming more and more a cultural elite in their efforts to outdo each other in finding 'exclusive' records, the pirates flourished. But, hearteningly, there were and are honest attempts to service the needs of the thousands of kids who danced to the rare sounds and welcomed a chance to buy them. Specialist record shops sprang up, where DJs – and fans – could discover those rare sounds which keep the scene turning over. Most get in 'exclusives', one or two copies of rare records which they sell to disc jockeys, but some of them follow it up and find large quantities of discs which have been exposed in the clubs. But importers have found that scouring American warehouses in an effort to find a particular in-demand item is very much a hit and miss affair. So as the 1970s moved on, and the obscurity of the sounds grew, pressers exploited the situation.

The Torch finally closed down in March 1973, but its proprietor, Chris Burton, was determined to move on to bigger things. He formed the

International Soul Club (ISC) and through frequent soul nights (first at the Top Rank and now the Heavy Steam Machine – both in Hanley) plus an expanding stream of 'special presentations' where the ISC takes over a hall for a night, he has done a lot to expand the Northern scene.

But in doing so he's grown fat (metaphorically as well as physically). And despite the major influence exerted on the Northern scene by the International Soul Club (grandiosely titled, since the activities of the ISC are unknown to London soul freaks let alone American soul brothers) Burton has failed in his self-confessed aim to totally control the Northern scene. Now, with his controversial pressing activities and his exploitive attitude to the music and the kids who dig it (40p for slogan badges – 'Keep The Faith' or 'The Torch' – which cost a few pence to produce) he has simply split the scene in two. Since the rise of the ISC, alternative clubs and venues have either sprung up or built on their existing popularity. The Northern Soul Club, based in Whitchurch, has a smaller, but more dedicated following than the ISC, while Burnley fans have formed the Soul Satisfaction Society. And the Blackpool Mecca still packs in an enthusiastic crowd every week to hear Ian Levine and Colin Curtis pour forth their ultra-esoteric obscurities.

But Andy Simpson, a dedicated fan of many years, is well aware of the scene's limitations as well as its strengths:

> For some people the Northern scene is a way to make a lot of bread. For others it's a big ego trip. But for some it's a love of the music situation. There are several major things wrong with the scene. There are the three ps, pressings, pills and pop, and the media doesn't understand what we're into. They either don't know about it (despite John Peel's recent accurate observation that it's arguably the largest underground following in Britain) or they treat it in an 'idiot-music-for-idiots' way. But with all its faults the Northern disco scene is a very exciting thing.

It's also a scene in which the relationship between record maker, DJs and record buyer is quite unlike anything else in pop – a difference symbolised by the practice of bootlegging. Bootlegging a record is the ultimate rip-off. The pirate cheats everybody: the artist, the record company, the composer, the music publisher, and ultimately the buyer. So why do they flourish, and particularly, why do they flourish on the Northern scene? The answer is, the climate is right ... in fact it's perfect, a pirate's dream.

The first Northern scene pirate was a Mr Jeff King. When the Twisted Wheel was flourishing Mr King began to import the sounds being played which weren't available on British release. And, as that kind of playlist became more the order of the day, so he found that the more obscure sounds were unavailable from the US distributors and one-stops.

So he hit on the simple and rather illegal idea of bootlegging. King would buy a copy of a top sound from a DJ (being prepared to pay the earth) and simply press up hundreds of copies on his Soul Sounds label. He didn't even need a retail outlet, he'd simply fill up his car boot with armfuls of Soul Sounds copies of 'At The Discotheque' or 'What's Wrong With Me Baby' and drive down to the clubs. When the kids came out, there'd be King selling his pressings from his car.

Apart from the immorality of his action, the sound was abysmal, a hissing, crackling, recorded-in-a-cardboard-box parody of the original goodie. But the kids bought them 'cause they were the sounds they wanted. Soon the Selectadisc record shop in Nottingham, which had specialised in the soul scene and had built up a formidable stock of UK and US soul, picked up on the idea. By 1971 the Greenlight bootleg label was being blatantly sold from Selectadisc. With an organised means of retail sale, they soon outstripped Jeff King who drifted off the pressing scene.

The music industry, or more specifically the copyright world, did little or nothing to discourage the growing trade in illegally pressed records. The main reason was ignorance. Copyright organisations like BPI and the MCPS were totally unaware of what was happening away from their sheltered London world. It was only when the blatant flouting of the copyright laws occurred on a massive, overground level with the sales of bootleg Dylan and Hendrix (and soon other) rock albums that the copyright societies were able to shake off their massive lethargy and internal inefficiency and begin fighting – with successful legal actions – the British bootleggers.

But that was rock and BPI would have to have been blind to have missed it. Somehow they continued to miss Selectadisc. As the Nottingham outfit put out more and more titles, they joined up with a renegade record collector Simon Soussan who from selling rare sounds at exorbitant prices in Leeds had gone to live in Los Angeles. Pressing discs in Britain was, with a tightening up of the British record plants, somewhat difficult now, so Soussan became the man Selectadisc needed. He ran a complete service. Find a rare, danceable sound. Press up three or four white labels and send them to key Northern DJs. Wait for the demand to grow and then press up a large batch and dispatch them to Nottingham. Selectadisc had by now developed a considerable mail order trade in the discs as well as supplying several other retail outlets. They are an enterprising company, and as far as their customers are concerned, they provide a good service. They stoutly deny that their pressings are bootlegged. Our investigations suggest otherwise – but the situation is complicated by the fact that Soussan puts out many of his pressings under the Canterbury and Soul Town labels which back in the 1960s were legitimate record companies. Perhaps Soussan (as he claims) bought the right to use certain labels, but the increasingly eccentric releases on the labels bear no relation to legal issues. Another confusing area of Soussan/Selectadisc's activity is counterfeiting ('piracy' as opposed to 'bootlegging' in copyright jargon) and over the last year or so a whole heap of in-demand sounds have been available, apparently on the original US labels – muffled sound and tiny differences in the label printing indicate otherwise. But the most mind-spinning activity of Soussan has been his taking unknown records by unknown artists and issuing them as by someone else who has a more commercial name (on the Northern scene). Therefore the Milestones become Butch Baker; and the Sunlovers become Eddie Parker and the Sunlovers (despite the fact that Eddie Parker – a Detroit-based in-demander – has absolutely nothing to do with the group).

Now Soussan has pulled off a new stroke. He's got his hands on studio session tapes minus the vocal tracks from existing popular vocal discs. So a vocal-less 'The Same Old Thing' by the Olympics, or 'Personality Theme' by Jackie Lee becomes the Fred Smith Orchestra or the Mirwood Strings. And Soussan's latest list now boasts the Soul Galore Orchestra – more instrumentals of big vocal hits.

Soussan's success depends on the specialised taste of the Northern soul fan but also, ironically, on the smallness of his market – if Northern soul records were all Top Twenty hits, bigger dealers than Soussan would be in on the action. But for the most part the in records are in with a small crowd as the obscurity of the following reveals: with the help of the Northern DJs we compiled a list of the biggest 'sounds' since 1967. The information in brackets indicates how the record was finally made available – either as a British reissue, a US import or a bootleg pressing.

1967

Tony Clarke: 'The Entertainer' (Chess reissue).
A classic, lilting Chicago dancer – recently reissued again.
Bobby Sheen: 'Doctor Love' (Capitol reissue).
An insinuating beat version of an early Whispers song.
Little Hank: 'Mr Bang Bang Man' (Monument reissue).
A bluesy dance disc whisked from the obscurity of an underpromoted Sound Stage 7 release.
Shirley Ellis: 'Soul Time' (CBS reissue).
The rather bland-voiced Miss Ellis pounded this piece of Motownesque into every dancer's brain.
Major Lance: 'Ain't No Soul Left In These Old Shoes' (Okeh import).
THE 'Okeh beat' record, a furious stomp of the Ronnie Milsap song.

1968
Chubby Checker: 'At The Discotheque' (Soul Sounds bootleg).
When Chubby stopped twisting, he tried a taste of the Motown beat.
Poets: 'She Blew A Good Thing' (United Artists reissue).
A floating, dancing goodie, a US success for Sue Records.
Flamingoes: 'The Boogaloo Party' (Phillips reissue).
An inane, mechanical stomper by a much loved group.
Contours: 'A Little Misunderstanding' (Tamla Motown reissue).
Even by 1968, Motown was a little too popular for Northerners. This stomper was obscure enough though.
Bobby Freeman: 'C'mon and Swim' (Autumn import).
Produced by Sly Stone. An old-fashioned rave-up.

1969
Invitations: 'What's Wrong With Me Baby?'(Soul Sounds bootleg).
A catchy, sing-a-longer from the Dyno Voice catalogue.
Tami Lynn: 'I'm Gonna Run Away From You' (Mojo reissue).
Started off as a years-old Atlantic obscurity, ended in the Top Twenty.
Tams: 'Hey Girl Don't Bother Me' (Probe reissue).
It took more than a year of Northern Soul exposure before EMI got hip enough to push this out; seven years after its original minor US success, it made number one in Britain.
Earl Van Dyke: 'Six By Six' Tamla Motown reissue).
An immensely popular, pulsating organ instrumental.
O'Jays: 'I Dig Your Act' (Bell reissue).
By the group's standards, a dull stylised record. But a big Northern sound.

1970
Alexander Patton: 'A Little Lovin' Sometimes' (Soul Sounds bootleg).
Despite the Soul Sounds bootleg, Selecta came up with hundreds of 'Capitol' copies with Patton's name spelt wrongly on the label.
Leon Haywood: 'Baby Reconsider' (Soul Sounds bootleg).
Pretty dull, despite its superfast beat.
Bob Bradey and the Conchords: 'More More More Of Your Love' (Chariot import).
An old Miracles song, sung by a clever Smokey impersonator.
Bob Wilson and the San Remo Quartet: 'All Turned On' (Tamla Motown reissue).
Boring Detroit instrumental and the start of an instrumental backing track Northern craze.
Ad Libs: 'Nothing Worse Than Being Alone' (Share import).
An infectious piece of Van McCoy.

1971
Prophets: 'I Got The Fever' (Smash import).
Blue-eyed soul, by team who became the Georgia Prophets.
Sandi Sheldon: 'You're Gonna Make Me Love You' (Okeh import).
Another Van McCoy dancer which was never off the turntables.
Richard Temple: 'That Beating Rhythm' (Jayboy reissue).
Fred Smith's 'Mirwood Beat' became a cult. The backing track (Jimmy
Conwell's 'Cigarette Ashes') was also big.
Bobby Hebb: 'Love Love Love' (Phillips reissue).
Sing along popsouler which eventually 'broke pop'.
Hoagy Lands: 'The Next In Line' (Laurie import).
A Sam Cookish dancer that had sold about three copies for Stateside.

1972
Sam and Kitty: 'I've Got Something Good' (Four Brothers counterfeit).
A repetitive, boring and obscure Chicago dancer.
Chubby Checker: 'You Just Don't Know (What You Do To Me)' (Out Of The
Past bootleg).
Another uptempo Philly/Motown fusion.
Lenis Guess: 'Just Ask Me' (bootleg and SPQR counterfeit).
A British cover by Etta Thomas is currently trying to catch the overground
disco sales.
Soul Twins: 'Quick Change Artist' (Karen counterfeit).
Underrecorded, Sam and Dave style vocal, Mike Terry production.
Archie Bell And The Drells: 'Here I Go Again' (Atlantic issue).
Atlantic quickly got hip to the disco spins and put it in the UK charts.

1973
Tony Clarke: 'Landslide' (Chess reissue).
Recently put out. The late Mr Clarke's memory lives on.
Damita Jo: 'I'll Save The Last Dance For You' (Ranwood import).
Re-recording of her old answer-to the-Drifters Mercury hit.
Tempos: 'Count Down Here I Come' (Canterbury bootleg).
Better known as the Younghearts, an infectious dancer.
Gems: 'I'll Be There' (Tru-Glo-Town bootleg).
Very, very fast girlie group. Put out in the States by Riverside.
Invitations: 'Skiing In The Snow' (Out Of The Past bootleg).
ISC's biggest seller, wonder if the group will ever know?

1974
Joe Hicks: 'Don't It Make You Feel Funky' (AGC).
Salvadores: 'Stick By Me Baby' (Wise World).

Watts 103rd Street Rhythm Band: 'The Joker' (Warner Bros).
Maurice Chestnut: 'Too Darn Soulful' (Amy).
Louise Lewis: 'Wee Ooo I'll Let It Be You Babe' (Skyway).
All ready to break overground. But will it be by legal or illegal means?

Tony Cummings

POP DISCOS

It's important to stress how small the Northern scene is (of its 40 biggest
sounds over the last seven years only three – those of Tami Lynn, the
Tams, and Archie Bell and the Drells – could be said to have made any
national impact) because every record which reaches the hit parade
without radio play is explained by reference to the power of the Northern
discos. The truth is that this power is limited; what Northern success may
do is convince a watchful record company that a single is worth trying
nationally, but it is the pop discos that will then make or break it – the
Coventry Mecca is more important than the Blackpool Mecca for the
commercial exploitation of discotheques that can create a chart hit.

The disco hit of 1974 was R. Dean Taylor's 'There's A Ghost In My
House' and its road to the top was long and winding. A staff producer
and writer at Motown, Taylor made occasional records as a singer in
the late 1960s and had two hits in the UK ('Gotta See Jane' and 'Indiana
Wants Me'). But he eventually decided that he wasn't getting as much
attention from the company as his black colleagues, and he left in
1972 to try his luck on another label. Meanwhile the English Motown
organisation had discovered the potency of their 1960s sound in the
North and had responded in two ways: first, they began to issue a series
of album anthologies of 'disco classics' – old tracks that were good
enough to dance to and obscure enough to satisfy Northern cultishness;
second, they employed a string of 'reporters' in the biggest discos, to
return a card each week indicating which Motown records (old or new)
were proving particularly popular. Early in 1974 Taylor's 'Ghost' was
issued on a budget compilation of his Motown recordings, and the cards
began to come in reporting its special popularity. Motown decided to
risk it on a wider audience and issued it as a single.

The point of Motown's subsequent promotion was to break 'Ghost'
as a national dancing record and they concentrated their efforts on discos
– not just the Northern ones which were playing the record already,
but the major dance halls around the country (mostly the Mecca chain),
sending the DJs the record, telling them that it was already a Northern

smash. The only radio station to get the full hype treatment was Manchester's Radio Piccadilly (on which Andy Peebles has an influential and broad-minded soul show for three hours on Friday evenings) and when the record first arrived on the national charts most BBC producers had not even heard of it. Their immediate response was to call up the British Market Research Bureau (BMRB) (who supply the chart) to check that everything was, uh, in order – was this unknown record for real? Were its sales genuine? The BMRB had triple checked already, equally taken by surprise – their sampling method (a careful geographical distribution of the shops whose sale figures they use) makes it virtually impossible for a local hit (even if the locality is as big as 'the North') to show on the BBC chart. But 'Ghost' had been selling nationally and by the time the BBC belatedly finished giving it their treatment (Noel Edmonds' record of the week, etc.) it was number one.

'Ghost' reached the public through three sorts of disc jockey: the Northern soulmen revealed its sales potential; the BBC jocks confirmed and enhanced its success; but it was the journeymen in the middle, the hundreds of commercial DJs with their mobiles and residencies up and down the country who really brought the sound to the people who bought it. Chris Bond, for example, one of Coventry's most successful DJs, plays records to a thousand people seven nights a week and must, in the course of this, reach a good proportion of Cov's single buyers – he covers teenagers at the Locarno, their older brothers and sisters in Mr Georges, and the young execs of the Villa Country Club.

Chris started playing records as a 16-year-old in 1968, saving up to buy some cheap secondhand equipment, playing the current and immediate past Top Twenty to whatever youth clubs would give him a couple of quid. This is the apprenticeship all DJs must go through, not just learning a mike manner but, more importantly, discovering disco taste – what to leave out of the Top Twenty, which oldies go down well, which new releases will be appreciated, how to balance the obscure and the familiar. By 1971 Chris had learned enough to be employed professionally by an agency, holding down spots around the West Midlands – Stratford on Friday, Smethwick on Saturday, Warwick on Sunday .... Stage Two of the DJ career and the lesson to be learned now was how to match an evening to an audience, how to vary a choice of records to suit different places and ages and styles. Chris extended his range even further by spending a year on the Continent (where DJs don't speak but English ones are in demand as they are chic) and learning the disco possibilities of heavy metal (Led Zeppelin make music which the Swiss like to dance to) and nonpop soul.

By August 1973 he was a full-time professional DJ, with residencies seven evenings a week, a wide range of experience and an expandingly comprehensive record collection. What most impressed record companies though (and guaranteed Chris a place on most of their mailing lists) was the number of people he played to, his selling power. (Bell, ever efficient, sends down spies to check he's still got the audience he claims.) This is not quite how Chris sees himself. He is an entertainer, putting on a show, and it's for the show that his records are selected. His audience want to dance (and sometimes smooch), they want to be surprised (by something new) and confirmed (by traditional favourites), they want to remember the past (oldies), and bask in the present (current hits); a DJ must put on a balanced show and the balance means different records for different audiences. Chris listens open-eared to every single he's sent but he'll only play it if it's right for his show.

Discos are vital for selling disco records (whether Gary Glitter or the Philly Sound) but they can't make any difference to the wrong sort of sound. The importance of a DJ like Chris Bond is that he's better able than most record company people to judge what is a 'disco record' (his livelihood depends on this) and intelligent promo departments treat him with respect and care (Phonogram, for example, regularly use their DJ letter to knock their own company's non-disco product – promising, one week, a Don Covay LP as a reward for breaking a single and threatening a Lena Zavaroni LP as a punishment for failure).

Compared with the Luxembourg DJs in the 1950s or the pirate/Radio One DJs in the 1960s, a 1970s disco DJ is knowledgeable about music and genuinely enthusiastic. His special concern is soul music, the source of most of the best dancing records. So another Coventry DJ, Pete Waterman, runs an excellent soul record shop where he and Chris Bond keep a permanently sharp ear open for soul album tracks or American imports with which to spice their acts. George McCrae's 'Rock Your Baby', for example, was a regular sound in the Coventry Locarno (and probably elsewhere) as soon as it was released in America and weeks before it was released in England. He won't play anything 'obscure' though, Chris Bond.

Monday night at the Coventry Locarno is teenage night and an ageing voyeur is made to feel clumsy. Dancing for these cool kids is in lines and there are precisely choreographed steps for each different record. A lot of chatting up is going on but not much pairing off and the clothes are slightly pre-rock 'n' roll (pony-tails are almost back). For a night like this Chris doesn't use more than 30 records, all played at maximum volume, highest energy. On the radio there's not much in common between the fake exuberance of the Rubettes and the elegant beat of the O'Jays; but here they are equal in their mastery of and mastery by dancing feet. The few oldies played are disco classics – 'Jimmy Mack' and 'Jungle Boogie' and 'Funky Nassau' and there's a smattering of reggae for the smattering of West Indian kids doing the splits (is that doing reggae in your jeggae?). There were two records I hadn't heard before – the Peppers' 'Pepperbox' and Al Brown's very fine 'Here I Am' – and the evening's newie was the Chi-Lites' 'I've Got Sunshine', at that time a track off an American LP. The evening's biggest surprise was discovering how much sense Grand Funk's lumbering 'Locomotion' made on the dance floor.

Except for some of the black records, though, the evening's music at the Mecca wasn't that much different from what you hear on Radio One – just confined to a dancing beat. The difference between Chris Bond's show and, say, Dave Lee Travis' is less one of tastes or values than of purpose – a disco has got a different use than a tranny. Chris wouldn't want to work on a radio station because he values his independence but he doesn't see that such a change would make a huge musical difference and certainly, from the other side, BBC DJs do a lot of work in discos. DLT and Stuart Henry are on the road more often than in the studio; the Rosko show is simply a broadcast of his live spectacular (only the go-go girls are missing), Noel Edmonds has a franchised mobile disco. Only the old men of the Beeb, Tony Blackburn and David Hamilton, confine their public appearances to supermarkets and pantos. There is a difference in what radio DJs do with records but this reflects not so much their own interests as the peculiar institution within which they are confined.

THE BBC

The basic constraint on the BBC is, paradoxically, the sheer size of its potential audience. There's hardly anyone in Britain who can't listen to the radio and as a public service the BBC is obliged to consider the needs and interests of all this population. (And so the Beeb's Audience Research department calculates audiences as percentages of possible listeners – everyone in transmitter range except the under-fives and over-80s!) Since 1967, Radio One has been confined to providing a pop service, but even that is aimed at a vast and varied market, and this affects what comes out in two ways: first, the BBC is obsessed with audience size and shape and satisfaction, and carries out endless research to discover who is listening to what and when and why. Secondly, the corporation can't escape consciousness of its responsibilities – its programmes are the product of an elaborate and cautious bureaucracy; there must be no scandal or uncertainty or offence. Underlying Radio One's use of records is an old slogan: Giving The Public What It Wants.

The public is divided into three parts – weekday daytime, weekday evening, and weekend – and the most important of these is the weekday daytime. The daily strip shows (Noel Edmonds, Tony Blackburn, Johnny Walker, and David Hamilton) are the core of the BBC's presentation of pop. Originally it was the responsibility of the producer of each show to put together an appropriate programme. There were constraints (needle time, the disapproval of the next man up the BBC hierarchy), but basically a producer could choose his own music. This system had to be dropped when it was discovered that some popular (i.e. best selling) records were never getting chosen. The charts are one of the best indicators of what the pop public do want and if Radio One was ignoring them then clearly the BBC was not fulfilling its obligations. Hence the playlist.

Playlist broadcasting originated on commercial AM radio in the States; the station manager would draw up a list of records, all the DJs would be required to play only records on the list. In 1973 the BBC began to organise Radio One in the same way. Each week the four producers of the daily strip shows meet to put together a list of 56 records – a playlist for them all. Add one oldie of the week (to be played in every programme every day) and a record of the week for each DJ and you get the 61 singles which take up about two-thirds of the 50 hours a week of daytime Radio One.

The remaining time is taken up with album tracks, oldies, and new releases. The album tracks and oldies are still chosen by the producers individually and are mostly used for audience participation – the various DJs all have spots for requests. New releases are used as a way of extending needle time. Playing a record for review purposes (which means both commenting on it and giving listeners the details of its catalogue number) exempts it from the needle-time statistics and at one time Radio One had a daily hour of What's New. This was unsatisfactory for both the BBC (who were stuck with a programme that was frequently lifeless) and the record companies (who didn't enjoy hearing their records being slagged off) and a new deal was made. The hour of new records would be spread through the strip shows in the form of new spins and the DJs wouldn't comment on them though they would still name their labels. There are now four or five new spins in every show and one of the four daily producers is responsible for selecting and placing all of them.

The needle-time agreement obliges the BBC to broadcast a proportion of its music in the form of specially recorded tapes but this makes hardly any difference to the playlist policy. For a start the tapes are used unevenly. Audience research shows that Radio One has its biggest audience at breakfast time and slowly loses listeners all day. Tapes are deployed accordingly: Noel Edmonds plays only records; David Hamilton plays hardly any apart from new spins. Virtually all the tapes are of groups and records that are on the playlist anyway and, as the BBC's studio facilities have improved, mostly you don't know you're not listening to the record. The only draw-backs of the tape system are that it benefits British groups at the expense of American ones (though visitors get very favourable treatment) and that it involves the use of a tape five days running, which limits the extent David Hamilton's show can vary from day to day.

The most startling thing about the way Radio One works is the insignificance of the DJs. They have nothing to do with the playlist and not much to do with the album tracks, oldies or even records of the week – the producers don't think they are of much help: 'Except for Johnny Walker, they're too busy opening shops and judging models to know anything about pop trends or tastes.' The BBC DJ's role is independent of the music he plays; he must have an appealing and individual personality and sell that to the listener. The format of all the strip shows is the same; in each half-hour unit there are two chart records and two others from the playlist, a new spin, an oldie, and an album track. What varies is the packaging, the DJ's spots and quirks. The idea is that Tony Blackburn and David Hamilton could play exactly the same records in exactly the same order and still have completely different shows.

For Radio One, as for disco DJs, playing records is just a means to the end of entertaining the public and both claim that it's their respective publics (which for Radio One vary from schoolkids to housewives to workers according to the time of day) who determine which records are played. But whereas a disco DJ has a clear idea of what his audiences want (to dance) and is in direct communication with them, can watch their reaction to his choices, the producers who compile the Radio One playlist are working with an imprecise notion of what pop radio is for, and know their audience and its reactions only secondhand.

Their surest measure is the charts and these are the basis of the playlist. Every Saturday the chosen dealers return their week's sales figures to BMRB; on Monday these are fed into a computer and on Tuesday morning the chart arrives at the BBC. The producers' meeting is straight-away – by Tuesday evening they have compiled the playlist that will determine their programmes from the following Monday (i.e. almost two weeks after the popularity of the records it includes was demonstrated). Their first rule of thumb is that every climber on the chart (they work with the Top Fifty) will be on the list, and that every record that has dropped out of the Top Twenty won't be. Falling records in the Top Twenty are treated on their merits – how fast are they falling? How long have they been on the playlist? Gutted this way the charts yield 30–35 of the records on the playlist, and there'll also be five or six new releases a week which are chart certainties – new records from big stars, follow-ups to big hits.

This leaves 15–20 records on the playlist with uncertain popularity – the producers have to use other criteria of 'good programme material'. These are rarely explicit; producers talk mysteriously of 'other indicators of public taste besides sales', and claim obligations to both record makers and listeners. They listen to every new single they get, and treat them sympathetically: four or five of each week's risk records are new releases and once on the playlist a record is usually given a chance to prove itself, being played for anything up to seven weeks even if not a hit. But at the same time the playlist won't include records that it's thought the public doesn't want ('we can't really play that to housewives') and this judgement tends to be narrow, and patronising – only in the evenings and at weekends will the BBC admit to an 'up market' for pop. Demographically they may be right, the bulk of the daily audience is housewives and children rather than students or rock fans; what's offensive is the contemptuous certainty with which this audience is satisfied.

The BBC can only be so certain because their argument is circular. A record on the playlist has a good chance of being a hit, a single not on it has hardly a hope. These results appear to confirm the producers' judgements, but they are equally a consequence of them. BBC people refer to a record which gets *Top Of The Pops* exposure but doesn't make the Top Fifty as a 'dog record' – it must be exceptionally unappealing to gain nothing from the industry's best promotional spot; but it's just as unusual for a record to get full Radio One treatment and flop and even more unusual for a record to get no Radio One play and make it. There are some alternative means of national promotion – films 'The Entertainer', TV 'She', the astute use of discos 'There's A Ghost In My House' – but these are so rare that Radio One is basically indispensable. Commercial stations are restricted to their areas so that, for example, while the BBC admit that Capital Radio was responsible for Prelude's 'After the Goldrush' being released as a single, they're still sure it only became a hit after they started playing it.

Radio One knows its importance for the record business and doesn't wear its responsibilities lightly. One reason for its elaborate organisation is to minimise the possibilities of payola, and while the BBC has 'good relations' with record companies (they're all part of the showbiz family), the business's direct salesmen, the pluggers, don't get much joy. The BBC isn't Luxembourg; there's no money to be made from playing a record or seeing it sell (unless it's on the BBC label, of course, and that's another story). But though the BBC's honour is intact, its account of its role in pop – as a sort of honest broker, benevolently selecting from the mass of weekly releases just those records its audience wants to hear – is ingenuous.

The Radio One DJs and producers may not be there to be bought, but they are involved in selling and record companies know it. The BBC moulds as well as responds to public taste, and record companies respond to as well as mould the playlist. Either way the effect on English pop is deadening. The no-risk policy, the firm control of every sound, means that the listener is rarely stimulated and that record companies can work out what is a 'BBC record'. The latter effect is the more dire. Given the pop that's available, the BBC doesn't do a bad job with Radio One (at least in terms of record selection – presentation is something else). The problem is its influence on what pop is available; the more cautious the BBC, the more predictable is the average British pop song, as record companies try to ensure their best access to the public. It was for this reason that the pirate radio stations, despite their own problems, were necessary for the creativity of British pop in 1964–67. Can commercial radio, the new rival to the BBC, make a similar impact?

CAPITAL RADIO

Capital Radio is the most significant alternative to Radio One because of its audience size (much greater than for its fellows in Birmingham, Manchester and Glasgow), its impact on the pop world (which is almost entirely based in London), and its brief as a music station (the rest of local radio, BBC and commercial, has to provide the whole range of broadcasting in a single station). It is worth studying Capital, then, as an example of how non-BBC pop radio can be organised.

Some of its attitudes are just the same (Aidan Day, the musical director, is an ex-BBC producer): the audience is similarly divided into weekday, evening, and weekend parts; needle time (nine hours a day out of 24) is concentrated on the daytime shows, tapes are only used as evening starts; programmes are adjusted as the day progresses – housewives come into their own at 9.00 a.m., students at 6.30 p.m.; there is a playlist. This is put together by Day alone, who selects 40 records a week, six climbers (new releases) and a few instrumentals and album tracks for occasional variation. The justification for the smallness of the list is that few people listen to the radio continuously; they mostly listen in a series of segments – while making the beds, or driving to work, or having a tea break. Day programmes his playlist accordingly, using the American AM 'Carousel system' to arrange the records in a repeated but varied pattern from 6.30 a.m. to 6.30 p.m. Nicky Horne (coming on at 6.30 p.m.) chooses his own tracks but Day keeps an eye on his plans and may advise him against too way-out music too early in the evening.

The object of the playlist is to achieve the 'overall sound' that Day believes will appeal to his audience. It is not clear how he comes to this belief. The Capital chart is no help; it is compiled by Day not on the basis of London's sales figures but as the chart that 'feels' right, that the audience 'seems to want'. Capital doesn't have to be comprehensive, it is confined to London listeners and can concentrate on the 'sophisticated pop audience of 15–40' as a potentially attractive market for advertisers. What this audience wants is not just guessed; Capital have done their research. So the music is adjusted to suit the different audiences that are dominant at different times of day; and when, after a few months on the air, it was discovered that the audience hadn't grown as planned there was 'a slight redirection' in music policy – Day decided he'd been too sophisticated too soon, had tried to change radio habits too suddenly. Previously sneered at pop hits were slipped into the schedules.

In musical terms Capital has two special characteristics: first, by having a small playlist it does avoid the more mindless and middle-of-the-road chart sounds – Capital housewives aren't as musically moronic as BBC housewives – but this defiance of chart values depends on good audience figures; Capital's policy has changed once and it could change again. But Capital's playlist is also much quicker on the ball than the BBC's – playing eventual hits much earlier. Aidan Day sees this as an indication of Capital's power to break records, arguing that 40 per cent of singles sales are in London and that, at the least, Capital gives the BBC an idea of what to play. But I think that what Day's playlist really reveals is his flexibility: he's not confined by a chart that's already more than a week out of date, he can back his hunches immediately (no committee to argue with), his pursuit of the sophisticated audience is an incentive to risk-taking. The only direct influence on Day's decisions comes from the DJs – they have an open meeting weekly and there is no evidence that record companies have any more power here than in Broadcasting House. Capital music is kept carefully separate from record commercials and Day treats pluggers in his best BBC manner – they are useful messengers but should be neither seen nor heard by programme planners.

In short snatches Capital is a more enjoyable pop station than Radio One. The commercials are less irritating than the banalities of Blackburn et al. and the music's better – less rubbish, more oddities. For longer or repeated listening, though, the short playlist is wearing – Top Forty radio only makes sense if you've got lots of buttons to push. On the other hand, Capital has established a distinctive feel. Maria Muldaur's 'Midnight at the Oasis' and Lynsey de Paul's 'Ooh Ooh Baby' were played on both Capital and Radio One but Maria's is a Capital record, Lynsey's a BBC one. It is this difference that could prove important for British pop – what matters is not that one station is better than the other but that they provide space for different sorts of music. How records reach the public isn't going to change much, but the range of choice might.

POSTSCRIPT

This account was written in June 1974; six months later and there have been some changes I should mention, though I don't think they affect the substance of my arguments. 1974 was a year of boom for soul music and of financial crisis for everyone else. The soul boom meant that the Northern Scene became increasingly important in record companies' attempts to keep up with public taste – this not only meant new labels and new promotion techniques (e.g. Pye's Disco Demand label) but also subjected the Northern discos to a new sort of commercial attack.

Meanwhile the financial crisis bit particularly hard on radio stations – both the BBC and Capital have had to reorganise their pop broadcasting to save money, although in practice their playlist and daytime policies have remained the same. As broadcasters' ambitions (and imaginations) are thwarted by economics it is not surprising that discos become an increasingly important alternative way of playing records.

(1975)

AFTERWORD

Twenty years on and the territory this article maps is still all too recognisable, despite the growth of 'specialist' commercial music radio stations and the emergence of exclusive club/rave culture. I'm interested that pirate radio didn't seem worth mentioning in the mid-1970s (and I certainly had no notion that classical music would become a kind of pop) but I doubt that anyone I talked to then would feel any differently about their job now.

Simon Frith

Back in 1973 I was able to document the birth of Northern Soul. What I never for one moment imagined was that 20 years on the Northern

Soul cultural phenomenon would still be with us. The back pages of *Echoes* and *Blues And Soul* still announce Northern Soul nights and all-dayers; specialist mail order companies are still toting Northern Soul 'classics', record companies like Kent and Ace release streams of compilation albums; and a new wave of DJs have emerged to 'keep the faith' and play dance music light years away from the house and techno of today's clubland. Maybe Northern Soul will never again spill into the pop overground. But it refuses to die.

For me, though, Northern Soul's most extraordinary and unexpected development has been the rise of record producer Ian Levine. Back in 1973 he was the top Northern Soul DJ whose residency in the Blackpool Mecca's Highland Room with his legendary 10,000 plus record collection made him *the* mover and shaker in Northern Soul. Over the years Ian moved on to become a highly successful record producer, starting with Northern Soul re-creations with artists like the Exciters and Elaine Thomas to eventually become the original producer for 1990's teen dance megastars Take That and East 17. Now *that's* another dizzyingly unlikely pop history saga waiting to be told!

Tony Cummings

5

The Philly Groove

Pete Wingfield

On a balmy night in the late summer of 1967, while the world was wearing flowers in its hair, I was sinking into my seat, trying to look inconspicuous amid hordes of black schoolkids and young mums in the middle of the stalls at the Uptown theatre, Philadelphia, Pa., two hours from the Big Apple by the mighty Greyhound. Philly, Doo Wop City; and the four young guys slithered around the stage, processes glistening as bright as their patent leathers, wearing orange suits with navel-length jackets and tapered bottoms so super-thin that, embarrassingly, their underwear showed through and ominous dark patches were appearing in the armpit region. They were direct descendants of those early, unwitting a capella pioneers, and were second on the bill (the Tempts were on top), riding high on a national hit with 'Cowboys To Girls' – I think – and they were singing it unerringly at the Uptown five times a day, seven days a week. The group was called the Intruders.

In winter of 1972, the wheel has turned full circle. The Intruders have created another monster, 'She's a Winner', and it's on the same label, Gamble. Both songs, and all the hits in between, were produced and composed by two men, Kenny Gamble and Leon Huff, at one studio, Sigma Sound, 212 N.12th St. Now, some 40 million singles since they kicked off together, the duo and their associates have made the city of Brotherly Love shine stronger than ever before on the musical map.

Not that it's ever been exactly dim. In 1956, local entrepreneur Dick Clark started a lip-sync TV show, soon networked through ABC, which enjoyed a heyday in the late 1950s/early 1960s, allowing Philly talent a golden opportunity for nationwide exposure, offering Dick Clark a golden opportunity for managers' backhanders, and ensuring that the city was always represented in force on the Hot 100 – at least until the English takeover in 1964–65. (Amazingly, 'American Bandstand' survives to this day.) The situation spawned outfits like Bob Marcucci's dreaded Chancellor Records, happily inflicting handsome non-talents like Fabian and Frankie Avalon on an eager public; such influential DJs as Jerry Blavat 'the geator with the heater', and Georgie Woods, 'the guy with the goods'; and the vastly successful Cameo-Parkway label, home of the dance crazes, whose boss Bernie Lowe gave us Ernest Jenkins, alias Chubby Checker (did he really marry a Miss World?), the Orlons ('South Street', 'Don't Hang Up'), the Dovells ('Bristol Stomp'), Bobby Rydell ('We Got Love', 'Wild One'), all of whom had some measure of chart action in the UK, and Dee Dee Sharp ('Mashed Potato Time', 'Gravy').

Dee Dee, born Dionne LaRue, is Mrs Kenny Gamble now; he'd written and produced a song or two for her on Cameo in 1960. Leon Huff, a pianist from across the bridge in Camden, New Jersey, with work for Quincy Jones in NY and a one-off national hit by hometown group 'Patti and the Emblems' under his belt, met Gamble, from South Philly, when the latter was working on and off for renowned shrewd operator Jerry Ross (recently of Bill Deal and the Rhondells fame). Pooling their experience and hope, Gamble and Huff set about going for themselves. Kenny had already laid a foundation for success to come by forming a group, Kenny and the Romeos; himself on vocals, Roland Chambers, from Marvin Gaye's band, on guitar, session organist Thom Bell, and Earl Young, who'd played drums for Stevie Wonder. It's these very guys that now form the backbone of the city's music industry, for they and a few others take care of the vital rhythm track on virtually every Philly-made hit.

The Intruders (naturally!) sang on the first independent Gamble–Huff creation, 'Gonna Be Strong' on Excel, but the G–H sound really dates from their second, the same group's 'United', Gamble Records' initial release. It was a respectable hit – even came out here, on London – with a trendsetting production, unusual for its time, employing swirling strings, cascading harps and, above all, vibes. As bells are to Spector, so are vibes (usually handled by one Vince Montana) to Gamble and Huff. Since then, the sound has been polished to a fine art, but the seeds were right there in 'United'. Later, less successful singles bore no resemblance to all this – the Madmen (Gamble 212) made an obscure goodie with lunatic sax on 'African Twist', and Bobby Marchan, of all people, lead singer on the classic Huey Smith New Orleans rockers did a comical funky rap about make-up – 'Ain't No Reason For Girls to be Lonely' (Gamble 216); but G–H's trump card lay with the Intruders' trite but endearing odes to city teenery: 'Me Tarzan, You Jane' … 'Love Is Like a Baseball Game' … 'Who's Your Favourite Candidate'. The titles speak for themselves.

As well as taking care of Gamble Records, the duo was working on a production company basis for major labels. Atlantic, hot with a master from Houston by Archie Bell and the Drells, forestalled the group's certain destiny as one-hit wonders by handing them over to Gamble and Huff, who obliged with a near-unbroken string of hits over the 1967–69 period (one of their oldies is, even as I write, in the British Top Twenty!); and Mercury got two-and-a-half albums' worth from G–H's collaboration with 'the Iceman', Jerry Butler: gems like 'Only the Strong Survive', 'Never Give You Up', and 'Brand New Me', just kept on a-coming, till Gamble and Huff got to carping over royalty percentages.

For many, the Butler material marks a creative peak in G–H's output thus far. Floundering after the demise of his previous label, Vee-Jay, and sliding reluctantly into a second-rate supper-club act, Jerry found the ideal complement for his relaxed vocals in the duo's sparkling production, and the sophisticated yet hip arrangements furnished by regulars Bobby Martin and Thom Bell. Such was the success of the team who, like Motown, relied on staff writers for strong original material, that a set of sessions at Sigma Sound became a kind of refresher course for artists in a musical or commercial rut. Atlantic sent Wilson Pickett (whose first G–H single, 'Don't Let the Green Grass Fool You', earned his first certified gold disc), the Sweet Inspirations, even Dusty Springfield. With the Intruders and Gamble Records temporarily quiet in 1969, G–H launched a new logo, Neptune, distributed through Chess and the GRT corporation, which before collapsing the following year put out some great sides by Sigler, the Vibrations, and the oft-recorded O'Jays – as well as a couple of killers by the late Linda Jones with George Kerr producing.

Annoyed at Neptune's relative failure, and sure that the music was all there in the grooves, Gamble and Huff started yet another company, Philadelphia International, this time through CBS/Columbia, which, with good distribution, scored straight off with the Ebonys' 'You're the Reason Why' and hasn't looked back since. The past year has brought two-million-sellers 'Back Stabbers', from the O'Jays, returning to the G–H fold, and Harold Melvin and the Bluenotes' 'I Miss You'.

So what's the secret? After all, Sigma Sound has no special assets. The sleeve notes to the Neptune LP *O'Jays In Philadelphia* describe it as 'unhip-looking' and the horns and strings are invariably local union dads. No, it's the rhythm section – the erstwhile Romeos, plus Ronnie Baker on bass, Leon Huff himself on piano, additional guitarists Bobby Eli and Norman Harris, and sometimes Len Pakula on organ, that have the magic musically. Earl Young, for instance, will often lay off everything but hi-hat pedal and bass-drum till the first 'hook' chorus, say a third of the way through a track, giving it a characteristic lift when he finally bursts in. Huff has an interesting percussive style with a tasty line in boogie left hand (check out the O'Jays' 'Looky Looky'). Roland Chambers, if indeed it is him, leans on light, octave-based, Wes Montgomery-esque lines to convey an impression of effortless swing. Meanwhile back in the control room, Kenny G. and engineer Joe Tarsia put their individual

Thom Bell

touch on what's coming through the monitors: punchy horns against smooth strings, imaginative percussion – claves, woodblocks, etc. – to beef things up, and that great drum sound, copiously spiced with echo. (And hell, a good gimmick always comes in useful – like the traffic noises that herald the Soul Survivors' 'Expressway to Your Heart', or the race track effects at the start of the new Intruders', 'She's a Winner'.) What comes out of all this is an airy, bouncy kind of a sound; tight, but not in the sense of clean and compact, as one might apply the word to Southern funk from Memphis or Muscle Shoals. And, like Motown again, custom-made for car radios.

Way down the bill that night in 1967 at the Uptown was a local trio, lisping slightly and resplendent in rose pink, the high-voiced lead singer mildly camping it up, to the audience's delight. By a year after that show, the Delfonics were Philly's hottest act. This was largely thanks to one man – the composer, arranger and producer for the group, Thom (Tommy) Bell, the third of the mighty triumvirate that now rules Philadelphia. While still working often for G–H and associates as arranger (he did those absurd 'Back Stabbers' charts), Bell created his own label, Philly Groove, distributed (confusingly) through Bell Records, exclusively for the Delfonics, notching up a run of hits that only stopped a few months ago when the group split with him, lamely carrying on under his partner, manager Stan Watson. Thom's songs are intricate and satisfying. He often will plant rich, moody intros, only to change to a different key and tempo when the song comes in; or lay out the verse in an unrelated key to the chorus. 'I'm Sorry', 'Break Your Promise', 'Ready Or Not, Here I Come', 'You Get Yours and I'll Get Mine', and for my money the best record of its type ever to emerge from Philly – the cataclysmic 'Didn't I Blow Your Mind This Time'. Every one was a short but grandiose epic, hugely commercial but at the same time ambitious and unarguably solid in musical conception. William Hart, lead singer with the group, would come up with the lyrics. Slight and unimportant in themselves, it was the soulful whine he delivered them in that mattered. But Thom Bell took care of biz on everything else: panoramic arrangements leaning heavily on instruments traditionally not used in R&B, like shimmering cellos and Wagnerian French horns. A lost LP track – 'How Could You' on the *Didn't I* album – is surely one of T.B.'s great moments. Beautiful, spine-tingling self-indulgence as a series of changes is repeated hypnotically, with increasing intensity, for five minutes, electric sitar in the lead over a hefty backbeat, with the voices coming in, softly, in the fourth minute. In 1971, on the Delfonics' departure, Thom Bell didn't blink an eyelid. Guided by Hugo and Luigi's Avco Records to a local Philly group, the Stylistics, just off a minor hit on a small label with 'You're a Big Girl Now', he moved to even greater heights both artistically and in terms of success proportionate to product, for the Stylistics' album yielded no less than four single gold records. It was the Delfonics revisited, and more. Russell Thompkins Jr, lead singer, has perhaps an even finer falsetto than Hart (this time out one Linda Creed does the words); he explained to me on a recent UK visit that Thom Bell goes through each song round a piano with the group, sketching out harmonics and topline, cuts a basic track with rhythm section, brings the group into the studio briefly for a few hours to add the vocal, then gets to work himself on the 'sweetening'. Next thing the Stylistics themselves know, the record is out! One could well criticise such a process on grounds of 'conveyor-belt soul'. But Lord, I'm not about to complain when the end result is so exquisite.

Bell's work on his own songs has the edge for me over the Gamble–Huff stuff. He goes for a different sound. Though using the same musicians, studio and engineer, he somehow contrives to make the final mix more integrated, with less sense of overdubbing and a greater corporate identity. He's as capable at the board as with the baton, churning out ingenious, even moving arrangements that are creamy but never sickly.

Totally committed until recently to the fly-by-night three-minute single, designed for saturation AM airplay and swift obscurity, men like Gamble, Huff and Bell have turned handicap to advantage by making almost every master a complete, concise statement in itself. But up to the last few months G–H and cohorts remained to the rock consumer remote, unfashionable figures. Happily, though, all three men are riding their current crest of a wave on singles without compromise. Bell's output with the Stylistics (he's also started to work with the Spinners)

The Stylistics

has got to be his best ever, track for track, while the O'Jays and H. Melvin smashes are among the most soulful sides put together by Gamble and Huff. No way are any of them flagging. (An attempt by G–H in 1970 to broaden their market via a Fifth-Dimension type 'class' group, the New Direction, was a dismal flop. Similarly, for example, Stax's pop product is notoriously unsuccessful. Moral: do what you do do good!)

You won't find any blues, not much country either, in Philadelphia; but it's the acknowledged centre for Northern black gospel and birthplace, with NY, of 'corner-boy' vocal groups. So it annoys me when rock experts seeking 'roots' should dismiss the things coming out of Sigma Sound as being too ephemeral and superficial, when the Philly men's respect for and inspiration from these origins is undoubted. Why, the Intruders had a hit in 1969 with a faithful revival of the Dreamlovers' 'We're Gonna Get Married'! Outsiders, unfamiliar with the idiom, can bypass it as not 'hard' enough, or laugh at the piercing falsetto, originated by the old 'bird' groups like the Flamingoes and now used by artists like Hart and Thompkins. But it is part of a living tradition, adopted without self-consciousness and as absorbing as anything in blues or country music. The records stand up by any contemporary standard in pop as a whole. To my mind at least, today's lush backdrops and technologically perfect productions, extend, rather than smother, that tradition. I know, even in these enlightened times, the black original still remains unnoticed until and unless copied in the white market – how else are the Osmonds as big as the Jackson Five? But the dwindling mass of punters who still wear blinkers making them blind to uptown soul, are missing the point, and a lot of wonderful music.

(1972)

AFTERWORD

Reading this stuff almost 23 years later, one's first thought is that what goes around surely comes around. Soulful vocal groups, after a long period out of favour, are once more in the mainstream of contemporary US black music, and the billboard R&B chart is awash in collective names to an extent not seen in decades. Any erstwhile fan, of, say, Blue Magic, will find much to enjoy in Boyz II Men; if you liked the Jones Girls, you'll probably like Jade, and so on. At last, harmonies are hip again, and a new generation of writer-producers is proud to wear their 1970s influences on their sleeve; L.A. and Babyface, McElroy and Foster and particularly Tony! Toni! Tone!, for example, all manage convincingly to harness the old musical values to the new technology.

The pendulum has swung back, not just musically, but sonically too. People's ears soon wearied of the in-your-face digital sound of the early to mid-1980s – stiffly programmed beat boxes, fizzy keyboard patches, tooth-grinding bell noises; at the same time, developments in sampling capability meant you could take a rhythm break from an old twelve inch, loop a part of it, and capture the looser feel of a real human drum track. Since then, everything's become murkier, more analogue-sounding (even to the extent, sometimes, of sprinkling on some vinyl-style crackle for added authenticity); so that in most cases, a typical 1974 soul track will tend in 1995 to sound less dated than one from 1984. Try it and see!

In one crucial respect, though, things'll never be the same. Geography has become irrelevant: no longer can you tell from listening to a record where it was made. Now it's the producer's library of sounds, samples, and grooves that matters, rather than the collective talents of particular local musicians sparking off each other as they play in the acoustics of a particular room in a particular town. (Antonio 'L.A.' Reid and Kenny 'Babyface' Edmonds, the Gamble and Huff of the 1990s, for example, recently moved their entire operation from California to Atlanta without any discernible change of sound or style.) Sure, Nashville still works triumphantly to the traditional method, and diehard Southern companies like Malaco in Jackson, Mississippi, still churn out tracks with their house rhythm section, on artists like Johnny Taylor and Denise Lasalle, for an older, regional black audience; but in the younger, nationwide chart-oriented R&B market, the old ways are gone.

Likewise, the sweetening, that orchestral element in the Philly sound that instinctively turned off the rock critics of its day, is largely a thing of the past. After all, why employ an arranger to write irrevocably for 20 expensive musicians, when you can raise an even larger section at the touch of a preset or two, run your ideas live through a computer via MIDI, and keep on tweaking the parts till the final mix (and after)? The trouble is, this often leads to little more than a pad, a cheesy string line, and a couple of 'sprangles' into the choruses, rather than the kind of rich and complex orchestral interplay once purveyed by the likes of Thom Bell (last heard of in Seattle, but – not surprisingly – unconnected with the grunge movement).

Gamble and Huff's empire, of course, went from strength to strength for some years after I wrote the above in 1972; but sadly, like Stax before it, it was eventually to sink into a morass of legal and financial sleaze. Philly today is no longer a major recording centre. The spirit of that joyous sweet soul music of the 1970s is unquestionably alive and well; but there is no more 'Sound of Philadelphia' – or, for that matter, anywhere else.

6

Johnny Cool and the
Isle of Sirens
Johnny Copasetic

NEW RUDIES BEGIN HEAR

This is about the words. In particular about some elements common to the lyrics of North American R&B, and Jamaican ska. So skinhead music jams a rude boot between the pages of this book, in an attempt to show that it has always been an adventurous and 'progressive' force in pop. But who cares who found it first? Who cares what the name is? RUDIES DON'T CARE.

NOW REEL ON

Ska – and reggae, rock steady, otherwise bluebeat – is the popular music of Jamaica. It and R&B, the popular music of Black North America, are two intimately associated and interacting branches of a common root. These two branches and their interactions are presented here as a coherent progressive movement in pop music. This is done by looking in depth at the work of two representative figures, one from each branch, and their innovations. These two figures are Curtis Mayfield on the R&B side and Prince Buster on the ska side. Such other figures as seem to be relevant to this development will be included as we go along, but it is not intended to write a history of the music, or an across-the-board survey of current developments, and the boring wastes of discographies and obscure records will be avoided.

For the purpose in hand it is best to consider the common origin of the two branches as being in the rock 'n' roll era of the 1950s. In fact the two branches were already distinct at that time, but it was then that the pop record became big business, and the use of electric instruments and amplification was widespread. At that time the heavy two-to-the-bar offbeat which was the legacy of boogie and blues really came into its own in the records of such people as Fats Domino and Chuck Berry. It was this feature of the increasingly widespread American records which was the initial influence of R&B on the musicians of Jamaica. Other influences on those musicians were of course not North American – there were plenty of indigenous ones, including a precursor of ska called mento. In North America too there were influences other than the blues and boogie, in particular gospel singing and jazz. Because of these differences the two branches developed differently; but the Jamaican musicians continued to be influenced by and to be aware of the developments of North American soul music and R&B.

To set the stage for the two developments we must look at their common ground, rhythm and blues around 1955–1960. Two records will do to establish this shared vocabulary. Wilbert Harrison's 'Kansas City' is a paradigm rock record, and could almost be ska, it has such a pronounced offbeat. But by far the more significant record is Chuck Berry's 1955 first hit record, 'Maybelline'. It also has the pronounced offbeat but most important of all it demonstrates another powerful influence that Chuck Berry had on all pop music, white and black, from that time on. Chuck Berry's statement is twofold. First, his lyric in this and all of his songs is full of object references, places, journeys and distance. None of that was new in itself: the white American folksong and the black American blues, and American literature in general are full of place-names, and journeys. Look at the songs 'Portland Town' and 'Highway 61', or at *Huckleberry Finn* for that matter. It was not new, but it was new for pop. Pop added its own definitive message – that you can speak about the generalities of life in terms of the precisely named objects that surround and delight those who live it – cars, juke boxes, creamsoda, hi-fi, hi-heeled sneakers, and freeways – and the activities of that life – driving, arriving, dancing and rhythm reviews.

His other influence is in his delivery. The best examples of this are in his later work, in for example 'Memphis Tennessee'. The scansion of Chuck Berry's lines is always exact, and his delivery matches this in its perfect attention to rhythm. In 'Memphis' it is this, coupled with his wry voice, his understatement, that gives the song its great sadness.

Chuck Berry was by no means the only bearer of this message. It doesn't matter whether it was he personally who brought the good news to those who followed or someone else. He stands as an outstanding exponent of the common source of these two developments.

STARTING FROM CHICAGO

In 1958 Curtis Mayfield and Jerry Butler formed the Impressions and began long and influential careers in the music. Both of them had experience in gospel groups and it was this training that was the prime influence on Mayfield's music, as it was on all the groups and singers in what is usually called soul music.

They made some records in Chicago, and Jerry Butler soon went solo. Curtis Mayfield wrote many of their songs in this Chicago period. The songs are mainly love songs of the 'won't you forgive me/look my way' kind, extremely well put together. At this time Curtis Mayfield started to write and produce records for other people. His first was for a woman called Jan Bradley and the song he wrote 'Mama Didn't Lie' serves to introduce the first of the themes which run through his work. The song is written from the point of view of a young woman who has found out that her mother was right all along – men are all the same, only after one thing. This simple tale reflects two of his themes: firstly the wisdom of age, secondly the sense of lost innocence. These two themes occur again and again in later development.

At this point the Impressions started to record for ABC Paramount, where their first record was 'Gypsy Woman', their first hit since the Jerry Butler days. This record introduces a third quality in Mayfield's work, that of allegory, and the appearance of archetypal figures, acting out a small story-like episode.

> From nowhere through a caravan
> Around the campfire light
> A lovely woman in motion
> With hair as dark as night
> Her eyes were like that of a cat in the dark
> That hypnotised me with love
> She was a gypsy woman
> She was a gypsy woman ...
>   Curtis Mayfield, 'Gypsy Woman' (1961)

She goes on to dance with all the men and finally vanishes, unaware of the love of the stranger.

Another similar record of that period is 'Minstrel and Queen'. In this a minstrel of low degree declares his love to 'the Queen with no King'. It doesn't say how it all works out. The song is not very good: Curtis Mayfield undoubtedly has a weakness for the 'I love you too/Honest I do' type of weak couplet. But the first line is striking – 'Queen Majesty, may I speak to thee,' where the doubling up of the royal title emphasises the distance and impersonality of the Queen. It has some of the irony of 'Duke of Earl', Gene Chandler's old hit. (Gene Chandler was later to record many Curtis Mayfield songs.) Both of these records were very influential in Jamaica. We'll come back eventually to that line from 'Minstrel and Queen'.

These few songs described so far already show themes strikingly different from the mainstream of R&B/soul music. The concrete imagery of Chuck Berry (wipe the windows, check the oil, check the tyres, dollar

Curtis Mayfield

gas) is a million miles away, but this is true of most soul music by now. The difference in Curtis Mayfield's songs is that a new imagery of 'classical' archetypes takes its place. Another difference is that Curtis Mayfield writes story songs, as Chuck Berry did ('Nadine', 'Johnny B. Goode'), a tradition maintained in country and western music but increasingly less common in R&B/soul music. These themes are all present in one remarkable song: 'Isle of Sirens'. He wrote it in the first Chicago period, about 1960, though he and the Impressions didn't record it until 1967. There is an absolutely awful Jerry Butler recording of it, made around 1960, which has Curtis somewhere in the background. Jerry Butler was completely at odds with Mayfield over songs like 'Minstrel and Queen' and 'Isle of Sirens' and obviously hated this one. The later Impressions recording of it is superb, with Curtis Mayfield's distinctive guitar rolling behind, and some beautifully restrained strokes of harmony from the other Impressions.

There's a story
Of beautiful women,
On an island in the sea,
Who called to me
Sailing by ...

And as we stayed on our course
I could hear them calling me,
And Lord, I can't stand
That beautiful cry.

Keep course,
Cried the captain.
Ignore them, let them be,
Straight ahead,
Cried the captain.
Sail on by and stay free,
Remember laws of mutiny.

And as we moved
The voices got louder,
They sing beautiful things in my ear,
I must go to that island of women,
I must see these creatures I hear,
Love is bright, and desires
Have no fear.

Keep course,
Cried the captain
Straight ahead, you stubborn man
We're all lonely cried the captain.
Take heed from an old man
For you don't understand.

Old man, your information
Makes no sense to me
Till the rock came
Of temptation,
And desires are heaven to me,
And off he leaped
Into the sea.

Keep course, cried the captain,
Keep course, cried the captain
Keep course.
           Curtis Mayfield, 'Isle of Sirens' (1961)

The three themes picked out above are all shown in this song. The archetypal figures of the Captain and the Sirens, the authority of the old man, and the inevitable loss of innocence in experience: 'and off he leaped into the sea'. It's the sort of thing that many people are trying to do these days, Van Morrison for example.

After the Gypsy Woman period two things happened. Firstly Mayfield joined forces with an arranger called Johnny Pate and produced some of the Impression's best work including 'Isle of Sirens', 'I'm Still Waiting' and 'People Get Ready', which harks back to his gospel singing experience. He also produced and wrote other people's songs. One of the first and greatest of these was Major Lance, who recorded many Mayfield songs. One of these, 'Um Um Um Um Um Um' is fairly well known. It was covered at the time by an English group. A young man comes across an old man sitting on a bench in a park who will say nothing but 'Mmm, mmm, mmm, um, um, mmm'. Later on in the song when the boy is older, he understands the reason for the old man's moan:

Now that I'm a man
I think I understand
Just why everyone should sing this song:
(Listen to me sing)
Mmm, mmm, mmm, um, um, mmm.
           Curtis Mayfield, 'Um Um Um Um Um Um' (1964)

Just as Chuck Berry in 'Memphis' conveys pathos by strict adherence to rhythm in a song with perfectly regular metre, so Mayfield and Major Lance between them do the same. Curtis also sings on the record, and the whole thing is so tight it sounds like double tracking. Another Mayfield/Lance cooperation which shows this is 'Rhythm'. This is a very simple dance song of the 'come on and do the-' kind. It is a type very common in R&B – an exhortation to dance some dance, the jerk, the pony, shotgun, boogaloo – there are millions of them, and it's a totally understood form of the medium. 'Rhythm' takes this familiar form and treats it as a totally abstract one. No dance is mentioned, just the abstraction of all dances: rhythm. The chorus, presumably Mayfield and odd Impressions, comes in on every other line with the exhortation. Major Lance weaves his way in and out of them with beautifully free phrasing, always coming back to the beat laid down by them and the orchestra, which plays a steady clip-clop beat like a syncopated cowboy horse.

> Chorus: 'You can beat the drum
> ML: Lord, all you want to
> Chorus: Let the bongos play
> ML: And dance all night and day
> Chorus: When the music flows
> ML: Lord I never want to go
> All: Rhythm, Rhythm, Rhy-thm
> ML: In my bones,
> Everytime the music carries on
> Lord, I feel like
> All: Rhythm ...'
>   Curtis Mayfield, 'Rhythm' (1964)

This control of rhythm – 'there can be no beat without rhythm' – and Major Lance's wistful voice make the song one of great sadness and loneliness. The contrast between form and message is as if a painter were to take some familiar and totally understood form in his medium, such as classical landscape, and paint a face with it.

Curtis Mayfield knows exactly what he is doing. He is a master, in complete control. Whether in his own recordings with the Impressions, or in other people's records, nothing in the vocal and instrumental arrangements is redundant, and the result is always a clean, spare sound. Even his weak cliche couplets ('Waiting for the rising sun / Everyone was having fun' – 'Gypsy Woman') have their place in his songs. (A couplet which looks weak on the page, may be perfectly right in a song if it occurs at a point of low tension or establishes a metre.) His command of harmony and antiphony of the gospel-influenced chorus is tremendous, and a fine example of this is in his production of the Fascinations' 'You'll be Sorry'. His more recent work carries all of this on. An interesting new factor is a political content in his recent songs, for example 'Choice of Colours', and 'Mighty Mighty, Spade and Whitey'. This social content has become predominant in his work now that he has started a solo career, and no longer records with the Impressions. In such recent works as 'We The People Who Are Darker Than Blue' the fantastical archetypes of 'Isle of Sirens' and 'Minstrel And Queen' are replaced by political ones. One example in particular shows that the new songs follow on from the old, the ironic 'Miss Black America', on his first solo album.

Meanwhile (Last Train To Skaville)

To consider the development of Jamaican music in the same period we must go back again to the source – the triple message of rhythm, content and delivery which was carried by Chuck Berry in the late 1950s and early 1960s.

The translation of this into Jamaican music placed huge rhythmic emphasis on the offbeat. The result was, in the early 1960s, the emergence of a lot of music using the same instrumental lineup as the American records – piano, bass guitar, guitar, drums and brass, occasional harmonica – but with a totally different sound. First of all, instead of having all the rhythm instruments playing the downbeat and maybe just piano providing offbeat, the position was reversed. Everybody played the offbeat, except maybe one instrument which carried the downbeat presumably so that the offbeat could be heard to be offbeat. Secondly they had beautiful horn players playing wonderful jazz-influenced solos using notes and scales which were strange to R&B and R&B-based pop, in particular in their use of the major seventh and sixth.

The forms they used were often based on the 32 bar pop song rather than on the North American 12 bar paradigm and its extensions; but the message of Chuck Berry and the early R&B performers had been absorbed. The songs were full of topical cultural references. Many of these were political. In particular many of these were connected with the Rastafarian cult.

This is a very diverse body of religious and political belief, taking its name from Haile Selassie, otherwise Ras Tafari, the Emperor of Ethiopia. It has its origins in the 'Back to Africa' movement of Marcus Garvey, and has some claim to be the origin of the US Black Power movement. Its adherents claim that they are the descendants of the people of

Abyssinia and that they should return to Africa, where Haile Selassie, the ruler of a Black Empire, has divine status in a promised land. It is often necessary to know about this phenomenon and the vocabulary of the belief to understand what the songs could possibly be about.

The songs themselves were generally either love songs of a kind familiar in the rest of pop music or songs with some kind of political commentary. This latter is to be contrasted with North American soul music (but not with blues). But this 'politics' is conveyed in the images of such beliefs as Rastafarianism, in the images of an isolated island nation and those of a culture of poverty. The images are of promised lands, exiles, messiahs, of strikes, working mornings and shanty towns. The Biblical imagery of the Israelites' exile in Egypt is also common.

In the period between 1960 and 1970 the music was referred to successively as ska (in the UK as bluebeat), rock steady and reggae. These refer to dances rather than to music and it is not always easy to say what the distinction is. Broadly speaking the later the record, the less the outstanding emphasis on simple offbeat and the more the other beats (except the first) are introduced, reflecting an increasing effect of indigenous influences and of 'uptown' R&B and soul. It was at the beginning of this period that Prince 'Buster' Campbell came to fame. Born in 1938, he was a boxer and a Sound System man, or DJ, before he became a singer.

THE YOUNG MODS' FORGOTTEN STORY

This chapter is above all about the relevance to people in this country of R&B and ska. It is therefore fitting to consider, before we go on, the people who were really responsible for discovering it and keeping it alive in this country. They were the mods.

In the early 1960s there was a revival of interest in R&B, which until then had been temporarily eclipsed. This rediscovery was not solely on the mods' part, but they were in the discotheques and bought a lot of the records, and were the driving force, though many other people took part. They were young, single, and relatively wealthy. In the main, they were Southerners, coming from the grey, outlying districts of London, like Watford and Harrow. They wanted the best and brightest things for their money, and they decided for themselves what they were. They had style. They were the first generation to have known nothing of the war and rationing, and this may have been what made them different. The R&B revival which they partly brought about was not a particularly radical innovation. R&B had always been there and was part of the accepted public musical vocabulary, despite its eclipse. The real right of discovery belonged to the previous generation. The Beatles and the Stones were the same music, albeit watered down and more acceptable, before they went off in their own directions, which are not our concern here. The real discovery of the mods was ska, which had been introduced to this country by Jamaican immigrants.

In about 1962, when the R&B revival was well under way and the Beatles were in full swing, there was a brief boom in Jamaican music. In the UK at that time it was called bluebeat. As far as the rest of the community was concerned it was fairly short-lived, though the papers made much of it – they were very concerned with the mod phenomenon at that time. For one thing, the Beatles had happened. For another the American R&B records were better made and in a fairly familiar idiom, whereas bluebeat records were issued in excessive numbers and were often badly made. Moreover, the music was pretty wildly unacceptable. The heavy offbeat made it sound like a parody of the crudest rock 'n' roll, the words were often unintelligible, and when intelligible were often either obscene or seemed to hint at some kind of political menace veiled behind extraordinary foreign imagery. To the populace as a whole, used as they were to post-Buddy Holly pop music, it was rather revolting. They could afford to ignore it because there was other good music around.

The mods, however, took it for their own for precisely these qualities that everyone else rejected, plus of course the fact that it was good music, fantastic for dancing to. The really remarkable fact is that unlike the rock 'n' roll revolution of the 1950s and the R&B revival of the 1960s, which were quickly assimilated into the musical vocabulary of the whole population, ska remained in isolation as the music of an outgroup minority. It has remained so to date. There are now some signs that the assimilation into the main culture is occurring – but that is getting ahead of the story.

Johnny Cool

From the beginning, Prince Buster was a most important figure in ska, and he spans practically the whole development. In the first bluebeat boom Prince Buster arrived along with many other people who are still going strong, such as the Maytals, Owen Gray, Laurel Aitken, and Millie. (Millie was the only one who had hit records. She was small, gorgeous and very good, but her hit songs – 'My Boy Lollipop' and 'I'm Falling In Love With A Snowman' – were not the sort of thing you theorise about.)

Prince Buster's early songs were purest bluebeat: a raucous offbeat and lots of good brass players (Prince Buster always had good musicians –

Georgie Fame's band did sessions for him). They were always well sung and clearly articulated, which last was unusual in records of that time. Two of them will do to introduce several of Prince Buster's characteristics. 'Sodom and Gomorrah' is a political tirade couched in the metaphor of the Israelites' exile in Egypt. The oppressor is addressed as Prince Pharaoh. 'Are you afraid to own your own name? You shall be destroyed like Sodom and Gomorrah.'

> ... Your kingdom was destroyed, because
> You were the son of King Pharaoh.
> And I was Moses
> Who led my people through
> The Red Sea.
> With a rod in my hand
> I will stretch forth my hand
> And the true king was delivered
> From the hand of the wicked
> Pharaohs.
>
> You ARE Prince Pharaoh
> Are you afraid to own your own name?
> You shall be destroyed, like Sodom and Gomorrah.
> C. Campbell (Prince Buster), 'Sodom and Gomorrah' (1963)

There are many other songs of this period which are directly political. 'Watch it, Blackhead' is about the allegedly unfair proportion of wealth in the hands of the comparatively recent Chinese immigrants to the West Indies. 'Ska School' – which begins with the Prince singing the alphabet to the tune of 'Auld Lang Syne', a forcible if not quite pleasing reminder of the breadth of his musical influences – is about illiteracy.

The second song, 'Madness', illustrates the elliptical nature of many of Prince Buster's songs. Like the situation between oppressor and oppressed in 'Sodom and Gomorrah' the relation between the accuser and the defender of madness is minimally described. (Though it was probably quite clear in a Jamaican context what the situation referred to was.)

> ... Madness, madness, they call it madness
> Madness, madness, they call it madness
> I'm about to explain
> That someone is using his brain
> Madness, madness, they call it madness

Propaganda ministers
Propaganda ministers
I've got an aim in view
I'm going to walk all over you

Madness, madness, I call it gladness
But if this is madness, man I know I'm filled with gladness
It's gonna be rough rough
It's gonna be tough tough
And I won't be the one who's going to suffer ...

              C. Campbell (Prince Buster), 'Madness' (1963)

But still more important, even these early songs illustrate the quality
of allegory that was brought out in Curtis Mayfield's work, the description of situations in terms of archetypal figures. We said that this was
a continuation of Chuck Berry's message that songs should be particular
and detailed, in terms of objects and individuals rather than generalities. This is the function of Prince Pharoah, Moses, and the Israelites
in 'Sodom and Gomorrah' as it was that of the old captain and the sirens
in 'Isle of Sirens'. The 'propaganda ministers' in 'Madness' have this
quality of definiteness in an otherwise very abstract song.

It is not just fanciful to identify this factor with the influence of Curtis
Mayfield. It is obvious that allegory in song is not a preserve of Mayfield
alone. It is also clear that its presence in both men's work owes a lot to
the influence of religion, rather than just to direct influence from one
to the other. None the less, Prince Buster's later development shows
explicit influence.

The development of ska as a whole was to greater complexity of
rhythm, and to certain content peculiar to it alone. In terms of content
there was among all performers a tendency to centre songs on archetypal
mythical figures. This tendency showed itself in two ways. First there
were lots of records taking as their titles films, and film heroes, and law-
breakers; these were mainly instrumentals with shouted catch-phrases.
An example is 'Lawless Street': 'John! Leave your guns alone! This is
Lawless Street'. 'Heartbreak Hotel' and 'Desolation Row' in a nutshell.
Prince Buster did one of these called 'Al Capone' (pronounced Kerpown)
interspersed with such cries as 'Don't call me Scarface! My name is
Kerpown! Al Kerpown!'.

The other way the tendency showed was in a figure unique to Jamaica,
the rude boy, or rudie. The rude boy is a supercool hooligan, and he
always wins, he's so cool. He is very dear to the Jamaican and skinhead
heart. James Bond is the rudie par excellence. So, by a strange equation,
is Andy Capp. Probably the best known ska record of all, '007 (Shanty

Town)', by Desmond Dekker, concerns Bond. The rudies' crimes in the songs are almost always looting, shooting and, curiously enough, 'bum showing'. Several records portray the court-room trials of rude boys. In one of these, 'Rougher than Rough (Rudies in Court)' by Derrick Morgan, the judge's opening remarks are answered by the chorused rebuttal 'Your honner … rudies don't care!' and they walk out free. Prince Buster portrays a similar scene in 'Judge Dread (Judge Hundred Years)', but with the roles reversed Judge Dread says 'I am the rude boy now … and I don't care'; and hands out enormous sentences to the accompaniment of a quiet, depressed sounding chorus (the jury?) 'You're rough … you're tough …'. In a stunning second episode he lets them all off again and comes down to dance in the court. All the time the band plays a steady tonic-subdominant-dominant riff very common in the ska of the time (compare '007' or 'Owe Me No Pay Me' by the Ethiopians).

> I want to see you dance
> Let me see you dance
> My name is Judge Dread
> And if I leave my chair
> And come down to dance
> I'm not going to look ashamed
> I am a judge
> And I know the dance …
>> C. Campbell (Prince Buster), 'Judge Dread
>> (Judge Hundred Years)' (1967)

Prince Buster's further developments are many. He continued to produce political songs ('Taxation'), and lewd songs ('She was a Rough Rider', 'Big Five', and 'Wind and Grind'). He used American soul influenced choruses, and always made fine music. He made versions of soul standards, including those by Curtis Mayfield ('Grow Closer Together'). The most important of these developments is shown by two of his best works, 'Ghost Dance' and 'Johnny Cool'.

The story songs with simple repetitious accompaniment like 'Judge Dread' and the instrumentals with elliptical occasional vocal interjections such as 'Al Capone' are the springboard for this development. Jokes as these songs are, the freedom of form that they afford is quite unusual. The isolated phrases in 'Al Capone' and the other songs of that kind like 'Lawless Street', which arrive completely without context, carry because of their ambiguity a great weight of image and meaning. This ambiguity due to ellipsis is a common thread throughout ska. Prince Buster's great innovation was to take the story song from the repetitive background – as in 'Judge Dread' or 'Ten Commandments' – and write songs in phrases and passages having the ambiguity and consequent impact of the isolated phrases of 'Al Capone' or the later 'The Scorcher' – of which the sole verbal phrase was 'Don't watch that, watch this. It's a scorcher ... Reggae child'. These new songs were made up of apparently disconnected passages of varying lengths. Some involved a sequential story-like character. Others were fragments from elsewhere. Yet others were more or less everyday phrases. Like William Burroughs and Bob Dylan, Prince Buster has a fine ear for the sound and rhythm of the casual phrase, the mainspring of rock 'n' roll.

You Dug Him Before. Dig Him NOW

The simpler of the two records in which he does this is called 'Ghost Dance'. It is simpler because it does have a main theme although no story as such. The theme is an open letter to his friends back in Jamaica, written/sung from abroad. The instrumental backing is a simple alternation of tonic and subdominant harmonies, a 'story song' backing even simpler than that of 'Judge Dread'. A ghostly voice in the background slides eerily from high to low notes and Prince Buster declaims. It is almost impossible to write down this song. For one thing it is full of proper names that I don't know how to spell. For another, from time to time throughout the song the Prince utters an explosive exhalation somewhere between a belch and a snort impossible to transcribe. The isolated phrase 'Ghost Dance' occurs throughout like the catchphrase of Al Capone and the other instrumental songs. The rest of it is in the form of a letter to a friend asking for messages to be sent. 'Give him my regards. Tell him Prince Buster says "Hello"'. At the end he sends the same message to two brothers: 'We grew together, please send them my regards. Tell them Prince Buster says "So long. Sorry we had to go, so soon." If music be the food of love, then I'll forever sing on, and fast as all, will soon get back my ship. Ghost Dance ...'.

Prince Buster's complete technical mastery has the same result here as Curtis Mayfield and Major Lance's 'Rhythm'. 'Ghost Dance', however inadequately represented on the printed page, establishes the kind of thing Prince Buster is doing. It shows the use he makes of the rhythms of everyday phrases, the effect of the phrase with no context, the effect of sequence without a story. An analogy that may supplement the very limited description possible in prose may be drawn between these songs and the strip cartoon Krazy Kat by George Herriman. In these strip cartoons three characters, Krazy Kat, Ignatz Mouse, and Offissa Pup live out their eternally triangular existence in a desert-like landscape which capriciously changes from frame to frame between day and night, flat and curved, near and far. They are surrounded by objects of character ambiguous as between vegetables and artefact, building or landscape, and by everyday things in incongruous juxtapositions.

'Ghost Dance' is as John the Baptist to 'Johnny Cool', the Prince's two-part masterpiece. It appears to be a 45 r.p.m. equivalent of the movie of the same name. In the first half we hear of the birth of Johnny Cool. There are two singers and the persona of Johnny Cool seems to oscillate between them. First it's Prince Buster who is Johnny Cool and who tells us of his birth and early life in a sort of Marlon Brando mumble.

> ... But my friends there,
> you know, they call me
> Johnny.
> They mean, you know, Johnny
> Coooool. Oh, so you mean Johnny Cool?
> Yes –
> Where are the girls?
> I mean, you know, Johnny
> Rough.
>> C. Campbell (Prince Buster), 'Johnny Cool' (1967)

The metamorphosis of Johnny Cool as Johnny Rough is only the first of successive guises. Next the first of several lyrical themes makes its first entry and is repeated:

> I beg you be cool
> Johnny Cool
> I beg you be cool
> Johnny Cool,

and the life of Johnnie Cool continues to murmured asides and encouragement from the second voice: '... everyone so hot and me feel so cool ... . The second, third and fourth themes then make an entry in succession, first:

> I wonder if you'll love me
> At the party
> Tonight
> Then meet me on Dark Street
> Everything
> is alright

followed by a scat theme, and finally the fourth theme: 'Queen Majesty, why don't you speak to me ...'.

This, slightly transformed, was the line that was singled out from Curtis Mayfield's song 'Minstrel and Queen' typifying Mayfield's use of archetypal figures. We saw that the double royal title is a device introduced precisely to underline the remoteness of the queen. This line constitutes a verification of the thesis of this chapter that these two developments in music are parallel and represent a single identifiable movement, for all their superficial differences. Prince Buster's song concerns the archetypal rude boy figure, Johnny Cool, and he has chosen as one of his contrasting themes a corresponding figure from Curtis Mayfield's work. We knew all along that he was aware of Mayfield's work, because he sang his songs. Here he affirms that he understands it and recognises its closeness to his own. Even the reversal of the second half of Mayfield's line is conscious – in the second entry the line is exactly as Mayfield wrote it.

A second entry of the first theme ('I beg you be cool, Johnny Cool') concludes the first part of the record. In the second part a second voice announces that he is Johnny Skolanski and that his friends call him Johnny Cool. A new entry of 'we all beg you be cool' is followed by a new theme:

Johnny music sweet
But dance can't keep
Johnny listen this
Sweet.

The various themes then repeat in altered forms and altered order. New relations between the themes are brought out. Finally a fragment of each of the five themes is stated in rapid succession and the record fades out on a final repetition of the Curtis Mayfield theme.

This work, with its combination of all of the factors discussed in this presentation sums up and concludes the argument. In effect, this record and the Curtis Mayfield/Major Lance 'Rhythm' are the argument.

ROUGHERENCES

Most of the facts (but none of the errors), concerning Curtis Mayfield's career were taken from: P. Burns, 'The Curtis Mayfield Story', in *Blues and Soul* magazine, 1968, nos 13 to 18.

An extensive account of Rastafarianism can be found in: M.G. Smith, et al., *The Ras Tafarian Movement in Kingston, Jamaica* (West Indies University College, Institute of Sociology and Economics, 1960).

(1972)

AFTERWORD (GOODBYE PORK-PIE HAT)

'Johnny Cool and the Isle of Sirens' was written 25 years ago, out of a conviction that there was a new global popular music, born of jazz, rhythm and blues, and ethnic musics, and nurtured by radio and the jukebox. I wanted to understand how the thrill and passion that is found in popular music from all parts of the world comes from tapping this universal source. (The piece was originally written for a special issue of *New Edinburgh Review* devoted to the counter-culture of the late 1960s – hence the 'I've-just-got-one-thing-to-say-to-you-hippies' tone of the opening remarks, which is of course entirely inappropriate to the present volume. I have let that stand, though I have silently corrected a few errors elsewhere in the piece.)

I chose two, not particularly geographically distant, musical cultures, and a particular pair of artists, to try to show this influence at work – black music of the US and Jamaica, because they were the major influences on the popular music of my youth, and the Impressions and Prince Buster because they made my hair stand on end, and seemed to embody the influence in a fairly direct way. I think the same point could have been illustrated in many ways with other examples.

Did I make too much of the sometimes slender threads that unite these works? Of course I did. Nevertheless, it is interesting to note that, in the subsequent period of Jamaican music, the Wailers recorded several Curtis Mayfield tunes, both with Marley ('Keep on Moving') and individually (Bunny Wailer recorded 'People Get Ready', and incidentally brought horns back from their post-ska eclipse in his albums of the mid-1970s). The influence is real, the global popular musical culture lives in these songs.

Something that I wish I had made more of 25 years ago is the influence in the other direction, and the widespread assimilation of Caribbean influences into popular music in the US and Britain that was already under way. Years before, Dizzy Gillespie had led the way for jazz, the compliment being returned in a sweet 1980s recording of 'Tin Tin Dao' by the legendary ska trombonist Rico Rodriguez. Georgie Fame's superb mid-1960s UK band included several Jamaican players who lent the horn section a sound that still sounds fresh today, and recorded ska material.

Taj Mahal's marvellous Caribbean fusion International Rhythm Band of around 1980 included the famous Trinidadian pan-player Robert Greenidge. This exchange continues to be one of the most exciting developments in popular music. Recent examples are the Cuban Gonzalo Rubalcaba (who has also recorded an extended tribute to Dizzy Gillespie) and the New York-based Myra Melford, both of whom combine contemporary jazz piano with a wilder octave-rich Hispanic Caribbean influence.

Many of the recordings discussed in the piece are available again on CD, including Major Lance's fine work and the Impressions' early recordings (although it is sad to know that Curtis Mayfield suffered a shocking stage accident in 1990, leaving him wheelchair-bound). Prince Buster's recordings are harder to find, although they crop up on compilations of ska material, along with the work of the great horn players of the period such as Rolando Alphonso and Don Drummond. Georgie Fame's early work with the Blue Flames is currently available in the UK on various budget labels. Bunny Wailer's *Struggle* was on the Jamaican Solomonic label. Taj Mahal's International Rhythm Band seems to be mostly stuck somewhere in the vaults (wake up, Warner Brothers!), but there are two exceptional (if uneven) live albums around on the Canadian Just a Minute label, and the US Laserlight budget label, with a very characteristic sound of this band. Gonzalo Rubalcaba's *The Blessing* is on (a Canadian subsidiary of) US Blue Note. Myra Melford's *Alive at the House of Saints* is on the Swiss Hat Hut label, and is my bet for something that will still be making my hair stand on end in another 25 years' time. Try this marvellous trio's live version of 'Frank Lloyd Wright Goes West to Rest'.

PART TWO: THE INDUSTRY

7

The A&R Men
Simon Frith

I've been surveying the year of singles again and come to the conclusion that 1974–75 was a dull year up in the charts. There was no dominant group or style but a series of over-worked formulae – white (Glitter Band, Mud, Kenny) and black (Barry White, Stylistics, George McCrae). The year's best singles were the successful outsiders; they refreshed simply by having charm (Billy Swan's 'I Can Help', Pete Wingfield's 'Eighteen With A Bullet', Ace's 'How Long') and vitality (Rupie Edward's 'Ire Feeling', Jim Gilstrap's 'Swing Your Daddy', Labelle's 'Lady Marmalade'). The year's only 'new' fad were the Bay City Rollers – and their success meant more to tartan patch makers than to the music biz; the year's biggest surprise hits, Tammy Wynette's 'Stand By Your Man' and 'D-I-V-O-R-C-E', were cut seven years ago; the only chart regulars to enhance (rather than exploit) their reputation were 10cc with 'I'm Not In Love'. For the rest, it was all grist to the nostalgia mill, and I can't hear 1974–75 as being very significant.

Part of the reason for this was that nothing much was happening to the taste for pop; audiences seemed happy enough in their various grooves and, with the exception of the hard-faced Roller girls, there was no musical fanaticism about, no uniforms that needed badges. By 1974 record companies had come to terms with the new selling media – commercial radio and discos. Commercial radio turned out to need little attention. It's clear what sound the major stations are trying for – progressive MOR, the easy-listening records from American FM – but, as yet, they seem to have little effect on singles sales.

Everyone, on the other hand, is now convinced of the selling power of discos. In 1974–75 there were more hits from more releases on more labels than ever before (so much for the economic crisis); it was a good year for American, and particularly black American records; pop reggae made a chart reappearance – all this can be attributed to the energy with which the disco audience was pursued. Disco DJs were swamped with singles and big English companies scurried madly through the catalogues of obscure American ones to find potential dancing hits. The results were various: Island, for instance, completely failed to find success with their USA Series, while Pye's Disco Demand Series managed to get the most mindless (and white) aspects of Northern Soul into the national charts; Jonathan King's UK label, a pioneer of the use of discos, didn't have a single hit and was joined in lack of success by Atlantic, Stax, and even Tamla and Philadelphia, the soul labels that were the first to get regular white sales; their places were taken by new names – Jay Boy, All Platinum – and the sharpest operator of all turned out to be Wes Farrell, veteran of family audience marketing (the Partridge Family), now making music for the New York disco crowds. Disco Tex, on Farrell's Chelsea label, was the cynical success of the year.

Disco Tex was a symptom: 1974–75 was a very pop year, very commercial. The music wasn't very interesting, nor was its audience; what was fascinating was the state of the record industry. No company had any particular advantage – no Beatles (Apple, for the first time, fell from the top), no secret mailing list; competition was real. And so the event of the year was the bankruptcy of the B&C/Trojan empire. Maybe *Rock File*'s surveys do reveal something – we recorded Trojan's lack of success last year, and Decca, bottom of 1973–74's Losers' Division with one hit from 110 releases, cut their output down to 45 (they still only managed two hits though – the anglicised version of Gilbert Becaud's 'Little Love And Understanding', and 'Hold On To Love', from Peter Skellern, who shortly thereafter signed with Island). Certainly the questions raised by the year's singles statistics are about the business: why did Phonogram have so much more success with its US labels (Avco, Mercury, All Platinum) than Decca with its releases on London? Why did Rak continue to thrive while UK faded? How did Magnet, a label established solely on the success of Alvin Stardust, manage to take off as an important all-round independent?

Rock critics are always looking in vain for musical trends, but the only continuing trend in Britain in the 1970s has been a business one, the diversification of the industry. Until (and during) the British Pop Explosion of the mid-1960s the music business was dominated by four companies (EMI, Decca, Pye, Philips); since then their influence has slowly been weakened. This process has had two sources: independent producers and independent labels.

Independent producers function, in creative terms, as mini record companies: the producer finds and contracts his own acts, records them at his own expense and brings the finished tape to a record company; the company presses and releases it on one of its own labels and pays a royalty on every copy sold to the producer. If the record flops then it's a cheap deal for a record company which has been spared the production costs; if the record's a success, the company has to pay out a higher royalty on every copy sold than if it had put the record together itself. Independent production was pioneered by the successful writer/producer/A&R men of the late 1960s – Roger Cook and Roger Greenaway, Tony Macaulay, Tony Hatch; there are now few successful pop operators who don't work as independents. The implications of this for the pop business are obvious. Even if the producers' records finally emerge on the major labels, the origins of pop singles are now much more diverse.

Independent labels began differently, as a response to the rock market. By the late 1960s Britain's major companies were aware of their ineptness with the new, album-oriented, audience and began to set up their own progressive labels – Harvest (EMI), Vertigo (Phonogram), Dawn (Pye), Deram and Nova (Decca) – to compete with the new rock independents – Island, Immediate, Chrysalis. The independents have had the better of this competition, but, on the other hand, the situation soon stabilised. The only new progressive label in the last couple of years has been Virgin and the most significant competition for rock acts these days is with American labels – RCA, for example, got Bowie, A&M Rick Wakeman, Warners Rod Stewart.

A second source of independence has been the musicians themselves. Inspired by business acumen (they'd give themselves a better economic deal) and claiming idealism (they'd offer fellow artists a better economic *and* creative deal), a number of labels have followed the Beatles' Apple – the Moody Blues' Threshold, ELP's Manticore, Deep Purple's Purple and Oyster, Rolling Stones, Elton John's Rocket, the Kinks' Konk, George Harrison's Dark Horse, and, most recently, Led Zeppelin's Swansong. Only Rocket and Swansong could claim to have had much success with their signings (Kiki Dee and Bad Company, respectively) and the major companies have preserved close enough ties with all these labels to continue to draw a share of the superstars' earnings.

But there is a third and more threatening source of new company-independent producers going the whole hog. Larry Page's Penny Farthing label, one of the earliest of these, had a bad year in 1974–75, but Mickie Most's Rak maintained its astonishing record and was joined in success by a sudden din of new labels – Michael Levy's Magnet; Gull, set up by MCA's A&R men when MCA decided to stop signing British acts; GTO, the label of Dick Leahy, Bell's ex-manager; Don Arden's Jet; State, run by ex-Polydor men John Fruin and Wayne Bickerton.

Apart from the progressive Gull, these labels are unashamedly pop oriented and their bosses have mostly worked in A&R – they know how the big companies operate. They also know that in an unashamedly pop year, with nothing much of musical interest going on, there is an even bigger onus than usual on A&R departments to come up with successful 'product' ... .

A&R MEN

A&R stands for Artists and Repertoire: an A&R man is responsible for what music goes out on a company's label – for getting artists signed to the label, for keeping them there (or dismissing them) and for the records that are issued in their names. Though in the short term a record company's success may reflect the effectiveness of its salesmen – pluggers, press office, distributors, sales reps – in the long run success depends on A&R judgments – who to sign, how to record and present them to the public. In 1971 EMI could still claim that: 'Using hundreds of promotion men and over a thousand salesmen EMI has the power to stimulate demand both in quantity and quality ...'.[*]

But in reply to the question 'What percentage of winners is a company like EMI looking for?' their Managing Director said 'If you got twenty per cent winners, real winners, of course you would be doing very well' and *Rock File*'s surveys show that EMI achieve nothing like that ratio, despite their army of salesmen. When it comes to the crunch it is the A&R men who, like football managers, have to carry the can for failure and their job (again like football management) requires diverse skills.

Talent spotting

The terrible warning that hangs over every A&R man's bed concerns the Beatles: Would You Have Turned Them Down? And certainly a large part of an A&R man's time is taken up with watching and listening to unknown acts, assessing their potential. But this is only one form of talent spotting. Another is poaching, picking up an act when its contract with a rival company runs out. There are various reasons for doing this; sometimes the hope is to revitalise a fading career; sometimes the move involves a complete change of musical direction; sometimes the new company simply offers an act a greater freedom to carry on doing what it's doing, in the belief that it has yet to reach its maximum market. In these deals an A&R department is offering 'sympathy' as well as money and this was obviously a key element in, for example, Island's 1974–75 signings of Kevin Ayers, John Cale and Peter Skellern. At a more cynical

---

[*] This is quoted in Michael Wale's *Vox Pop: Profiles of the Pop Process* (Harrap, 1972), from which I have also taken the comment on success rate.

level a company might simply outbid its rivals for a known successful act; the decision is based on a straight calculation – what is the act's earning power? What can we afford to offer? A big label can always outbid a small label (and so Mercury got 10cc from UK) but can't always avoid over-bidding (as I'd bet RCA did for the Kinks). These signings are the equivalent of transfer deals in soccer – even with the most established stars judgements still have to be made about future playing potential.

A&R men don't just judge acts, they've also got to be able to spot *records*, and this, again, in various contexts. First, there are all the tape deals being offered – are they worth it? Jonathan King's skill, for example, has always been with sounds rather than acts – who else would have heard the possibilities of 'Wave Your Knickers In The Air'? Then, there are the US catalogues to go through. The master here is Nigel Grainge at Phonogram, who's interested not just in what might hit but also in what *won't*, he doesn't like releasing records needlessly and so, for instance, did not bother to release All Platinum's American follow up to Shirley's 'Shame, Shame, Shame'. Third, record companies are now aware of the profits to be made from an astute re-release. It was nifty work on Anchor's part to issue Brian Hyland's 'Sealed With A Kiss' just in time for the summer of 1975, and Decca's good judgement got the Chi-Lites' 'Have You Seen Her?' into the Top Three twice in four years, but the re-release of the year was 'Stand By Your Man', as CBS found an unexpected source of wealth in their back catalogue. There's less money lost if an oldie flops and the profits of a successful re-release are consequently greater – going through back numbers is now part of the A&R routine.

Accounting

All A&R decisions are basically financial (that's what they mean by 'potential') and the calculations have to be precisely made. Companies don't just sign a group and leave them to get on with it, they have to weigh the necessary investment against the possible returns. There are obvious questions to be asked; how ready is the act to record? How much rehearsing time does it need? What advance should it get for equipment? What recording costs are necessary? How much help should the company give with organising gigs and tours and publicity?

The answers are not absolute but depend on one simple considera-tion – how much is the act going to earn? And this is where the problems start: not only may companies calculate this all wrong, but they can't avoid (though they rarely admit this) splitting their acts into potential divisions, and a future Division One act is going to get more investment than a possible Division Three-er. The latter musicians inevitably feel neglected and this becomes one of the major causes of transfer deals – a Third Division act with one company hopes to be treated as First Division with another (perhaps the clearest example of such neglect, and the misjudgement that it involved, was Apple's treatment of James Taylor). Meanwhile, a potential First Division act which fails involves a company in such heavy losses that it is often loath to admit it and merely redoubles its efforts (and expenditure). It's not unknown for an A&R man to become so obsessed with an act which he and no one else believes in that he not only neglects his other signings but even gives up the search for anyone new. Even if such an act does eventually sell records, its success may not be profitable – too much money has been spent in getting it there. This year, for example, A&M got a hit with Supertramp, and Vertigo scored with Alex Harvey, but their future sales are going to have to be long lasting to make up for their past records of failure.

It is in this context that competition between record companies is unequal – some have much more capital to risk than others. John Peel was an excellent talent spotter for his Dandelion label but never had the necessary money to bankroll his proteges. Clifford T. Ward, Kevin Coyne, Medicine Head have all had greater success with their subsequent, wealthier labels, and Peel couldn't even afford to *sign* Roxy Music and T. Rex – he knew they were Division One acts but couldn't provide the production and promotion costs they'd need to prove it.

Another calculation A&R departments have to make in signing an act concerns the balance of their label. There are two strategies. Some companies like to dangle a finger in every pie – if teenybop idols are selling they'll sign a teenybop idol; if it's drug-crazed hippies then they'll have one of them; if discos are a market then they'll make disco music. The problem with this is that a label's identity may become so diffuse that it can attract neither musicians nor audiences from the special scenes it's trying to cover; and so companies have created their own special labels (Harvest, etc.), while others have tried to change identity with huge, well-publicised, signings (CBS with rock acts in the 1960s; a number of pop labels with black acts in the 1970s).

The alternative is to begin by developing a specific identity and only sign acts that match it. The independent rock companies are an example. Island and Charisma's hopes were to build up an audience that trusted the label and would listen sympathetically to any act on it. But Tamla Motown has been the most successful 'identity label'; Tamla music became identified as a specific genre. Trouble arises when tastes change – specialist labels have nothing to fall back on. Some are content to remain specialist, catering for their small but sure soul or folk or jazz minority; but any company which has had a taste of mass success is under pressure to diversify. In America Motown developed its own progressive (Rare Earth) and pop (Mowest) labels, to add white and non-soul acts to its lists; Island have deliberately built up an A&R team with diverse tastes, in order to widen their spread of music.

All these calculations rest on assessment of the market, on an understanding of how records get sold. A&R men have to know about Radio One and *Top Of The Pops*, about discos and the college circuit. A record is rarely made without reference to who it's being made for; A&R men are inevitably involved in the problems of publicity and promotion.

No wonder that their recording contracts go into such detail: 'The Company shall have the right to choose which tracks shall be issued as singles, which on albums, and which not at all; the Company shall have the right to decide when recorded material shall be released; the Company shall have the right to decide how an album shall be presented – the order of the tracks, the design of the sleeve; the Company shall have the right to decide the title of an album and of all the tracks thereon; the Company reserve the right to rearrange, remix, re-record the Company's product ...'.

The fact is that A&R men are operators, dealers. Talent spotting is the easy part; then come the years of handling the acts (and their managers), of coming to terms with independent producers (and their tapes); of negotiating the rights to American tracks. It all needs careful thought, careful calculation, careful accounting (and over their desks hang the balance sheets).

Producing

The A&R man is responsible for transforming the potential of the talent he's signed into a saleable product and traditionally his most important role was as record producer. At EMI, for example, Cliff Richard was the responsibility of Norrie Paramor, the Beatles of George Martin; both men were part of the A&R team, both were expected to supervise recordings, to arrange and engineer and realise their acts' music. These days an A&R department's production role need not be so direct, the job is still to get the right sound but this means, more and more, getting the right outside producer and studio and engineer. Derek Green of A&M explained the 18-month gap between signing Andy Fairweather-Low and recording him, this way:

> The reason the first album took so long was because we were searching around for the right producer. We approached all the big names, but none of them

could hear the potential in the music. They all said no. Then we finally got through to Elliot Mazer, Neil Young's producer. Although he liked some of the stuff, he wasn't too sure about it at first. We eventually persuaded him ... .*

(This is also a good example of a company's desperate faith in an act for which they've just paid a lot of money. If I'd been told by 'all the big names' that they couldn't hear 'the potential in the music' I think I'd've given up.)

Management

An artist is bound to a record company by a contract which demands so much 'product' per year; the A&R department have to ensure that the terms of the contract are met. But, in the end, there's no way to force a musician to make music, and certainly no way to force an act to make good (or commercial) music. Enforcing a contract means keeping everyone happy; preventing freak-outs and piss-abouts, papering over group cracks, having the lads (or lasses) on the road when they should be on the road, in the studio when they should be in the studio; keeping the costs down, the spirits up. Man management (with the help and hindrance of the acts' own managers) – it's like football again and just as important a part of the job. I'm convinced that Island's success, for example, has rested on its patient coping with the occasional way-wardness of its acts.

Talent spotters, accountants, producers, managers, and all the time with one eye on the market and one on head office, it's not surprising that A&R men pop up from a variety of backgrounds: writers (Richard Williams went from *Melody Maker* to Island, Pete Frame from *Zig Zag* to Charisma, Andrew Bailey from *Rolling Stone* and the *Evening Standard* to Bell): musicians (Dave Dee is with Atlantic, Muff Winwood, ex-Spencer Davis Group, with Island); disc jockeys (ex-BBC man Alan Black is with Polydor; Nigel Grainge of Phonogram and Pete Waterman of Magnet both ran discos); promotion men and salesmen (the internal route, followed by Ian Ralfini and Martin Wyatt of Anchor, by Peter Summerfield of Pye, Robin Blanchflower of CBS).

The variety of people in A&R makes for a variety of company styles. I have been describing A&R in general terms, the outline of the job. But the job gets done differently, well and badly, with different emphases. Different companies experience different pressures.

---

* In an interview with Rob Partridge, 'The Glitter Passed Us By', *Melody Maker*, 19 October 1974.

PYE

Pye is best described as a middle-of-the-road company; a long established British pop label, it had its share of success in the 1960s (the Kinks, Petula Clark, the Searchers) but never picked up a superstar and has been singularly unenterprising in its rock signings – the only big success on Dawn was Mungo Jerry, signed through a tie-up with Red Bus Productions. The A&R director is Peter Prince, the A&R manager Peter Summerfield; the way they work provides a clear picture of the state of mainstream British pop, 1974–75.

They still get the tapes trickling in ('99 per cent rubbish'), they still travel the country viewing acts, following up tips, but the basic signing the A&R men do these days ('a couple a week') is on a package deal with an independent producer/writer/artist team. Pye claim a special advantage in these deals – many of the most successful independent producers (Tony Hatch, John Schroeder, Tony Macaulay) are ex-Pye men. So Pye got the Hatch/Des Parton/Sweet Sensation singles, and so they landed the world's biggest selling single of 1974, Biddu's production of Carl Douglas' 'Kung Fu Fighting' (on the other hand, they didn't get the Biddu Orchestra album – he did that deal with Epic).

The second A&R task is sorting through American material. Pye have the rights to a number of American labels and a variety of ways of dealing with them. Some tracks simply appear on the Pye International label, one-off arrangements; some US labels – Buddah, Kama Sutra, Stax – retain their identity. With Buddah the English A&R men decide on what and what not to release – Gladys Knight's hit 'Try To Remember'/'The Way We Were', for example, was not an American 45 until Pye had it in the British charts; with 20th Century, by contrast, Pye had to follow the Americans' release policy and 20th Century now has its own British office.

Pye have also had a long-time (and rather surprising) access to obscure soul singles, through the passion of John Abbey and his Contempo label. The company were comparatively slow to appreciate the full potential of the disco market, but when they did, they had the contacts, the understanding, the material, to do it full justice; Pye's Disco Demand series run by Dave MacAleer, succeeded with its odd combination of straight soul, doctored backing tracks ('Footsee'), and English made-for-disco products like Wayne Gibson's 'Under My Thumb'. The label's mixture of cynicism and purism seems a basic part of Pye's attitude to soul; their latest venture is the Right On label, whose releases will be decided by Dave Godin, an obsessional soul collector/writer.

Pye has had reasonable success with its tape deals and American labels but the hard point remains that the label has few successful acts of its own and has a very poor hit-to-release ratio (both Pye and Pye International are low in our Losers' Division). The A&R department claim that this reflects the essential MOR character of their music, that some of their singles function simply to get a bit of Radio Two play, to keep an artist in the public ear so that they'll buy his albums; but the majority sink without trace. They also dismiss the British market as being of diminishing importance in world sales (Des O'Connor, I was surprised to learn, is 'big in Japan'). Maybe so, but it sounds as though Pye is becoming a minor, specialist, MOR label, its pop success confined to the tape deals negotiated with shrewder operators than its own A&R department.

CBS

CBS is a telling contrast to Pye, a major American label which not only smoothly added rock to its distinguished classical and pop catalogues but in doing so became, with Dylan and Sly and Paul Simon and Janis Joplin, a leading rock label. In England the A&R director, Dan Loggins, is an American, and his team have divided responsibilities: Robin Blanchflower, A&R manager, is the traditional English showbiz figure; Alan Bown works as talent scout and artist liaison; Nicky Graham, Paul Phillips, and Michael Gane are staff producers. The English A&R men make none of the decisions about the company's American material, have no interest in one-off or short-term contracts, and are wary of tape deals with independent producers (though two of their biggest sellers, David Essex and the Wombles, reached them this way).

Their basic brief is to sign acts which are going to last, and what they have to remember is that CBS has got an amazing lineup already – there's no point in signing anyone who's not different or better than the company's existing talent. The tapes come in, as everywhere else, but for CBS these are a minor measure of potential. How does the act perform live? How does it look? Has it got the material/appeal/originality/guts on which to base a career?

Behind these questions lies an attitude that clearly comes from American CBS: the relationship between a record company and all its artists should be very close; a record company has responsibilities beyond the formal terms of a contract – to be involved with promotion and publicity and management, to look after its musicians. And so CBS has one of the few British A&R departments in which everyone can (and does) still produce; it has one of the few to appreciate the importance of local radio as a source of tour promotion (making special interview and jingle tapes, tying single releases into this strategy).

But CBS remains a schizophrenic company: it is essentially American (two-thirds of its releases) and has American, album-oriented, attitudes – careful and tactical talent spotting, supportive production and management, well organised tours, and so on; singles are thought of as album fodder. But at the same time CBS is an old-fashioned English pop label, with the Wombles and Tammy Jones and a manipulative appreciation of the importance of *Top Of The Pops* and the centre-spread in the *Sunday Mirror*. The consequence of this is not that CBS does particularly badly, but that it should do better! The company has signed a number of rock acts (Kokomo, Starry Eyed and Laughing, A Band Called O) which have the right style for pop (Top Twenty) success – the question is whether they will get it with CBS. So far they've fallen through the hole in the middle of the company: the pop A&R men aren't comfortable with rock, the rock A&R men aren't comfortable with singles. And so the most successful CBS pop act is the Wombles.

EMI

EMI is big like the BBC, and still recovering from the Beatles. Big means complex: Harvest and Capitol have their own staff, some American labels have their own logos, other American material is issued on EMI International, the EMI label is left with 'everything from Queen to Cilla Black'. The Beatles were such a huge success that the company only realised later that they'd been carried through the 1960s despite an archaic organisation. The EMI label has started again from scratch, shedding the over-large team of staff producers and talent scouts and faded stars, trying to change the image from grand old man of British pop to a new and thrusting young label.

EMI's A&R team (Nick Mobbs, Martin Clark, Ian McLintock) is genuinely obsessed with talent spotting. They don't believe that anything much is going to come in and so they go out – on the road, round the clubs, glued to *New Faces* and the *Melody Maker*'s folk/rock contests. Cockney Rebel were watched in clubs; Be Bop De Luxe (who ended up on Harvest) created a local (Yorkshire) buzz which reached EMI via a record shop's enthusiasm to a company salesman. The importance of these signings (and Pilot and Queen) wasn't just for themselves but also to encourage others. EMI would now like a couple of really heavy acts (and privately the A&R men believe that Harvest has lost its way – neither commercially successful, nor convincingly progressive; they'd like EMI to move into its territory).

The label is happy to sign tape deals, take one-off records, but they're more interested in the long term and here their talent-spotting instincts pull two ways – on the one hand it's safer to deal with established acts ('if they've been together for a long time they must have something') who've got live experience, their own management, a 'professional' outlook, but on the other hand it's more exciting to develop a talent from nowhere, and the department has its own eight-track studio and the dream of finding something on the rough tape that will turn out to be magic when the right knobs are pulled.

For acts that are signed, EMI's A&R department plays the same supervisory role as in any other company – getting the right producer, thrashing out release policy – but they are much more cost conscious than anyone else I spoke to, everything has to be accounted for. Not because EMI is hard up (no signs of a recession there) but because it is so rich it is so easy for a group to lose a thousand quid on a silly single that the A&R department have a special duty to make sure that they don't. The weekly A&R conference is joined by marketing men – the A&R department has to justify what it's been doing.

Maybe in consequence EMI are open in admitting that far too many of their singles flop and that *Rock File*'s surveys are an accurate guide to a company's success. They try never to release a single that they don't believe will be a chart hit and the only exceptions are for occasional 'political' reasons (which I take to mean that if one of their major artists sends in an appalling track as his next single they have to take it) and the few 'catalogue sellers' – records which make a five-figure sale but over a long period to a steady market – Cliff fans, Northern Soul regulars.

Singles success is not, of course, the major concern of a record company – there's far more money in albums; but the overall aim is to have successful acts, who will sell records of all sorts. This includes singles and EMI well know that the top twenty is still by far the best break for an act. Their failure with singles is a failure of A&R judgement and they'll only make one additional comment: for them, Radio One remains the essential medium for singles sales ('we are their slaves'); they experience the 'subcultural pressure' to pre-guess the BBC's taste, and they believe that the station is slowly drifting towards an MOR sound – just when they're trying to shift the EMI label the other way.

MAGNET

Magnet was started when writer/producer Peter Shelley played his tape of Alvin Stardust singing 'My Coo Ca Choo' to accountant Michael Levy and persuaded him that it was a chart cert and the good basis for a new record company. Within two years Magnet has become one of Britain's most successful independent labels, ambitious enough to handle more than just its own productions. The company's day-to-day A&R man is Pete Waterman, an influential Midlands DJ who came to Shelley's attention when he helped break Alvin Stardust. His original job was to find soul and reggae singles for possible Magnet release, but now it's he who goes through all the tapes, goes out spotting (he found Adrian Baker). He takes anything interesting to Shelley and they take their joint thoughts to Levy's weekly decision-making conference.

Magnet follows the A&R strategy developed by Dick Leahy at Bell in the early 1970s: Limited Output, Intense Promotion. They are looking for hit singles, reject all offers of heavy bands, don't even pretend to be able to handle someone like 10cc. They want a record; they don't care who the performer is, how they look, if they perform live (Magnet knew nothing about Susan Cadogan, for example, when they bought 'Hurts So Good' from Dip), they're not even interested in potential – they want the hit now. Their only questions are: is it good material? Does it come across? Does it sound right?

Pete Waterman is one of the few A&R men who has direct contact with the kids who buy his company's records – he plays to them in his disco, sells to them in his soul shop. His kids buy records, not acts, and Magnet's 'servicing' role is performed accordingly: so, 'Hurt So Good' was remixed to bring the voice forward, ethnic reggae was turned into disco-pop by astute knob-fiddling; now Waterman produces Susan Cadogan himself – the result is no longer reggae, but given what happens to other women in reggae (nothing) I doubt if Susan minds.

As a small company Magnet can't afford many failures, they haven't got enough of a cross-subsidy effect from established artists' steady sales – hence the intense promotion. They don't believe that Radio One is everything (though they're good at Radio One games: Adrian Baker made special jingles for Tony Blackburn and Noel Edmonds to support 'Sherry', having played the jingle the DJs followed through with the record, an effective ploy with a distinctive sound. Pete Wingfield used the same tactic with 'Eighteen With A Bullet'); they have an extensive disco mailing list (probably the most effective there is, except for Nigel Grainge's at Phonogram) and claim to get about 400 very valuable reaction letters on everything they release. Four of their 1974–75 hits were 'cross-overs' – i.e. they enjoyed radio play as a result of their disco popularity.

Success brings its own pressures. Peter Shelley, with his own musical ambitions, no longer has time to look after Alvin Stardust so Magnet went outside, to Roger Greenaway. The result, 'Sweet Cheating Rita', was Stardust's first flop. Independent producers also come in with

unsolicited tapes which clutter Pete Waterman's office, some of them
good (Guys and Dolls), some of them unusable.

There are foreign affairs: Epic handle Magnet material in the United
States, Germany is the company's best market. Already new calculations
are being made: does it sound right for Europe? As the output increases
will promotion become less intense? Can Magnet continue along their
single-minded way?

LAST WORDS

There are getting on for 150 A&R departments in the British record
industry; four is a tiny sample, unrepresentative, etc. But I wasn't
looking for laws or patterns; I was simply trying to find out what A&R
men did, which was the best image – evil genius? Showbiz hack?
Musicians' friend? Office stooge? All of these, I suppose, and I am
tempted to generalise.

One of the few laws of pop sociology says that the quality of the music
is in direct proportion to the number of record companies producing
it. The argument is most clearly developed in Charlie Gillett's *The Sound
of the City*: he shows that rock 'n' roll emerged from the studios of competitive independent labels and was emasculated as these labels were
absorbed into the majors. But the emergence of the new pop labels in
Britain over the last few years has not improved anything. I admire Rak
and the early UK, Bell and Magnet, for their success, but in musical terms
their output is rubbish, lowest common denominator pop; they've
hardly issued a single between them that I've kept. The same goes for
all those independent producers: these days people go out on their own
not because they can't make it with the majors, but because they can
make it only too well – what's at issue isn't taste but profit. And so my
new law goes: the bigger the company, the more likely it is to sign
someone original, issue something interesting.

The essence of A&R is risk-taking, nothing is certain except, maybe,
that if the Beatles got back together again, their first album would go
straight to number one (but would their first single?). A lot of an A&R
man's time is taken up with weighing odds; like any race-goer he's got
to judge conditions and form. The A&R man is constrained by the
condition of his company, of his market, of his selling media, and his
form book has a list of every hit, everything that's already worked. There
are very few real gamblers in British pop, the music only develops when
a loony comes along and rewrites the form book. Virgin are the only
company gambling a bit madly at the moment, experimenting in the

singles market, with little success so far – if they ever win big, other A&R men, their risks reduced, will suddenly turn out to share Virgin tastes.

The gambling metaphor rests on the peculiar relationship between music and money that is the heart of the record industry. Hang around company men, get involved in company concerns and you start talking (as I have in this piece) in company terms: music = product, audience = market, success = sales. What music actually is – notes and words, passion and energy – gets lost in the analysis of company policy, market breakdown, media exploitation. And yet … . Hang out some more and you find that it's the rare A&R man who isn't really into music as music – it's how he got into the job in the first place. And what's weird is that the music he's into is not usually the music he's putting out. I can forgive the enthusiasm for trash hits (spoiled by success), and I can understand not signing acts (too risky), but I can't understand the extraordinary amount of trash flops that come pouring out of every label on singles and albums. The only possible explanatory concept is 'professionalism'. There's a great mystique in the business about the professional approach (getting it together) to performing, managing, writing, recording. And, as in football, the 'great professional' is usually the great bore.

In *Rock File* I wrote a piece on Holyground, a studio in Yorkshire that was trying to work as a collective record company. One of Holyground's aims was to break up the usual division of rock labour, to give musicians greater control, to avoid making music product. The studio's best musician was Bill Nelson, he now leads Be Bop De Luxe, signed to Harvest, just beginning to dent the American glitter market. There's less idealism about these days. Odd eccentric labels do still appear (Oval, Rubber, Rampant) but I don't know what happened to Holyground and I now see the future somewhere else: the essence of a healthy rock scene is what's happening live. I've concluded that most records (and all discos) are bad for music. A good example: the pub rock story, when it comes to be written, is going to be most instructive and I'll bet on this conclusion in advance: every pub group gave more pleasure live than any of them has or ever will on record.

I dunno where that leaves A&R men.

                                                        (1976)

AFTERWORD

The names have changed (some of them); the processes described here
haven't. Punk gave 'independence' a new ideological inflection;
technology confused the distinctions between musician and producer
and engineer; and if I were writing the piece now I'd be more interested
in the implications of this industrial system for black musicians and
entrepreneurs. But the biggest difference between the British record
business then and now is its place in the global music market: no A&R
man now could afford to be as provincial as they seemed back then.

8

In Praise of the Professionals
Charlie Gillett

Here's a list of the twenty most successful producers in the British record industry over the past eleven years, in which perhaps half-a-dozen names will be more than vaguely familiar. Paul McCartney, David Bowie, Jimmy Page of Led Zeppelin, and Brian Wilson of the Beach Boys are self-producing artists who are known primarily as performers, secondarily as writers, and only incidentally as producers. Of the others, Mickie Most has made himself a household name as a panellist on the *New Faces* TV show, rather than as producer of 63 hit singles, and the two most famous producers as producers are probably George Martin of Beatles fame, and Bob Johnston, producer of Bob Dylan when it mattered. But what about those names at the top of the list – Peter Sullivan, Tony Visconti, Felton Jarvis and Gus Dudgeon – or, further down, Glyn Johns, Mike Curb and Mike Leander?

In one sense, maybe it is right that the producers remain virtually anonymous; after all, it is the performers who take the risks of laying themselves open to the public, and who deserve whatever fame they can acquire. The successful producer is usually paid well for his efforts, and should not covet public recognition too. But producers are not simply ignored; there is often an undertone of suspicion and mistrust in music paper coverage of producers, resulting in a negative image of some kind of bureaucratic Svengali, who makes the artist conform to his company's concept of commercialism. At best, the producer is portrayed as a benevolent layabout who keeps the musicians supplied with booze or drugs, and does his best to keep the tapes rolling.

As an ex-journalist with some of those prejudices towards unseen 'manipulators', I have found my attitude towards successful producers shifting from hostility to awed admiration since I joined the ranks of producers myself. Formerly derisive of records which achieved their aims so simply and easily, I now marvel at Mickie Most's deceptively casual and uncannily accurate productions for Hot Chocolate, am entranced by the sounds on Abba's records (put there so neatly by Benny Andersson and Bjorn Ulvaeus), and yearn for a return of the energy that was captured by the Beatles under George Martin's watchful eye but never recaptured by any of them on their own without him.

Table 1: The Top Twenty Producers 1967–77

| | | Singles | | Albums | | |
		Top 30 Hits (1)	Chart-Toppers (2)	Top 10 Hits (3)	Chart-Toppers (4)	Weighted Total* (1+2+3+4)
1	Peter Sullivan	24	2	16	2	84
2	Tony Visconti	24	4	11	4	81
3	Elvis Presley/ Felton Jarvis	29	2	13	2	80
4	Gus Dudgeon	24	2	10	4	74
5	Mickie Most	63	1	1	–	68
6=	Chas Chandler	20	6	7	3	65
6=	Bob Johnston	6	–	13	5	65
8	George Martin	19	5	7	3	62
11=	Paul McCartney	19	2	7	3	56
9	Jimmy Miller	9	3	5	5	59
10	Gordon Mills	21	2	7	3	58
11=	John Franz	17	1	11	1	56
13	Glyn Johns	13	–	9	3	52
14	David Bowie**	15	–	8	3	51
15=	Nicky Chinn/ Mike Chapman***	26	5	3	–	45
17	Brian Holland/ Lamont Dozier	29	–	4	1	44
15=	Jimmy Page	–	–	7	6	45
20	Mike Curb**	18	5	3	–	37
19	Mike Leander	23	3	3	–	38
18	Brian Wilson	6	1	9	1	39

* Weighted total reached by ascribing one point for every Top Thirty entry, two points for every singles chart-topper, three points for every Top Ten album, and four points for every album chart-topper.
** These producers worked with various co-producers.
*** Chinn/Chapman figures include two singles produced by Chapman alone.

The standard word used to describe a producer's distinctive sound is 'formula', which carries a pejorative meaning, as if it is somehow easy to keep doing the same thing, and easier for a producer to get away with repetition than for an artist. The figures based on the logs in this book suggest that it is almost as hard to survive as a producer as it is for an artist. There were 49 producers who had ten or more top 30 hits in the period covered, compared to 44 artists with ten or more. The log of producers shows many names who had only one hit, and of course does not list the legion who tried and never succeeded – including, at the time of writing, this writer.

There are no easy routes to success in the music industry, and no safe ways to sustain it, but one of its greatest attractions is that there are no established training programmes which qualify an applicant; in every section, you learn by doing, absorb the lessons of mistakes, repeat them, and try again. The paradox for producers is that it is often unclear exactly what they did, and therefore what they should repeat or change.

The essence of the producer's role is to be the catalyst for the other participants in the studio, the person who sparks them off into delivering their best, together. In some cases, the producer is doubling up some other role, as songwriter, arranger, recording engineer, or performing musician, in which case he (producers are rarely women) can lead by example and physically control what happens. But more often, the producer is there strictly as a producer, and has to coax or bully the team into an inspirational performance.

The term 'producer' has come into widespread use in the record business only in the past 20 years, and it has a different meaning from film and theatre producers, whose main role is to raise money and support ventures financially while a 'director' controls the creative process. The record producer is a close equivalent of the film director, who juggles actors, script-writers, camera crew and sets, much as the producer works with singers, songs, musicians and engineers.

Before they were known as producers, session supervisors were called recording managers or A&R men, whose job was to 'marry' an artist ('a') to a song ('r', for repertoire). Most of the time, the singer was established on the company roster, and the A&R man's main decision was to assign the song best suited to each singer's particular style. This kind of producer has become almost a minority figure in the record industry these days, but six of the top 20 are basically traditional A&R men – or were at the time they scored the hits logged here. Peter Sullivan (number one on our list) found the right songs for Tom Jones and Engelbert Humperdinck at Decca before going independent to form the AIR production company in partnership with other producers including EMI's George Martin (8); a contemporary of theirs, Johnny Franz (11=), stayed at Philips where he prospered during the 1970s with Peters and Lee among others until his recent death; in America, Felton Jarvis (3) sniffed songs and scouted musicians for Elvis Presley, for years without any credit on either singles or albums until the last few releases before Elvis' death, which listed Elvis himself as 'executive producer' and Felton as 'associate producer'; at MGM, Mike Curb (20) was vice-president for a while, when he kept Donny Osmond 'hot' by the apparently simple expedient of retrieving songs from the 1950s for him to revive; Bob Johnston (6=) was US Columbia's man in Nashville, where he helped Bob Dylan to find the musicians and moods he needed.

The A&R man was usually on a salary, rather than a royalty 'commission' on his work, which may account for why most successful staff producers go out on their own to be freelance operators; as independent producers, they can not only expect a royalty, but have more freedom to select compatible artists to work with, and are more likely to achieve recognition for their work, at least within the industry, if not with the public at large.

In America, the independent producer became increasingly common during the 1950s, either working for established companies, or setting up their own small labels and competing directly with the major companies. Jerry Leiber and Mike Stoller were among the pioneer songwriters who established that producing was an art in itself that should be rewarded with a slice of the income, and 25 years later they still have the knack of finding commercial frameworks for such diverse British hit-makers as Stealers Wheel, Procol Harum and Elkie Brooks.

In Britain, the drift towards independent production did not become conspicuous until the early 1960s, when Joe Meek is acknowledged to have been the leader (as freelance producer of John Leyton, the Tornadoes and others). The real surge of independent activity here followed the emergence of groups who played their own instruments and often wrote their own material, several of whom were still in full flight at the start of the period covered by our logs in *Rock File*: the Beatles, the Rolling Stones, the Kinks, the Who, Manfred Mann, the Hollies.

In contrast to previous generations of singers, these groups did not depend on Tin Pan Alley tunes and studio orchestras, but sought their own particular sounds, and needed help rather than instruction from their producers. In the absence of an available pool of qualified producers to choose from, they made do with men instantly converted from a variety of other roles: probably the least qualified but best-placed to take on the role of producer were artists' managers, several of whom also started their own labels: Andrew Oldham (manager of the Rolling Stones, owner of Immediate Records), Robert Stigwood (manager of Cream and the Bee Gees, owner of RSO), Kit Lambert (manager of the Who, owner of Track), Chris Blackwell (manager of Traffic, owner of Island), and – in a different field of music – Gordon Mills (10: manager of Tom Jones, Engelbert Humperdinck and Gilbert O'Sullivan, and a director of MAM Records). Also in our list, Chas Chandler (6=: manager of Slade and their producer for Polydor), and Mike Leander (19: manager of Gary Glitter and the Glitter Band, and their producer for Bell).

For a while in the mid-1960s, to be an American producer in Britain was to be in a distinct category, as Americans were recognised to have more adventurous production styles, and among the most successful and influential were Shel Talmy (the Kinks, Manfred Mann, Amen Corner) and Jimmy Miller (9: Traffic, the Rolling Stones), both of whom played an important role in educating our engineers in American production techniques. For artists who write their own songs and play their own instruments, engineering is usually the one part of the recording process they are prepared to leave to somebody else, so an engineer-producer is the ideal person for them, resulting in high places in our top twenty for Tony Visconti (2: producer of T. Rex and co-producer with David Bowie), Gus Dudgeon (4: Elton John), and Glyn Johns (13: several different artists).

For some artists, the long-term aim is to become their own producers, having learned all they can from working under A&R men, managers, engineers, and anyone else who might have been appointed to help them. Brian Wilson of the Beach Boys (18) was far ahead of most artists in achieving this goal, writing, arranging, and producing the Beach Boys records from 1965 onwards, and it may have been a determination by some of the individual Beatles to achieve comparable autonomy that caused them to break apart and stay apart; John Lennon and George Harrison both started strongly and then lost momentum, while Paul McCartney (11=) gradually revealed himself to be a 'stayer' with apparently limitless ingenuity and perseverance.

Of the other artist-producers, David Bowie (14) has almost always credited a co-producer, usually one with engineering expertise (Tony Visconti, Ken Scott), and although most of his work has been with himself as performing artist, he has also successfully produced other people (Mott the Hoople, Lou Reed). Of all the producers in the top twenty, Jimmy Page (15=) is probably the most narrowly-focused, limiting himself exclusively to producing Led Zeppelin, the fourpiece group in which he is lead guitarist.

One way or another, we have identified categories for 17 of the top twenty producers, leaving Mickie Most (5), Nicky Chinn/Mike Chapman (15=) and Brian Holland/Lamont Dozier (17) to be accounted for. They stand apart from the others in several ways, having an immediately recognisable production style which they applied to several artists with equal success.

Mickie Most is a phenomenon without parallel. His 63 hit singles in this period is more than twice any other producer's total, impressive proof of his ability to adapt to changing dance rhythms and visual images. Yet he had only one chart-topping single in the whole period ('You Win Again' by Hot Chocolate) and his only Top Ten album was a greatest hits compilation (again by Hot Chocolate). It is hard to avoid the conclusion that he was better at following trends that initiating them, that he could be quick to cash in on a market or an idea but could not be bothered to be as relentlessly perfectionist in following them through.

Mickie's critics would accuse him of being purely 'commercial', yet his lack of thoroughness suggests a different conclusion – he produces records for fun, rather than for maximum financial gain.

The most striking aspect of the roster of artists listed against Mickie Most's name in the index of singles producers is that none of them have been major on-stage attractions, working the college and town hall circuits to back up their hits. Mickie's tastes and instincts take him towards the 'showbiz' side of the business, aimed at the very young kids who watch Saturday morning TV and their parents who watch the variety shows on the same box in the weekday evenings. From 1970 onwards, Mickie produced exclusively for his own Rak label, and in many ways functioned like an old-fashioned A&R man, finding songs to suit singers who were marketed towards distinct audiences. He had worked with more authentic artists like Donovan and Jeff Beck, but rarely tangled with them on Rak, where his main and enduring act was Hot Chocolate.

Featuring the instantly recognisable, chalk-on-the-blackboard voice of bald black Errol Brown, Hot Chocolate had 14 Top Thirty hits (13 produced by Mickie Most), which put them among the top twenty artists for the period; yet without a big current hit they could never be sure of filling a provincial town hall. Effective and appealing as their records often were, they did not generate an impulse among listeners to want to explore further, to buy albums or go and see the act on stage. There seems every chance that Mickie Most will soon feel obliged to find an act with those qualities, but who respect his flair for hearing compelling dance grooves and insistent chorus hooks, and that he will still figure high in the list of top producers in ten years' time.

As if his log of hits as a producer were not impressive enough, Mickie Most also cultivated the period's most successful production team, Nicky Chinn and Mike Chapman. As producers who wrote their own material, Chinn and Chapman belonged in a tradition of British producers which includes Roger Greenaway, Tony Macaulay, and the Phil Coulter/Bill Martin team; but Chinn and Chapman managed to create a quite distinct identity for each of the artists they worked with – principally Mud, Suzi Quatro and Smokie – which helped to make them potentially enticing as album and live artists. But the association with Rak may have served to diminish their credibility as 'rock' artists in Britain,

Songwriter–Producers
Nicky Chinn (left) and Mike Chapman

where the press is strongly suspicious of artists who do not write their own material, even if they deliver it in a style which sounds as if they could have done. Mud broke away from both the label and the producers (but did not enjoy anything like the same kind of success on their own), leaving Suzi and Smokie still with them, and still looking for that elusive 'credibility in depth'. Whatever Chinn and Chapman's status in ten years' time, it seems very likely that there will have been a critical re-evaluation of their hits in the 1970s, which put strong rhythms under interesting songs with enough originality to carry five singles right to the top of the charts.

In the case of Brian Holland and Lamont Dozier, such a re-evaluation is already taking place. Their high placing on the top twenty is particularly remarkable as their active career as producers was confined to the first four years covered here, having begun earlier, in 1964. Having been originally hired separately as staff writers for the Detroit-based family of labels owned by Berry Gordy (including Tamla, Motown, and Gordy), Brian and Lamont struck up a working studio relationship in which Brian was mainly engineer and Lamont did the musical arrangements; working primarily on songs co-written with Brian's brother Eddie Holland, the team strung together long series of hits for the Four Tops, the Supremes, and the Isley Brothers with such regularity and apparent infallibility that their operation became known as a hit factory. But although their success in America was instant and huge, conservative radio programming in Britain delayed the impact, and they had several big hits with reissued releases.

The first impact of the Holland–Dozier productions came through their irresistible danceability and their penetrating vocals; only years later did some of us more casual listeners begin to absorb the contributions made by loping bass lines, momentous drumming, and all the surreptitious effects from tambourines, hand-claps and other percussive additions. Countless British producers paid sincere homage by stealing every idea they could identify and reproduce, and it seems that every year a different song incorporates the bass-line riff from 'I Can't Help Myself' by the Four Tops and makes the Top Ten ('Black is Black' by Los Bravos and La Belle Epoque, 'I'm on Fire' by 5000 Volts, 'Love Really Hurts Without You' by Billy Ocean among them), and 'Where Did Our Love Go' by the Supremes attracts a new cover version virtually every month without ever losing its own appeal.

Brian Holland and Lamont Dozier helped to establish production as a craft which merged the inspiration of art with the method of a profession. Everyone who has followed owes them some debt of gratitude.

(1978)

Afterword

We have not systematically kept score of the production successes of the past 20 years, but it is safe to say that none of the top 20 from 1967–77 would challenge for a place in an equivalent table for 1985–95. But while the names have changed, most of the same types of producer are still there. Although they are less common in the UK these days, the song-writer-as-producer is still a viable role in the US, particularly in black music where Minneapolis-based Jam and Lewis (working with Janet Jackson and others) and Atlanta-based L.A. Reid and Babyface (Bobby Brown, TLC and others) have taken over the mantles of Holland–Dozier and Gamble–Huff. The artist as self-producer had emerged 20 years ago, and is now an industry norm (Prince, Phil Collins, Sting), often in conjunction with an engineer-turned-producer or co-producer like Hugh Padgham (who worked with both Collins and Sting) or Steve Lilleywhite (with U2), now the most common type of producer.

Almost extinct now are manager-producers and entrepreneur–producers. Pete Waterman was the exception that proved the rule. Noted throughout *Rock File* in his successive roles as a Coventry club DJ and A&R man at Magnet Records, Pete later went freelance to form successful production relationships, first with Peter Collins (producing Nik Kershaw), and from 1984 with the engineer–musician partnership of Mike Stock and Matt Aitken.

The team of Stock–Aitken–Waterman would undoubtedly head the league table of producers of UK hits in the past ten years. After providing hits for other companies, notably with Dead or Alive, Mel and Kim, and Rick Astley, Waterman formed his own PWL label to release productions by his team for the Australian soap opera stars Kylie Minogue and Jason Donovan. But the more successful Stock–Aitken–Waterman became, the more Waterman was derided and reviled by fashion-conscious commentators in the British media. He was understandably mystified by the venom of the attacks: 'I couldn't have had a worse press if I had spent every night killing grandmothers.' His sin? To have infected – some would say infested – British radio with catchy phrases set to irresistible melodies, performed by singers who did not write their own songs. This last point seemed to be the most culpable of all possible crimes – pop music journalists only liked performers who wrote their own songs, as an expression of their own experience and angst, and they mistrusted a process which involved singers interpreting another writer's material. Such journalists seem unperturbed by the fact that many of the records they love best were made through this process (such as 'I Heard It Through the Grapevine' by Marvin Gaye or 'Mr Tambourine Man' by the Byrds). But that was then, and this is now, and now, it seems, such a method is irredeemably suspect. Managers behind recent 'pop' projects have taken note, and are careful not only to ensure that each project contains at least one member who is a song-writer (for example Take That and East 17), but that the managers themselves keep their heads down, in contrast to highly visible managers of the 1960s like Brian Epstein (the Beatles) and Andrew Oldham (the Rolling Stones).

Ironically, the politically-incorrect Pete Waterman was actually a forerunner of the hippest new category of producer, which has become steadily more prevalent since the period covered by *Rock File*: the DJ–producer. A case of poachers-who-turned-into-game-keepers, club-based disc jockeys, frustrated by records which didn't meet the criteria demanded by their audiences, set out to metamorphose existing records into what they wanted. Speeding records up or slowing them down, combining snatches of drums from one record with catchy hooks from another, DJs created a live 'mix' in their clubs which they subsequently sought to emulate in a recording studio. Linking up with an engineer, they provided themselves with customised versions of the records they wanted to play.

The next step was to press up a few pirate copies of these in-demand, but unauthorised, 'remixes'. Sometimes, these pirate releases were suppressed by the record companies which owned the rights; but more often, the applicable record companies authorised the remixes, either by officially releasing the do-it-yourself efforts, or by commissioning remixes along the same lines. Working with multi-track tapes of the original recordings, the DJs became familiar with the procedures of making records, and some took the final step of initiating recordings under their own project names. During the late 1980s, the British charts were awash with projects whose producers were more the 'artist' than the singers who nominally fronted them: Coldcut, Bomb The Bass, S'Express and the Beatmasters. For precedents, we would have to go back to the 1930s, when the big bands were named after their band-leaders, and vocalists took secondary billing.

Despite attempts to take these projects out on tour as if they were 'real artists', neither the press nor the public could get to grips with the anonymity of the concept, and subsequent generations of DJ–producers took note and kept their heads down below the sniping line. In Europe, where there was no equivalent music press to pour scorn on any sign of commercial ambition, unembarrassed producers were delighted to supply the market which the British pioneers had revealed. The doors to the UK Top Ten were left wide open to DJ–engineer producer–partnerships from Germany, Sweden, Italy, Belgium and Holland. Apparently disqualified from playing the game, the canny-as-ever Pete Waterman licensed the Dutch project 2 Unlimited, produced by the team of Wilde and De Coster, and had several huge hits in the UK on his PWL label.

In my 1978 piece, I confidently predicted that in ten years' time there would be a critical re-evaluation of the role and contribution of producers like Chinn and Chapman (Mud, the Sweet, Suzi Quatro) and Holland and Dozier (Four Tops, Supremes). In the event, Mike Chapman went on to to become even more successful, as an American-based producer of Blondie and the Knack, without being acknowledged as a significant figure in his own right. Holland and Dozier's contributions have been more widely appreciated, along with those of fellow Motown producer Norman Whitfield (the Temptations and Marvin Gaye, before he started to produce himself). But ironically it has been the Motown session musicians operating under their direction, rather than the producers, who have achieved 'legendary' status. Drummer Benny Benjamin and bass-player James Jamerson are properly revered, but although Norman Whitfield went on to substantial success as writer–producer of Rose Royce for his own Whitfield label, he still remains an enigmatic, unexplored figure.

It is difficult to explain why producers come in for such a 'bad press' while film directors, in many ways their equivalent, are treated as 'auteurs' not only in specialist film magazines, but by the film reviewers in national newspapers. In many cases, directors are given more credit (or blame) than they deserve, since the contributions of actors, writers, editors, cameramen and producers are also vital to the final result. By contrast, record producers often have a vital influence on the final result, and yet are consistently over looked in many discussions. In all the fuss about the recently successful albums by Blur and the Cranberries, hardly any mention is made of the fact that both albums were produced by Stephen Street, who was also engineer and/or co-producer on most of the records by the Smiths and Morrissey. He must be doing something right, but nobody seems to care what it is.

Is it simply that different kinds of journalists write about film and music? Or that journalists think they understand what a film director does, but have difficulty understanding and appreciating the role of a record producer? Does the job defy evocative description, or are producers all uninteresting journeymen? I still think that record producers achieve a miracle every time they capture the spirit of a song or an idea, when they make it 'work' for the rest of us who listen to the record; and that they will eventually be recognised as having been more important than many of the artists who received all the attention at the time. But I must admit that this recognition is taking longer than I expected!

9

In a Week, Maybe Two, We'll Make You a Star

Stephen Barnard

I think it's great, the parents would say,
I think it's great you've got someone,
Someone to idolize, who must look twice his size,
I think it's great you're going through a phase
And I'm awfully glad it'll all be over in a couple of days
   Harry Nilsson, 'Mr Richland's Favourite Song' (1971)

On 4 October 1973 the BBC television programme *Top Of The Pops* celebrated its 500th birthday with a special edition. Much was made of the occasion; the Jackson Five, the Osmonds, Gary Glitter, Mick Jagger and Slade were all seen on film paying, in the latter two cases at least, somewhat dubious tribute to the big daddy of all television pop programmes, and twice the usual number of artists were featured. Extended to an hour's length, the show quickly developed into an orgy of self-congratulation. But the *pièce de résistance*, as far as the show's producers were concerned, was the 'surprise appearance' of American teen idol David Cassidy. At the beginning of the programme viewers saw what they were led to believe was Cassidy's plane still in flight over the Atlantic and about 40 minutes later saw the plane actually land and the lad himself disembark. After skipping down the steps to exchange a few pleasantries with the show's co-host Tony Blackburn, Cassidy then mimed both sides of his new record, right there at the airport.

In fact, Cassidy had been in Britain for several days prior to his *Top Of The Pops* slot, staying at some secret hideout in the country. The segment had been recorded a day prior to transmission and the plane had taxied in from a private airfield. All that Cassidy's October visit did in fact consist of was that one television appearance, a brief press conference, and a phone call to BBC Radio One's childrens' request programme, *Junior Choice*, on the following Saturday morning, intended

120

primarily to mislead fans over the time of his departure and so avoid chaos at the airport. No concerts, no interviews, and at first sight hardly worth the time or money involved in making the 6000-mile trip from Los Angeles to London.

Ostensibly, the visit took place just to plug the new record and pay homage to *Top Of The Pops* on its grand anniversary; but its true importance lay in re-establishing Cassidy in both the hearts and minds of British teenyboppers. The attention of the teen magazines and Radio Luxembourg, whose importance in helping to sustain the whole teenybopper phenomenon cannot be over-estimated, had turned away from Cassidy towards the Osmonds, and young Donny in particular, in preparation for the concert tour of Britain planned by the Osmonds for late October. In this situation, Cassidy's management saw it as crucial that he should put in an appearance on these shores, however briefly, to steal some of the limelight. But there was more to this visit than simple oneupmanship. The facts facing the Cassidy camp were that no record released under either the Partridge Family name or by Cassidy solo had made the American Top Fifty in the past 18 months and that latest ratings showed that the series was losing viewers at a considerable rate. There could be no doubt in anybody's mind that as a teen idol David Cassidy was over the hill, while the Osmonds and the Jackson Five were still managing to hold their own. In Britain, however, the situation was different; Cassidy's records were consistent bestsellers and popularity polls still rated him highly. Hence the importance of the British market to Cassidy's management, and hence the lightning visit.

Six minutes singing to a pre-recorded backing track on a drizzly night at an airport did the trick: Cassidy's record, 'Daydreamer', bounced into the British Top Fifty at number eight just one week after release. A week later it was number one. Shrewdly timed, brilliantly executed, the visit was public relations engineering at its most effective.

> Do I have to do this all over again,
> Didn't I get it right the first time?
>> Peter Tork, (for the Monkees) 'Do I Have To
>> Do This All Over Again' (1967)

David Cassidy is a television star, and the success of *The Partridge Family* marks the first time that television has ever come to terms with pop music to its own satisfaction. *The Partridge Family* is produced for American television by Screen Gems, who are owned by Columbia Pictures (who also own Cassidy's recording company, Bell). The Screen Gems organisation itself supervises all those aspects of the pop business that are usually decentralised: marketing, networking, promotion, publicity, records, concerts, the lot. The Screen Gems principle is to exploit pop music through the medium of television, and the Cassidy enterprise is the latest and by far the most efficient and successful manifestation of that principle.

The problem all along in presenting pop music on television has been that television itself has never been a particularly teen-oriented medium. American television is regarded as family entertainment and has to appeal to the widest possible cross-section of the American public to satisfy both the public themselves and advertisers and sponsors. Rock 'n' roll was too violent, too raw and too overtly sexual for family viewing and so for some time was only allowed the minimum of coverage on television variety shows, and even then producers insisted on Elvis Presley being photographed from the waist up as a built-in safeguard against complaints from the Mothers' Union. Dick Clark's *American Bandstand* gained advertising sponsorship by diluting the music itself, by making it clean, presentable and safe – in short, making it acceptable for family viewing, to young children and adults as well as record-buying adolescents. Ricky Nelson was 'accidentally' launched as a record star out of *The Ozzie and Harriet Show*, which featured his parents in a typical family soap opera. But television was never as important to the popularisation of rock 'n' roll as Hollywood films were and it was only in the late 1950s that promoters began to explore the possibilities of hype by TV, although in those days all it consisted of was three minutes' miming on nationally networked television programmes: needless to say, a lot of payola was usually involved.

This was television coming to terms with pop music but still failing to appreciate the vastness and, it must be said, the potential gullibility of the teenage market; all the major hype operations of the late 1950s were instigated by people from within the pop industry itself, not from within television. Younger kids had *Huckleberry Hound* and *Captain Kangaroo*, while adults could sit back and enjoy *Peyton Place* and *Bewitched*; but for teenagers there was nothing but groups miming to their records on American Bandstand or its mid-1960s equivalents *Shindig* and *Hullabaloo*. This was a legacy that pop music was saddled with throughout the 1960s; what pop music there was on TV was computerised, mechanical and totally harmless, and this was itself a major contributing factor to the sterility of the entire American pop scene at this time. It should be remembered that even the Beatles only made it in America after one of the biggest pre-visit hype operations ever, and still owe a considerable debt to Ed Sullivan for giving them their first national exposure on his show.

The potential role of television as an image maker was belatedly realised after the Beatles' success. Teenybopper magazines in the early

1960s had tended to drool over television stars as much as they did straight commercial pop idols, and there were passing crazes for, among others Richard Chamberlain of *Dr Kildare* fame; David McCallum, the star of *The Man from U.N.C.L.E.*; and Robert Fuller, co-star of *Laramie*. Some of these stars even made records and had hits but they were never followed up and their popularity was not sustained. This was a mere extension of the filmstar syndrome in a televisual context and the records were strictly one-off propositions, gimmicks, novelties, not to be taken too seriously even by the artists concerned.

Enter the Monkees, in the summer of 1966, with a television series at peak viewing time, networked nationally, and a number one hit record. The group was the creation of two producers at Screen Gems–Columbia, Bob Rafelson and Bert Schneider, whose intention it was to produce a new situation comedy series about the life of a pop group. They hired scriptwriters Paul Mazursky and Larry Tucker and handed the musical supervision of the series over to Don Kirshner, head of Screen Gems Music and a tremendously influential figure on Tin Pan Alley in the early 1960s. Needing actors and preferring not to use established stars because of the ego troubles that might ensue and because of the money involved, they advertised in *Variety* for four unknowns. Five hundred and thirty-seven answered the ad., from whom Mickey Dolenz, Mike Nesmith, Davy Jones and Peter Tork, were eventually chosen. Dolenz was a former child star who'd fallen on bad times; Nesmith was a native of Texas and an accomplished folk musician; Jones was an actor living off a contract he had signed a couple of years previously with Screen Gems and Tork had played blues in Greenwich Village. The Monkees were, of course, modelled on the Beatles, and the film techniques used were imitation Dick Lester, obviously cribbed from *Help!* and *A Hard Day's Night*, but they were new to television and certainly new to a second generation of teenyboppers for whom the Beatles were just a group their elder brothers and sisters liked. Initially, the concept of the Monkees was not particularly mercenary, cynical or exploitative; all four members were contracted as actors and not as musicians, with a suspension clause should any member of the group become uncooperative once the show was under way. To its makers, *The Monkees* was, at first, just another television show.

The show was an immediate hit and so there was pressure for a single. 'Last Train To Clarksville' reached number one two weeks after release and there were demands for an album. But putting the show together each week proved to be a full-time job, which left the producers with only two hours each week to spare for recording. The group were told what to sing and how to sing it, with everything else done for them, and the crushing blow to both Nesmith and Tork, the musicians of the group, was to find that not only were they not required to play their instruments on their recordings, they were not even *allowed* to. Worse still, the publicity men actually tried to pass the instrumentation on the records as that of the Monkees themselves. In time, the Monkees' records were making far more money for Screen Gems–Columbia than the show was, a situation the makers had never anticipated. For Don Kirshner this was fine. All the material that the Monkees recorded came from his publishing house and from the nucleus of writers who had been working for him since his days in the Brill Building in New York – Gerry Goffin and Carole King, Neil Sedaka and Howie Greenfield, Barry Mann and Cynthia Weil included – and the royalties from Monkees records were the company's biggest source of revenue. Finally, however, the question over who plays what became too much for Mike Nesmith. Stuck in a hotel room one afternoon he called up all the magazines in town and told them to send reporters down for an 'unofficial news conference', without consulting either Screen Gems or the other Monkees. Only *Look* and *Time* sent people over, but that was enough. He told them the full story, about the extent to which they had been hyped as a group, how they had been taken advantage of all the way down the line, about how they never played on their records because they weren't allowed to, and how he felt it was the right time 'to draw the line as a man'.

It had the desired effect. Within days it was the major news story in all the American trade papers and started a raging controversy over the whole question of manufacturing groups and the exploitation involved in selling them to the teenage market. Kirshner argued that pressures on the group were such that there was no time to help them develop musically and that people obviously liked the records, otherwise they wouldn't buy them. Others in the Screen Gems camp doubted the group's ability, and pointed out that they had a responsibility towards the musicians they employed to provide work for them, i.e. they had a union agreement to uphold. Soon after the story broke, Screen Gems called a meeting at a Beverly Hills hotel and reminded Nesmith of the suspension clause in his contract. Furious, he walked out and put his fist through the door, glaring at one of the company's legal advisers and saying, 'that could have been your face'. He could have been suspended and sued for every penny he had, but Screen Gems really had little choice but to accede to his demands and allow the group to do their own backing tracks. There were also practical considerations behind their decision: soon the Monkees were to make concert appearances and it was therefore essential that they develop some kind of musical proficiency beforehand.

After that episode, however, Screen Gems quickly lost interest in their property. The Monkees made only one more series, although a string of commercially disastrous albums followed that did establish their credentials as musicians. As a final parting gesture, the Monkees made a film, *Head*, with Bob Rafelson directing, which took the rise out of the pop business itself. Rafelson, who was concerned solely with the television side of the Monkees and had nothing to do with their musical output or the publicity machine, co-wrote a song for the film with musical coordinator Jack Nicholson (the film director), 'War Chant' which summed up the recent events:

> Hey, hey, we are the Monkees
> You've heard it all before
> The money's in, we're made of tin
> We're here to give you more
> > Bob Rafelson and Jack Nicholson, 'War Chant' (1967)

Peter Tork was the first to leave the Monkees, in mid-1969, as soon as his contract expired. The rest followed in quick succession. In 1970 Tork began legal action against Screen Gems–Columbia for alleged non-payment of royalties. At the same time, Davy Jones and Mickey Dolenz issued a joint writ against Screen Gems charging breach of contract; fraud; deceit; misrepresentation; conspiracy to deny them royalties for discs, merchandising, songwriting, and producer royalties; and also personal appearance coin. Both court actions remain, at the time of writing, unresolved.

The four members of the Monkees were paid a weekly salary, nothing more. According to Gloria Stavers, the editor of *16* magazine, quoted in an interview in *Rolling Stone*, income from merchandising the Monkees was the one factor that saved Columbia Pictures from bankruptcy. But, apparently, the Monkees saw very little of that money. The point was that Screen Gems never expected the Monkees to last. They were not prepared, until Nesmith forced their arm, to give the group the chance to develop musically, and it was this lack of far-sighted management that brought the Monkees enterprise to such a messy close.

> Always the same routine
> I never change,
> Not funny ho-ho
> Funny strange
> > Tony Romeo, (for David Cassidy) 'I Am A Clown'

The importance of the Monkees was twofold. First, they set a precedent in the method of pop music presentation on television, and demonstrated the degree to which the medium of television could be used in selling that music, even if this was not the original aim of the series.

Hype took over when the Monkees' managers realised just what a good thing they were on to, but attempts to cash in on the Monkees' success in 1966–67 failed without exception, even though groups like the Cowsills and the Spectrum had extensive TV backing. It was too soon after the Monkees' collapse to try it again, the Monkees had come just at the right time, two years after the Beatles and in the middle of an American pop renaissance that included such groups as the Lovin' Spoonful, the Mamas and the Papas, and the Turtles.

Second, the Monkees, entirely through their appearances on TV, created or at least discovered a new market: sub-teenagers, very young kids whose previous interest in pop music might just have extended to Burl Ives singing 'Big Rock Candy Mountain'.

The Monkees reached their peak in 1967, the year that Pete Fowler describes in 'Skins Rule'[*] as 'the great divide', the year pop music seemed to split into two distinct camps, leaving on the one hand the music of the underground, incorporating acid-rock and head music, and on the other, mundane bubblegum, pop at its most blatantly commercial and at its most hideously banal. Bubblegum was tots' music, literally, distinguished by its crude, pip-squeak rhythm and nursery-rhyme lyrics, conveyor-belt music at its lowest level ever. Groups like the 1910 Fruitgum Company and Ohio Express catered for the market that the Monkees had unearthed and had then forsaken but, paradoxically, this new form of bubblegum was essentially faceless. Buying an Ohio Express single to a young kid was just like buying a scribbling pad with a picture of Yogi Bear on the front. The members of the 1910 Fruitgum Company or the Kasenetz–Katz Singing Orchestral Circus never made the centre spread of *16* or any of the other teenybopper magazines. Bubblegum represented the very first time in pop's short history that it succumbed to total lack of image.

Image or no image, television was there to exploit the new music, and it was Screen Gems yet again who set the pace via cartoon series about a mythical pop group called the *Archies*. The mastermind behind the series was Don Kirshner, and all the songs were written, played and sung by the Monkees' ex-producer Jeff Barry and a select band of session men. All the records were put out on the Monkees' former label Colgems. Cartoon characters couldn't complain about not being able to play on their records, even the hype machine was unnecessary. And *The Archies* was a kiddies' show in the traditional mould, *Atom Ant* plus music, that wasn't even highschool revisited, but a product of the culture of the nursery rhyme or the summer camp. This particular legacy is still with

---

* See p. 153 of this volume.

us today, witness *Josie and the Pussycats* and the crude cartoon versions of the lives of the Osmonds and the Jackson Five.

But in pop the situation continually shifts. Love and peace at Monterey and Woodstock gave way to fear and loathing at Altamont and out of it all came the twin developments of an acoustic revival and heavy rock. Rock was still largely pseudo-intellectual, wordy, 'sincere', and strictly non-danceable: students and hip adolescents in their middle teens lapped it up. The new heroes were not pin-up idols, not stars in the old pop sense, they were mostly younger versions of Dylan aimed at those too young to have caught the man himself first time round. For the less intellectual, the void still existed, however, and attentions temporarily turned to the contrived gut rock sound of groups like Grand Funk Railroad.

But the appeal of Grand Funk's 'heavy metal' rock was almost wholly male orientated, which left the American female pop audience looking for something to call its own. Bubblegum was still going strong but it was still pre-teen music, pop at its very lowest common denominator, and there was another factor to consider. The girl who was nine years old in 1967–68 at the start of the bubblegum craze was now 12 going on 13 and going through her first pubescent pangs. And there was nothing, no love symbol, no one on whom to focus her adulation. Having grown out of bubblegum, the music without image, the post-Monkees generation were finally finding they needed a Monkee-type figure to fill the idol vacuum. Grand Funk were too rough, James Taylor was too complex. The teen magazines pushed a kid called Bobby Sherman, but after four Top Ten hits, 1969–70, his popularity waned. So enter, in the spring of 1970, *The Partridge Family*, David Cassidy, and the teenyboppers.

Television was almost wholly responsible for starting the teenybopper bandwagon rolling, and again Screen Gems–Columbia were the instigators. Conceived, as *The Monkees* had originally been, as just another situation comedy series, *The Partridge Family* merged the plots of *I Love Lucy* and *Ozzie and Harriet*. But this time the company made absolutely sure of handling the business efficiently and, however coy it may sound, responsibly. They gathered members of Cassidy's family and close friends to handle his personal business affairs, and from the start adopted a benevolent, if somewhat patronising attitude towards him. The idea appeared to be that if he was cosseted enough he would never have anything to complain about. And it seemed to work.

David was only 18 at the time. He was the son of Hollywood actor and musical comedy star Jack Cassidy, had acted briefly off Broadway and had a number of small acting roles in shows like *A Man Called Ironside* and *Medical Center*. When his stepmother Shirley Jones, herself an

David Cassidy

Oscar-winning actress of considerable experience, was signed to play the mother in *The Partridge Family* it was only natural – and perhaps inevitable – that her actor stepson should join her in a co-starring role. Cassidy's appeal, like the plot of the series itself, was more fundamentally old fashioned than that of the Monkees. If the Monkees were based on the Beatles, Cassidy was based on the typical star of the highschool period before the arrival of the Beatles, right down to the song material for which producer Wes Farrell resorted to reviving old chestnuts like 'Walking In The Rain' and 'Breaking Up Is Hard to Do'. The show couldn't really fail. David had a ready-made clean-cut image as a typical all-American boy, he could sing, and the publicity machine behind him was the most efficient in Hollywood.

The show achieved very high ratings but, inevitably, Cassidy became bigger than the series, and his records put out under the Partridge Family name were soon bringing in more revenue to Screen Gems than the show was. This had all been anticipated, so the next step was to record Cassidy as a solo artist in his own right, not just in his guise as Keith Partridge. With the release of his first solo album, *Cherish*, in 1971, Cassidy-mania reached its peak, but although Screen Gems went to great lengths to keep their artist 'happy', the pressures on Cassidy soon began to show. An interview that David gave the magazine *Rolling Stone* in March 1972 very nearly ruined his career, exposing as it did not only his frustration at the role he was being forced to play out in public as well as on TV, but also his own attitudes towards sex and drugs, which were too far for comfort from the image of Keith Partridge. For one thing, the article exploded the myth of his virginity. Worse still, the pictures used to illustrate the article were mostly nude or semi-nude, pictures that Cassidy had had taken at his own request but which were never intended for publication. Cassidy only just survived the onslaught of condemnation and derision that followed and the whole episode may well have precipitated a decline in his popularity.

But this was only in America. In Britain in the spring of 1972 Cassidy was still very much an unknown quantity, for while *The Partridge Family* had been networked by the BBC a year previously at peak early evening viewing time on Saturdays, it had been taken off soon after because of lack of response. It took some effort on the part of his record company and the newly-formed British branch of the David Cassidy fan club to persuade Independent Television to buy the series and network it. Of the records, the Partridge Family's 'I Think I Love You' had been a British Top Tenner, but solely on the strength of radio play, and Cassidy's successful British solo singles, 'Could It Be Forever' and 'How Can I Be Sure', were never featured in the television series. What the television series did do in Britain was create a hard core of Cassidy followers, but the responsibility for making him so big as a teen star lies not with TV but with the publicity machine employed by Cassidy's management in this country. On his first visit here, Cassidy could be found on a boat moored strategically on the Thames near Tower Bridge; girls jumped into the water to try and reach him. It all helped. Cassidy became news; such incidents even made the nine o'clock TV bulletins, usually renowned for their staidness and lack of sensationalism. By skilful manipulation of the teenage press and a number of short well-publicised visits, David Cassidy was established in Britain. Nevertheless, his popularity in this country can never be taken for granted, hence the Screen Gems decision to send him over in early October, for his record sales are undoubtedly heavily dependent on his TV exposure.

David Cassidy has now left *The Partridge Family* and is ostensibly planning a career outside television but within pop music – or more appropriately, within show-business. He is in rather an anomalous position. In interviews and on television he comes over as a nice guy thrown in at the deep end of something he did not personally create and only just about keeping his head above water. He admits to feelings of insecurity and unlike his 'rival' in the teen stakes, Donny Osmond, he's old enough (23) to appreciate exactly what he's going through. Yet in a way he is trapped. He is not in the business for money particularly, for kicks, for sex or even for simple egocentric pleasure. He is in the business because the choice not to be is not his. Even now, with his popularity in America very definitely on the decline, he has a contract with Screen Gems to fulfil. They still see him as a long-term investment, in contrast to the Monkees, and they will presumably develop him as a singer in the Andy Williams–Jack Jones tradition. Whether he has the talent to achieve that status remains to be seen.

David is a fair singer, a good actor and a likeable personality, but it could be that none of this is enough to enable him to survive longer than the customary three years a teen idol can expect. At the time of writing David Cassidy is number one.

(1974)

AFTERWORD

David Cassidy's star waned quickly. He was eclipsed by the younger, homelier Bay City Rollers; a teenage girl died at one his shows; and *The Partridge Family* was dropped by BBC TV. His supposedly more 'grown-up' albums flopped, a renewed acting career misfired and he followed a minor chart comeback in 1985 (with 'Last Kiss') by publishing a seedy autobiography.

If individual pop idols rarely last, television's capacity for making and breaking them is one of pop's constants. In the 1970s glam rock floundered, not on a tide of punk, but on the mundane matter of a *Top Of The Pops* technicians strike that kept all the pretty faces off screen for ten weeks during 1975. John Travolta may have made his name in the films *Saturday Night Fever* and *Grease,* but it was television showings of clips from the latter on *Multi-Coloured Swap Shop* that turned him into pop's biggest post-Cassidy teen star.

It was Saturday morning shows of the *Swap Shop* ilk (*Tiswas, Superstore, No. 73, Going Live*) – not *Revolver* or *The Tube* – that made the real pop stars of the early 1980s onwards, with their seamless combinations of games, interviews, cartoons, pop videos and live performances. These shows defined pop not as part of teen culture alone but as children's fodder; they were springboards for Culture Club, Duran Duran, Wham! and a clutch of others, and a new wave of pics-and-songwords magazines, such as *Smash Hits.* They helped turn soap operas like *Neighbours* (with more young characters than any other soap) into national cults and their stars (Kylie Minogue and Jason Donovan) into pop singers, setting a precedent for children's soaps like *Byker Grove* (come in PJ and Duncan) to follow. Every promotion person knows that even extensive radio play can be worth little if it isn't backed up by promo video slots on prime time kids TV.

Pop commentators used to delight in pointing up the circularity of pop – how old sounds and even old stars came back in re-invented form, how the marketing lessons of the past are re-learned by each successive generation of star makers. The fact that my nine-year-old daughter's favourite single is Boyzone's revival of the Osmonds' 'Love Me For A Reason' (backed by a note-for-note re-tread of the Monkees' 'Daydream Believer') does give the point some credence. But the idols of the 1990s do face different expectations to those of two decades ago: every kid-appeal band knows that the first rule of pop survival is to mature musically with their audience, and that there is credibility to be gained from writing one's own material (Take That, East 17, Wet Wet Wet) and/or taking control of one's own stage projection and particularly choreography. In this, at least, today's white pop heart-throbs have learned much from black predecessors like the Jackson Five and New Edition (featuring Bobby Brown) and latter-day counterparts like Boyz II Men and All-4-One. Whatever Michael Jackson's problems have been in recent years, his success is a staggering testament to his ability to keep an audience by means of disciplined musical changes, creative use of new media and to some extent the creation and perpetuation of his own myth. Most astonishing of all, he has achieved this while still retaining a significant constituency among pre-teen music buyers.

In general, however, new technology and new media force the pace in pop as much as anything or anyone within the pop industry itself: no one could have foreseen, back in 1974, the impact of video as a promotional medium, nor the growth of a huge child-centred leisure industry (encompassing cable channels, computer games and theme parks) that would take the Ninja Turtles, the Simpsons and Mighty Morphin' Power Rangers to number one and prompt countless merchandising spin-offs. While teenage culture remains as difficult as ever for television to pin down and please, the pre-teen market can be catered for and exploited with relative ease. Some decent records apart, the Monkees and David Cassidy still have a lot to answer for.

10

Have Pity for the Rich
Bob Edmands

Maybe the basic problem with the rock industry in the mid-1970s is that too many people are earning too much money. Are rock million-aires the acceptable face of capitalism? The *Daily Mail* recently informed its readers: 'One hundred young music men acclaimed last night as "the new aristocrats" – each earn at least £100,000 a year from British pop. The executive journal, the *Director*, discloses the vast wealth accumu-lating for pop stars, composers and managers.' And under a headline which read 'The Millionaires of Pop', the *Mail* named the likes of Jimmy Page, Keith Emerson, Elton John and Rod Stewart.

Another report, in the *Business Observer*, revealed that more than 50 rock artists made between two and six million dollars each during 1972. With British rock acts acknowledged as the biggest crowd-pullers in the US, perhaps the *Mail* and the *Director* underestimated the amount of loot in circulation. Is it good for musicians to earn all that, and is it good for us to help them? According to the *Observer*, a top album can sell eight million copies, and bring in 40 million dollars. After the first top album, what incentive does a rock millionaire have to work on his second? It's no surprise the biz goes through 'superstars' like a flu victim with Kleenex tissues.

John Lennon is one of the survivors, but only just. His last album was called *Mind Games*, which sounds like some sort of fashionable cerebral sport for hip business executives. Maybe that's one reason why it sold in substantially less numbers than his product prior to the 'New York City' disaster. The question of why Lennon appears to be on the slide commercially seems worth considering.

Possibly he's become too remote from his audience – the Howard Hughes of rock 'n' roll. With his puritan crop-top and his Himmler specs, Lennon is an austere figure. At a glance, he might be an alienated Marxist intellectual, bitter over the number of copies of *Workers Press* he's failing to sell. Alternatively, he could be one of those jaundiced airport lounge lizards – a flashbulb fetishist whose main contribution to entertainment consists of stepping on and off jets. The working-class hero looks increasingly like a prisoner of his own private war.

That's one problem a rock millionaire has to face – imprisonment. Life under mansion-arrest must be a debilitating experience. Once the novelty of your personalised pinball machines runs out, what is there left? Mind games seem to have been Lennon's answer ever since he became a student at the Yoko Ono School of Conceptual Philosophy.

For a card-carrying cynic, Lennon proved an eager pupil, happily confusing the most simple-minded gibberish with cosmic paradoxes. Yoko's stock-in-trade seemed to be not so much playing on words as dozing on them. No wonder the public got angry and then bored with the visual equivalents, all those draggy bed-ins and bag-ins.

Try some of the mind games on Lennon's album. One track is called 'Nutopian International Anthem'. It lasts 0.3 seconds, which is another way of saying no time at all. If Nutopia is a negation of utopia, maybe that's appropriate timing for its anthem. Who knows? Or, indeed, who cares? And if that doesn't tickle your cortex, how about the album sleeve? Our hero is pictured in the foreground, a tiny figure. His wife is huge in the background, apparently lying on her back – an unusually submissive pose. Her profile is a sort of visual pun on a mountain range. Perhaps it's a comment on Lennon's humility. Maybe Mahomet was leaving his mountain. Possibly Yoko's sinking behind the horizon. Or she's buried up to her neck in sand. Intriguing?

Well, as intellectual exercises go, these seem somewhat less stimulating than *The Times* crossword. John Lennon probably has a rather more boring life than the average, unliberated housewife, if that's his idea of a vigorous cerebral work-out.

Some critics claim to have detected a deterioration in Lennon's music. But this album displays few inadequacies in that department. Play 'Revolution' from the *The Beatles* album back-to-back with 'Bring on the Lucie' here, and you would be hard pressed to spot the decay.

If anything, Lennon seems to have his talent on a tighter rein than before. The love songs on *Mind Games* are among his best. 'One Day (At a Time)' and 'Out of the Blue' would have been hailed as Beatle classics, had sympathies not been alienated way back. Lennon still has that perfect raw, rock voice, custom-built for the echo-chamber. He puts it to good use on 'Meat City' and 'Aisumasen (I'm Sorry)'. He also seems to have become an adept producer, coaxing many neat touches out of the back-up band.

Lennon's ear for word-play remains intact. He sings, in 'Out of the Blue': 'Every day, I thank the Lord and Lady'. It's a modest little joke about religion and women's lib. As modest, in its way, as all those little puns in *A Spaniard in the Works*. On this album, he even cocks a restrained snook at his radical sloganising. 'Bring on the Lucie', one of his jolly political singalongs, has a line about 'Freda People'. If you guffawed in 1965, why isn't your face cracking now?

Lennon's music and lyrics have changed very little since 'Abbey Road', so his declining popularity has its roots elsewhere. Lennon has lived with his loot longer than most rock millionaires. He's had longer to adjust to his status, but so has the public. Eccentric millionaires tend only to be tolerated if they're aristocrats. Lennon's ham-fisted adoption of radical causes hasn't helped close his personal credibility gap. There has always seemed something bizarre about millionaire revolutionaries, and he's no doubt suffered as a result of the scepticism generated by the record industry's exploitation of radical sentiment.

The biggest marketing coup of the 1960s was undoubtedly to sell pop music to an age group which might otherwise have been embarrassed to admit to the trappings of adolescence. Pop music was transformed from something as unwelcome post-puberty as acne, to a medium which endowed a kind of intellectual status on its adherents. This was done in a number of ways.

One method was to associate the product with current political and social controversies. The album market was generated in part by the deliberate identification of rock music with young people's views on the massive issues of the 1960s. Rock was sold as soundtrack to The Greening of America. The blatant appeal of advertising campaigns like 'The Revolutionaries are on CBS' made it quite clear that the business was anxious to exploit political energies. Vietnam protest, Black Power, and campus confrontations were all grist to the industry's mill. Revolutionary spouting by the major rock musicians was always either ambiguously metaphorical (e.g. Bob Dylan) or banally simplistic (e.g. Lennon), allowing bets to be hedged on most occasions. Perhaps it was silly to expect otherwise: too many great expectations were built on flimsy foundations. Records like the Beatles' 'Revolution' and the Stones' 'Street Fighting Man' were thoroughly conservative statements; but young radicals were obligingly willing to suspend disbelief. No wonder Richard Neville, former editor of *Oz*, is herding sheep in Australia. It's the nearest he could get to role reversal.

If politics had been more than a sales gimmick, we'd hear plenty from rock stars about 1970s issues. But apparently it's no longer hip to churn out lyrics stuffed with third-hand dialectics. Rock is supposed to be outselling both Hollywood and organised sport in the US, so you might think there was an enormous opportunity for big-league rockers to provide a moral lead for the kids who provide their incomes.

Lennon is one of the remaining few who apparently takes that kind of responsibility seriously, despite the odium created by all those industry hustlers who turned radicalism into a fashion accessory to wear round the office. And Lennon has never perpetrated anything as crass as Chicago's war graves poster, or the Groundhogs' *Thank Christ for the Bomb*, or Jefferson Airplane's 'Up Against the Wall' routine. But when he sings on *Mind Games* 'Stop the killing now', is there anyone who would disagree with such a broad appeal? This is a form of commitment that commits him to nothing and sounds like an easy cut-price gesture.

All millionaires have a common failing. Their view of life is inevitably different from that of the average bum on the street. Social isolation is deadly for a creative artist, dependent on sympathetic feedback from his public.

Pete Townshend of the Who is one rock millionaire who seems acutely aware of the dilemmas of his position. It's perhaps worth considering what prompted him to invite the Sweet to play the Who's gig at Charlton Athletic football ground. The Sweet are the 1970s' answer to the Tremeloes. No doubt you remember the Trems, fans. They were the leading exponents of scapegoat rock, the people you bashed if you wanted to show intellectual muscle in progressive music circles. Every junior pop pundit cut his teeth on the Trems' reputation. The Trems were scapegoats because that's how attention is diverted from the shabby rhetoric that turns musical fashions into radical crusades. They were sitting ducks for the snobbery and elitism of the hip establishment. The Trems used to come on the telly, looking like a Benny Hill send-up of *Top Of The Pops*, waving big meaty hands, and shouting 'yippee'. All very uncool. They always looked too comfortably working class, somehow, and that was deadly. Rock 'n' roll proles have to wear their alienation like glitter and look thuggish, or bisexual.

Working-class pop stars shouldn't look like something out of *Come Dancing* in a wig. Not like they've got a train set in the attic back home. When rock music is a gesture against your prep school background, or a substitute for your neglected adolescence, the Trems were not really in the right class of rebellion.

And six or seven years on, neither are the Sweet. Or, at any rate, they weren't, until a careful piece of image-building blurred the issue. The Sweet are a vehicle for two hustling songwriters, Nicky Chinn and Mike Chapman, whose songs apparently sold more singles in one year than the Beatles managed in their best twelve months. Chinn and Chapman began writing cretinous novelty songs, like 'Co Co', 'Funny, Funny' and 'Poppa Joe' – which were all hits for the Sweet. This made the band ideal cannon-fodder for a Tremeloes routine from the critics.

Happily for the Sweet, they were a little more self-aware than their forerunners, they could manage a half-hearted sneer for publicity stills, and they were fortunate with Chinn and Chapman, who really began coining it, by adopting the simple ploy of adding up-front drums and guitars to their cosy singalong routines. This led to some degree of bewilderment among reviewers, who were faced with the familiar ingredients of a hard rock sound added to teenybop novelties. The issue was really clouded by David Bowie. His single 'Jean Genie' was put out at the same time as the Sweet's 'Blockbuster'. And both ripped-off the same Yardbirds riff. To praise one and put down the other presented a considerable challenge to typewriter gymnasts. The Sweet were left with some slight degree of begrudging acceptance, at least from people whose careers are based on awarding those kinds of points.

As for the rock audience, it remained largely unimpressed. And for Pete Townshend to invite this calibre of artist to appear with the Who, that was verging on blasphemy. It represented a head-on collision with a consensus opinion carefully nurtured for almost ten years. Happily for Townshend, and perhaps for the Sweet, they never made it to the gig. Brian Connolly, the Sweet's singer, is perhaps the most self-conscious about his punk image and was apparently the victim of a street attack. He bravely soldiered on to complete the Sweet's next single, as well as an album aimed at the rock market. But it was reported that a live gig was considered too risky for his vocal chords.

Still, Townshend's invitation remained an important event in its own right. It was probably the most significant gesture he's made in the last seven years. Here's a description of the Who, written by Nik Cohn in 1969: 'Mod had died, and the Who had got to be one of the truly established groups, almost like the Beatles or the Stones, almost as rock-like and as ignorable as that. Simply, they'd become solid citizens.'[*] If that was true then, how much more true is it now? The Who recently celebrated their tenth anniversary in showbiz by playing to a total of 80,000 people over four nights at Madison Square Garden. Pete Townshend was the man who wrote that line about 'Hope I die before I get old'. Some people thought he meant it at the time. Others thought he was writing on behalf of a generation that meant it. Riches and respectability are powerful antidotes to gut rebellion. The Who are growing old as gracefully as is compatible with selling records. The evidence is in their music. *Quadrophenia*, Townshend's attempt to exorcise the ghost of *Tommy*, was a plush, smooth production, without sharp edges. The flailing, raw energy, which propelled the Who along ten years ago, has been almost entirely dissipated. In its place, there's only artful self-parody. Townshend, who's cynical about his decline as a writer, might well agree.

---

[*] Nik Cohn, *Pop From the Beginning* (Weidenfeld and Nicholson, 1969).

A back-track through the Who's music clearly reveals that Townshend's music peaked well before his earnings. By the time *Tommy* appeared, to excessively fulsome praise, it was already evident something was amiss. No doubt Townshend has suffered from the euphemistic rigours of life on the road. But his muse has also been hurt by the social distance he moved from the source of his original inspiration. Townshend was never a real mod, but he was a middle-class voyeur close enough to the phenomenon to hide the difference. Once he closed the front door of his plush Thames-side home, he shut out the stimuli which kept his work coherent.

If Townshend has opted to prolong his earning potential for as long as possible, it's hard to blame him. But it's also apparent he's not entirely happy with the situation. He said, in a 1972 interview, that fees demanded by top rock bands were 'the highest manifestation of gross, flamboyant capitalism ... let's face it, they give you gold records and in America they don't say for selling a million records, they say for selling a million dollars. So it's a tricky situation to wake up one morning and pretend that money's got nothing to do with it, because it has.' It's an onerous responsibility, having too much money and too much prestige, particularly if you're doubtful whether you deserve either. Townshend added: 'If a group's got money it's going to pay off on tax, rather than spend it on insane press receptions or farces like Apple Corps, they could put their money into a place like the Rainbow.'

In the event, Townshend's chosen gesture to his conscience was his invitation to the Sweet, gambling his prestige, rather than his money. He talks in terms of causing 'some feedback to help people coming up'. But why the Sweet? Brian Connolly's reported theory was: 'I think maybe it was Townshend's way of saying the Sweet is underrated musically ... I mean the Who were a singles band once; we've got so much in common with them I think.'

This opinion is guaranteed to wring howls of anguish from Who freaks, and with good reason. The Who never depended on slide-rule professionals like Chinn and Chapman. Their singles were all Townshend's own work, and if there are such things as pop masterpieces, that's the category they were in. Townshend's considered to have captured the mood of the 1960s as effectively as the early rockers reflected the spirit of the 1950s. If Townshend sees the Sweet as natural successors, he's become very jaded and self-disparaging indeed. But it's arguable he's survived with his artistic integrity almost intact.

There are other exceptions which perhaps prove the rule. The most obvious example are Emerson, Lake and Palmer. They're so anxious to hang on to their riches, they've said they'll live permanently in the US – to escape the clutches of Mr Dennis Healey. This blatant materialism ought to be offensive, but it isn't. ELP come as near to giving value for money as it's possible for rock millionaires to get.

They played a recent three-night residency at a theatre in Liverpool in what seemed to be either a generous gesture towards their fans, or a finely calculated tax write-off. The amount of electronic hardware the band carts round hardly makes a UK tour financially viable. Their audience sported campus chic and army surplus, and if it was moved by the music, it didn't let on; but since the whole show was in brain-melting, 2000-decibel quadrophonic sound, reactions tended to be smothered. ELP are a band with whom reviewers feel uncomfortable, despite their apparent massive success in the US. Maybe it's time for a critics' moratorium on the subject. Writers stuck for a put-down of ELP tend to compare them with the well-publicised technology they deploy as a means to their musical ends. The band are said to be sterile, clinical, lacking in emotional commitment. One daily newspaper critic described them as 'dispossessed of humour and warmth'. Strangely, this sort of description appears totally at odds with the evidence of the ELP stage show, which is heavily underpinned with emotional commitment. Contrary to the familiar hostile verdict, Emerson displays a great deal of personal warmth towards his audience. True, he's no Hughie Greene, but that brand of friendliness is hardly what's required.

Emerson has an easy rapport with the faithful, based on a quaint kind of humility, and the success of this approach is evident midway through the set. He performs a ludicrously clever amalgam of classical themes during his solo spot on the Steinway, firing off musical puns with a casual virtuosity that's undeniable. The audience is utterly transfixed. Emerson sits with his back to the fans, and his only gesture to showmanship is nicely calculated, drawing friendly laughter. He swigs a wine bottle with his right hand, while continuing to play with his left. The house creases up, aware that it's a joke that's being shared.

But that's somewhat of an aside for Emerson. The music carries the weight. Emerson no doubt enjoys applause. He would be perverse if he didn't. But that barely explains why he works his imagination so hard at every gig. Ego-tripping comes easier than that.

Lake and Palmer also seem committed to their music in a way which goes beyond self-indulgence. Palmer looks like he's flown in from Muscle Beach; but narcissism is not his main preoccupation. The guy works harder on his ten-ton drum kit in two hours than most people manage in a day. His technique is the nearest to impeccable in rock, and like his spectacular gallops round the kit, it's thoroughly sub-servient to the music. By the end of the evening, all his expensive ironmongery, like Emerson's keyboards, looks no more than adequate for the occasion. Palmer is probably obsessive about his own expertise, and it's absurd to suggest there's no emotional commitment with artistry so disciplined.

Lake's solo spot is as immaculate as his white suit. His songs are clearly at odds with the ferocious instrumentals which are the trio's obvious speciality, but it looks as though he could have made a living of sorts without the other guys. His lyrics are not particularly inventive, but he's got a good ear for a plaintive melody, and a talent for projecting it.

The meat of the show is naturally the ensemble work, and the band only takes as much pleasure in overkill as other big-league heavies. Musical effects which sound uncomfortably contrived on vinyl seem totally in context on stage. Emerson used to hump his keyboards as though in imminent danger of confusing music shops with brothels. But the musical resources now at his command have made that type of touting for audience acclaim unnecessary.

Emerson, Lake and Palmer could hardly go through the motions at every gig, even if they wanted to. The motions are so complex, lethargy would simply get killed in the rush. Ecology freaks should be delighted with these guys. They demonstrate at every performance that people can successfully control an advanced electronic environment. The machines will not take over, if ELP have anything to do with it. They've successfully harnessed all that power in pursuit of their musical ambitions, exploring the outer limits of rock technology, and the moogs still can't walk around on their own.

The achievement of ELP is remarkable given the context in which they find themselves. The effect of all the huge rewards available within the rock industry has been mainly to abort the careers of those artists who're only in it for the money, and to provide a sinecure for those who're in it for the music. It's odd to think of the Rolling Stones in the second category, with their heavy decadent image. Perhaps they can't think of anything better to do. All that sitting around in mansions playing with yourself must get boring. But despite the undiminished vigour of their stage act, their vinyl output is displaying increasing lethargy. It's perhaps no surprise. The Stones are now on the wrong side of the generation gap. Their last TV appearance in the UK was on a lip-synch show called *Lift Off With Ayshea* which is aimed firmly at kids. There's a tendency these days to forget that's who rock – or, more honestly, pop – is for.

The Stones were plugging their single 'It's Only Rock and Roll'. They were dressed as sailors, like Alice Cooper on the *Muscle of Love* LP cover, and they were slowly disappearing under a flood of crazy foam. The appearance was made even more ignominious by their place on the bill – just after the adverts, just before Ayshea Brough did her supermarket

Top Ten routine. The stars of the show were the Bay City Rollers. The kids must have wondered who exactly those daft old jerks were.

Rock millionaires lose out all round. They haven't even got the freedom to enjoy their gains. How do they spend it? Yachts, private jets and investment in capitalist enterprises are presumably out of the question for radical rockers. Some, no doubt, invest in the pharmaceutical division of the Mafia, as though that was somehow morally worthy. But shoving a million dollars up your nose takes a long time. And time is the one thing a self-made rock recluse has too much of. Boredom leads to intellectual stagnation, and if your one pleasure in life is that annual album, you must get pretty bored. Even the tiniest ripple of thought must take on the dimensions of a brainstorm.

John Lennon's problems are surely being experienced by increasing numbers of culture-shocked victims. If there were more than 50 people earning two million dollars in 1972, how many were there in musicland's booming 1973? The idle rich have always had time on their hands. The record industry has created a pampered elite for whom time must seem an intolerable burden. If the recession has whittled down 1975's new millionaires, it may be no bad thing. Playing those mind games for ever sounds a heavy sentence.

(1975)

AFTERWORD

Success and excess drive away the muse in rock music, as elsewhere, and this was a conclusion many people were reaching on the eve of the punk rock phenomena in the mid-1970s.

I thought initially that John Lennon's *Mind Games* album was clear evidence of musical ennui resulting from being super-rich, but life and Lennon were more complicated than that, and it seems his wealth was just one of the many factors at play. Perhaps the public perception of his peculiar, isolated lifestyle coloured the view of his music.

At the time, I wondered what history would have made of the best of the songs on *Mind Games* if six of them had been leavened by half-a-dozen from McCartney and a couple from George Harrison, with George Martin in charge of cosmetic surgery.

Twenty years on and, given a rather greater instinct for survival, the Beatles might still have found themselves playing Wembley Stadium and churning out pastiches barely distinguishable from the originals. Not unlike the Stones, in fact.

Would we care now how rich they are if they'd stayed together (and John Lennon was still with us)? Indeed, if the surviving trio are successful in doing a Brandon Lee with ancient demo tapes, we might yet find ourselves looking through a glass onion with rose-tinted spectacles.

PART THREE: THE AUDIENCE

11

Youth Culture/Youth Cults: A Decade of Rock Consumption

Simon Frith

1967 was, and will for ever more be, the Year of Rock. On 1 June Procol Harum's 'Whiter Shade of Pale' entered the singles chart and the Beatles' *Sergeant Pepper* entered the album chart. Procol Harum were number one for six weeks, the Beatles were number one for the rest of the year. Both records were perfect 1967 artefacts, with classical references, drug hints and obscure lyrics, both were simultaneously realistic and mysterious. These records were fun but serious too. Pop was not the right word for them at all: there was something here that was going to transform our lives. What was involved was not just music, and certainly not money, but a whole cultural caboodle. 1967 remains the nostalgic high date for Western cultural revolutionaries, just as 1968 does for Western political revolutionaries, 1967–68 remain the high years for all revolutionaries. As Bob Christgau wryly observed, the catechism went Q. Why is rock like the revolution? A. Because they're both groovy.

In 1967 Marc Bolan formed Tyrannosaurus Rex. In 1977 he died, an ex-mod, an ex-hippie, an ex-glam rock idol. He was, I guess, always a punk. There's no particular reason why a decade should be a neat historical package but the 1967/1977 comparison is obvious: the same energetic burst of groups and labels and gigs and audiences, the same easy-spoken anti-commercialism, the same hopes for music as politics. The pace was different – it's the record companies who won't get fooled again, and Mark P. moved rather more speedily from his magazine, *Sniffin' Glue*, to his record company, Step Forward, than Richard Branson managed, a decade earlier, to make the same trip from *Student* magazine to Virgin Records – but it was surely right that the Sex Pistols should end their brief life as a Virgin group. The decade finished as it began: the hippies' tragical history tour being repeated, this time as punk farce.

All rock fans are obsessed by patterns and precedents, and punk revived all the old arguments about pop's political and social significance. After years of being a business, rock was youth culture again. And that's what I want to write about here, because although it's been obvious, ever since Elvis Presley first jived Ed Sullivan, that rock 'n' roll was youth music, I've never been sure what this meant for either music or youth.

The music business itself appears to operate according to contradictory assumptions. On one hand, there is the notion of a single teenage culture, its experiences, aspirations and values naturally expressed by and through rock; on the other hand, there is a model of disparate youth cults, each of which needs its own particular form of musical servicing. In 1967 the rock business was clearly dominated by the idea of a unified youth culture, a newly liberated generation, but the rest of the musical decade revolved around fragmentation, as rock became heavy metal and folk-rock, country rock and teenybop, progressive and disco, singer/songwriters and glitter. The market itself was divided into hairies and skinheads, smoovies and greasers, teenyboppers and students, boys and girls, and rich and poor. From this perspective, punk, rather than being a re-expression of the old ideals of youth as counter-culture, was just another narrow cult. But then again the 1967 pattern re-emerged – the music press went haywire, A&R men began a flourish of punk signings. Punk was not just a cult but a culture too; it was, in fact, a cult of youth culture – everyone was remembering the mods, the golden age, 1967. I must start again.

YOUTH, MARKET AND CLASS

The usual sociological story of rock and youth goes something like this. The first decade of rock 'n' roll (1955–64) established it as a music for working-class teenagers. Rock 'n' roll's good qualities were spontaneity, vitality, wit and honesty, its bad qualities were banality, crudity, cynical exploitation. It was music for dancing, courting and hanging about – silly love songs with a more or less insistent beat.

This pioneering period (in which the music got worse as record companies made formula teenage pop out of the original rhythms and passions) was succeeded by the golden age of teenage music, 1964–67, in which the good qualities of rock 'n' roll were rescued from commerce and supplemented with new musical elements. Rock 'n' roll became complex, interesting and artful, lyrics took on poetical and political concerns, the audience sat down to listen. The Beatles and Bob Dylan met up with Elvis Presley, rock 'n' roll and teenage pop got mixed up with ideas and sounds from blues and soul and folk and protest, the resulting records were at once exciting, intriguing and real. In *Rock File*

3 we listed the best hundred singles from 1955 to 1975; 38 came from this golden period.

By 1967 pop had become rock – no longer working-class teenage music, but a form of expression for youth in general, for a generation. Youth was now an ideological rather than a chronological category. It was no longer enough to enjoy being young until we grew up, the idea was to stay young for ever – 'hope I die before I get old!' – and to use music as the source and expression of this ambition. If there had been a *Rock File* then, listing the charts from 1957 to 1967, its conclusion would have been unshakeable: 1967 marked the end of the beginning. Rock 'n' roll, commercial teenage pop, had become rock, an art form which bound a community and articulated its freedom from previous generations' hang-ups about work and sex, safety and settling down.

But, so the argument goes on, this conclusion would have been false. 1967 was, in fact, the beginning of the end of the grand ideology of rock and youth. The chart clues to the future weren't 'Whiter Shade of Pale' and *Sergeant Pepper*, but Cream's 'I Feel Free' and the Jimi Hendrix Experience's 'Hey Joe' (they entered the charts, appropriately enough, on the same day, 21 January). These were the intimations of what was really to come – rock as a commodity for the 'intelligent' consumer. What the industry learned in 1967 was that rock could be marketed as a specific genre – not integrated with rock 'n' roll and pop, but sold in a deliberate isolation from them.

The rock/pop distinction is now taken for granted, but was established quite slowly and through two separate stages. Rock forms of production and consumption were perfected between 1967 and 1971, as an increasing number of bands and performers aimed their music at an album-buying market of hip, mostly male, music freaks. This was the period in which Jethro Tull, ELP, Pink Floyd, Yes and the rest of the rock super-groups established their popularity; it was the period when Led Zeppelin became the world's number one concert attraction and album band without releasing a UK single. Rock, it became evident, was to be sold on elaborately packaged LPs, to be performed on the college and concert circuit, it was world music – as successful in Japan and the US as in Britain. It was a music of lengthy studio and concert work-outs, technically, lyrically, instrumentally and electronically rich and elaborate; it was music to be played on expensive stereos and FM radio, on TV shows like the *Old Grey Whistle Test* (which first appeared, as *Colour Me Pop*, in 1968). It was released on progressive labels (EMI's Harvest, for example, and independents like Island), sold by Virgin mail orders (from 1969) and shops (from 1970), and praised in the transformed *Melody Maker*.

Rock File's figures tell the rock success story succinctly enough, but as this music and its marketing became increasingly cut off from mainstream teenage taste a vacuum was left. It was filled in the 1971–73 revival of pop. Again, the charts tell the story: the parallel success of T. Rex and Slade, the rise of manufactured teen stars – Sweet, Mud, Suzi Quatro, Gary Glitter, Alvin Stardust – and teen idols – Donny Osmond, David Cassidy. This music was marketed through dance-halls and discos and posters and pin-ups; it was written up in *Jackie* and *Fab 208* and *Record Mirror*. It was made by independent producers like Chinn and Chapman, Mickie Most and Jonathan King, and sold on *Top Of The Pops* and Radio Luxembourg. It was bought, in Woolworth's and Boots, by a mass market of dancing, chart watching, mostly female, mostly British, pop fans.

By 1972, the mid-point of the decade, the rock/pop division was as absolute as the gloom of ageing 1967 ideologues. The critical mood was captured in the original *Rock File* by Pete Fowler's piece, 'Skins Rule'*. His conclusion was that the division among music consumers reflected their essential class differences. On the one hand, there was the culture of middle-class rock – pretentious, genteel and professional, obsessed with bourgeois notions of art and the accumulation of expertise and equipment. On the other hand, there was the culture of working-class pop – banal, simple-minded, based on the formulas of a tightly knit body of businessmen.

What was depressing was not the fact of this division itself, but the resulting vacuousness of both forms of music. Pete's point was that neither rock nor pop expressed anything of interest at all. Youth culture had become a marketing device and the only lively youth cult, the skinheads, had no musical interest whatsoever. They were football fans.

In the mid-1970s the class analysis of the youth market was as common in the record business as it was among rock sociologists, but its very neatness was suspect. The argument rested on the assumption that consumer class = musical taste = pop genre, and problems emerged when this assumption broke down. Two musical movements, in particular, resisted such simple analysis. Firstly, the rise from 1971 of the loosely defined genre of glam rock (David Bowie, Roxy Music, even Rod Stewart and Elton John) defied the marketing conventions – these performers were successful in both rock and pop terms. Similarly, as the decade developed, it became increasingly difficult to make sense of heavy metal (originally, as with Cream and Jimi Hendrix, rock's core form) as middle-class music. Bands like Black Sabbath, Uriah Heep and Deep Purple had their own armies of scruffy working-class fans and in America, in particular, it was obvious that a band like Grand Funk didn't appeal to the readers of *Rolling Stone*. If British fans never went as far as their

---

* See p. 153.

American peers in their devotion to Kiss, a heavy metal teenybop band, they did make it impossible to classify Status Quo, one of the 1970s most successful groups, as either rock or pop.

Punk owes debts to both glam rock and heavy metal so it's not surprising that in 1977 the class market model broke down altogether. Punk was simple three-minute music which claimed a working-class audience. It explicitly opposed hippies, artistic complexity, techno-logical grandeur and the rock establishment; it was, from one perspective, primitive British dance music. But, on the other hand, pogo isn't disco and punk rockers also claimed to make their audiences think. Punk lyrics meant something; punk had an ideology that opposed the pop notion of passive teenage consumption – if punk's targets were working class, its aims were usually taken by middle-class, art school bohemians. Punk certainly wasn't pop, Tony Blackburn music, but neither was it rock, Bob Harris style. When commentators tried to pin down its class significance all sorts of confusion and ambiguity emerged. Rock ideologues like the *NME* and John Peel championed punk against pro-gressive rockers like Genesis and Joni Mitchell. The question ceased to be who consumed music and became how they did.

IDEOLOGY AND PROGRESS

In September 1969 *Melody Maker* celebrated the first annual poll results to reflect its new rock policy (i.e. Scott Walker and Cliff Richard were replaced by Emerson, Lake and Palmer) with this comment: 'The poll results generally were proof of the tastes of the vast majority of young people in Britain today – they want pop that is progressive played by musicians who are honest. And they don't want old-style showbiz type pop.'

'Progressive' was the key rock concept in the late 1960s, and musical progress was understood in two ways. First, it was believed that rock musicians were getting better and better as they mastered more instru-ments, more rhythms and more sounds, as they invested more and more capital in sophisticated technical means of reproducing these sounds on stage and record. Rock fans were offered the prospect of ever more complicated music, as avant-garde bands blazed the trail that the future rock mainstream would follow. Rock, in other words, was expected to be cumulative. Not only was each record of each artist going to be better than the one before, but each new performer was going to start from a new plateau of existing achievement.

The problem with this argument (still common in the pages of *Melody Maker*) was its assumption that rock musicians were artists in the traditional bourgeois sense, that rock expression was the result of individual creative needs, insights and reflection (hence the emphasis on rock honesty as opposed to commercial deceit). But the unfortunate fact was that most rock musicians had nothing interesting to express and having expressed nothing once proceeded to go on expressing it for ever. Far from being more authentic than showbiz pop stars, most successful 1970s rockers were engaged in the usual pop process of repeating and refining a winning formula. The 1967–77 chart statistics show little sign of musical progress.

The second progressive belief was that rock was no longer just a youthful form of expression but had become as ageless as any other form of art. Musicians and their audiences, it was asserted, would grow old, progress, together. (An example of this argument in practice is Derek Jewell's BBC Radio Three show, *Sounds Interesting*. He removes rock records from any context of consumption and presents them as 'interesting' works of art in their own right.) The assumption was that rock, once concerned with youth, would develop the musical and lyrical means to express adult concerns too.

The chart details undermine this argument as well. Twenty-five has continued to be the cut off age for rock interest and involvement, and rather than developing their musical tastes, most rock fans' tastes freeze at the age of 18. 'Progressive' rock taste has turned out to mean buying another Led Zeppelin or Rolling Stones record every year and the most successful rock groups base their success on not progressing – one of the obvious features of the *Rock File* figures is that the supergroups which emerged at the beginning of the decade still dominated album sales and concert receipts at the end.

There have been hints, since 1974, of an adult rock music, but it is hardly progressive. Hip easy listening is, rather, a new form of traditional middle-of-the-road pop. The most successful HEL musicians are Fleetwood Mac and the Eagles, Cat Stevens and the Moody Blues, Pink Floyd and Genesis. It is not so much their music that these people have in common as their approach to their music. Listen to their records one after another and what you hear is perfect productions and hi-fi sounds and technical expertise. Their songs quote with effortless flexibility from every 1970s rock genre; they are grown up love songs – about breaking up and starting over and loyalty and responsibility and not being young and foolish any more. Everywhere there are harmonies, warm and soothing like mother's milk; this is LP music, best heard for hours at a time, worst heard in three minute jerks. There's no passion involved, no personality, nothing to shock or startle or irritate. Nothing to change anyone's mind.

By 1977 it was difficult to discern a progressive rock taste; it was more instructive to consider the Virgin Records story. In 1973 Richard Branson launched the Virgin label on the basis of his shops' success in servicing the progressive rock consumer. His first signings were Mike Oldfield, Henry Cow and Gong; the company did not issue singles or obvious commercial sounds but offered itself as an 'alternative' label, an outlet for the counter-culture, rock progression and, on the Caroline label, avant-garde experiments. Today, scarcely five years later, Caroline is dead, Henry Cow gone, and Virgin is a commercial record company with its fingers in every pie. Its signings are still more enterprising than those of most other record companies but it is no longer possible to classify Virgin acts as 'progressive rock'.

By 1977, in short, the record business's class-based market distinctions between pop and rock, singles and albums, *TOTP* and the *Old Grey Whistle Test* still operated, but they could no longer be expressed in ideological terms, as commerce vs authenticity or easy listening vs progression. Rock had turned out just as calculatedly commercial (and more profitable) than pop, the rock audience consumed its music just as passively. In as far as the ideological distinctions could be made at all they had to be applied within both markets: on the one hand, there is challenging and original music to which an audience must make an active response; on the other hand, there is conservative and routine music, to which the audience reaction is passive pleasure. If we apply these distinctions to the marketing model we get this table:

Table 2: Passive–Active Distinctions (Marketing Model)

	working class	middle class
easy listening	teenbeat/pop	hip easy listening
progressive	punk	avant-garde rock/ the underground

THE YOUNG CONSUMER

Punk's peculiar position in rock history is now clearer, but this model is still too neat. It combines marketing distinctions (whom companies aim their music at, teenagers vs students etc.) and musical distinctions (music as challenge vs music as formula) but it ignores the consumers themselves and what they do with their music. It can't explain, for example, why certain forms of music get taken up by particular youth cults (e.g. reggae, briefly, by skinheads) or how such cults fit into the general market model. From this perspective, the most interesting divisions in the youth market are between degrees of musical commitment, and these differences reflect not class but age and sex and attitude (the music press, for example, and rock radio shows draw their predominantly male consumers from all classes). Only a small minority of rock and pop fans focus their leisure attention on their music; the majority of the young, whether working class or middle class in market terms, use their records as background for their important activities – dancing, partying, courting, homework, study.

This background audience is most obviously divided in sexual terms. Take the contrast between cock rock and teenybop: by cock rock I mean music making (which crosses conventional genre distinctions) in which performance becomes an explicit expression of male sexuality – it's the style of rock presentation that links a rock 'n' roller like Elvis Presley to subsequent stars like Jagger, Roger Daltrey, Robert Plant and all their imitators. Such performers are aggressive, powerful, boastful strutters; their acts are explicitly metaphors for sexual performances. Cock rock is loud, rhythmically insistent, structured round techniques of arousal and climax; the cock rock image is of the rampant male traveller, smashing hotels and groupies alike. In such rock, musical skills become equated with sexual skills; rather than being bound by conventions of a song form, cock rockers use their instruments to show 'what they've got' – hence the guitar hero.

Cock rock's consumers are predominantly male. Teenybop, by contrast, is consumed almost exclusively by girls. What they're buying is also a representation of sexuality resting on a particular combination of sound, image and lyric, and the performers involved are just as much male idols. But their sexual appeal is different. The teenybop idol's image is based on vulnerability, self-pity, need; his songs are about being let down and stood up; his form is the pop ballad, a less physical music than cock rock, drawing on older conventions of romantic fantasy. In teenybop cults live performance is less significant than pin-ups and posters and TV appearances.

The resulting contrast between, say, Thin Lizzy fans and David Soul fans is obvious enough but my point is more general. What is involved here is the sexual division in the mode of appropriation of all background music. While boys identify with the performers in terms of power and control and ability, girls become the ideal respondents to their idols' needs; similarly, while the male musical experience is essentially collective (this is most obvious in the live shows of acts like Led Zeppelin, Status Quo and Slade, with their football atmosphere of all boys together), the female musical experience is essentially individual, each girl becomes potentially the star's special partner. Even in the middle-class world of student and sixth-form music, it is the men who get drawn into the rock world of shared knowledge and technique, the women who retreat to the bedroom culture of sensitive listening to singer/songwriters and Angst-filled poets.

Whatever the exaggerations of this analysis, it is certainly true that the small group of young consumers whose lives do revolve around rock is mostly male. For this group music is a cultural focus: there is a direct relationship between the values believed to be expressed on record and the values sought to be expressed in the listeners' ways of life. Music can be such a focus in more or less articulate ways: at its simplest the relationship just involves adopting a musical style as a symbol for a particular cult (e.g. rock 'n' roll for teds) – the relationship is purely conventional; in its most developed form the relationship involves a youth group being inspired and instructed by the values expressed in a rock genre and adapting their lifestyles accordingly (e.g. underground for hippies). The consumer model now looks as follows:

Table 3: Rock/Pop Consumer Model

	Pop (teenage market)	Rock (youth market)
Focus	A. Cult Symbols glitter/glam rock 1960s reggae punk as power pop heavy metal Northern Soul	D. Value Carriers underground avant-garde 1970s reggae punk as politics
Background (collective)	B. Dance Music teen beat disco Tamla/soul	E. Party Music Stones pub rock/cock rock HEL with a beat
Background (individual)	C. Bedroom Music teenybop	F. Bedsit Music singer/songwriter HEL without a beat

Most of these categories are clear enough and punk, for instance, fits into both A and D, operating as a symbol for a youth cult as well as, for a minority of its fans, a carrier of specific cultural values. D is, indeed, the source of progressive music. All the other categories involve easy listening: they are used for leisure whose meaning and structure are determined elsewhere – by people's lives at work, at school, at home; it is the point of the music in these categories to be comfortable and familiar fun. Only the consumers in category D expect more from music; only they expect more from leisure, experiencing it not as a relief from work but as an alternative to it. The challenge of progressive music is a challenge to the whole notion of passive leisure consumption. Music in this category is a threat to the normal workings of the record industry, which, as in both 1967 and 1977, moves quickly to control it, to reduce it to the easy listening categories of the other rock uses.

But there remains a paradox for the industry even in this process. Its safest way of making money is to understand the various consumer groups involved and to cater to their tastes accordingly – record companies have become highly sophisticated in differentiating between the various audiences in their promotional uses of the press, radio and TV, discos, concerts and so on. But, at the same time, the most profitable performers are those who cross such categories – the decade's biggest sellers (Rod Stewart, for example, or David Bowie) became big by bucking the normal market structures. The paradox, then, is that the most successful rock stars tend, at least at the beginning of their careers, to be the least obvious commercial creations: it is precisely because they are not marketed for a specific audience that they are able to transcend the usual youth divisions.

(1978)

AFTERWORD

It says something about my 1960s sensibility that I could confidently describe girls' 'individual' and 'passive' pleasure in pop even after watching tartan hordes of Bay City Roller fans laying siege to Coventry's Leofric Hotel. But then I no longer know what I meant by 'active' and 'passive' consumption. This was an attempt to combine my academic and journalistic interests (the arguments here were developed in my book *The Sociology of Rock*) and my own love of music seems strangely absent.

12

Skins Rule

Pete Fowler

THE ROCK AND ROLL JAMES DEAN

> Of course, the whole thing is a game of seduction between me and the
> audience. My act is very sexual. I know it. I mean when you've got this guitar
> between your knees, putting out a lot of energy, strong or soulful music, it's
> going to be erotic whether you like it or not. I give them excitement, energy
> and my time. But it's not only an orgiastic exercise – I can be quiet and poetic
> too … . I've sort of become a rock and roll James Dean.
>
> Marc Bolan (talking to Donald Zec,
> *Daily Mirror*, 13 April 1972)

Strong stuff from the Metal Guru himself – Bolan is clearly convinced
that he'll be the one down in the annals of rock history as far as the
1970s are concerned. And, more important, everybody seems to believe
him. It's not just in the pop press that we can find the interminable
Bolan interviews and photographs of the golden boy in his latest lamé-
suit – they're in the nationals too. Over the past couple of months, I've
lost count of the number of features on T. Rex – and most of these features
follow the same corny format pictures of screaming teenyboppers, a long
description of the effect of Bolan on his audience ('And of course at the
end of it all a pair of pink panties thrown at the stage' the *Daily Mirror*
again), and an in-depth analysis of 'the unquestionable phenomenon
in this year of Pop', usually written by Bolan himself.

This, really, is the starting point in the difference between Bolan-as-Idol
and his predecessors. Bolan knows all the answers. There's no need for
the Maureen Cleave type of journalist at all because all the reporter need
do is to listen to the words of The Man himself and get it down in writing.
He really does write their features for them. Looking back to Presley and
the Beatles, the change of direction is startling. No doubt about it, the
Beatles were verbal, but on the question of their popularity, they were
dumbfounded. Not once did they come up with anything approach-

ing articulate. Elvis, of course, was even more reticent. He simply thanked God and his Mother in the best American tradition. Bolan's confidence in himself makes me more than a little suspicious, though this in itself doesn't add up to much of an indictment. Yet, other things do.

First, it must be obvious to all that the appeal of T. Rex isn't anywhere near as broad-based as that of the Beatles (or even the Stones) nearly a decade ago. There're just far too many kids who hate Bolan, and far too many who laugh him off. The Beatles were notable for the lack of teen-opposition (they cut right through the existing barriers in the 12–25 age bracket) and their only enemies were the old rock purists who couldn't stand to see some bum English group getting a success out of old classics like 'Roll Over Beethoven' and 'Twist and Shout'. By eliminating an effective opposition, they helped to create a solid, united teen-culture – which lasted in England from 1963 through to 1966. The divisions that did 'exist' were fake divisions dreamed up by the press ('Dave Clark 5 ousts Beatles' etc., or the 'Stones vs Beatles dilemma'. No one would admit that most of the kids who bought the Beatles' records also bought the Stones'.). There were no real schisms; the concerts given by the Stones in London in 1963 and 1964 at places like Ken Colyer's Studio 51 and the 100 Club were attended by students from London University, spivs from Soho, and kids up for the day from the council estates in the suburbs. As the old sign used to read, 'Even GOD digs the Stones'.

Second, some awkward, damning facts. At the beginning of this year, BBC Radio One presented a new kind of chart on the Tony Blackburn Show: the 100 best-selling number-one hits in Britain over the past decade.

1.   She Loves You (Parlophone 1963) Beatles
2.   I Want To Hold Your Hand (Parlophone 1963–64) Beatles
3.   Tears (Columbia 1965) Ken Dodd
4.   Can't Buy Me Love (Parlophone 1964) Beatles
5   I Feel Fine (Parlophone 1964–65) Beatles
6   We Can Work It Out/Day Tripper (Parlophone 1965–66) Beatles
7   Release Me (Decca 1967) Engelbert Humperdinck
8   Green Green Grass Of Home (Decca 1966–67) Tom Jones
9   The Last Waltz (Decca 1967) Engelbert Humperdinck
10   The Carnival Is Over (Columbia 1965) Seekers
11   I Remember You (Columbia 1962) Frank Ifield

12 Stranger On The Shore (Columbia 1962) Acker Bilk
13 The Young Ones (Columbia 1962) Cliff Richard and the Shadows
14 Sugar Sugar (RCA 1969) Archies
15 Cinderella Rockafella (Philips 1968) Esther and Abi Ofarim
16 Needles and Pins (Pye 1964) Searchers
17 Bachelor Boy/The Next Time (Columbia 1963) Cliff Richard and the Shadows
18 I'd Like To Teach The World To Sing (Polydor 1972) New Seekers
19 Two Little Boys (Columbia 1969–70) Rolf Harris
20 Telstar (Decca 1962) Tornadoes
21 Glad All Over (Columbia 1964) Dave Clark Five
22 Help! (Parlophone 1965) Beatles
23 Anyone Who Had A Heart (Parlophone 1964) Cilla Black
24 Lovesick Blues (Columbia 1962) Frank Ifield
25 My Sweet Lord (Apple 1971) George Harrison
26 You'll Never Walk Alone (Columbia 1963) Gerry and The Pacemakers
27 Hey Jude (Apple 1968) Beatles
28 Hello Goodbye (Parlophone 1967–68) Beatles
29 Hard Days Night (Parlophone 1964) Beatles
30 I'll Never Find Another You (Columbia 1965) Seekers
31 The Last Time (Decca 1965) Rolling Stones
32 Distant Drums (RCA 1966) Jim Reeves
33 Those Were The Days (Apple 1968) Mary Hopkin
34 I'm A Believer (RCA 1967) Monkees
35 Return To Sender (RCA 1962) Elvis Presley
36 Ernie (Columbia 1971–72) Benny Hill
37 From Me To You (Parlophone 1963) Beatles
38 Rock-A-Hula Baby (RCA 1962) Elvis Presley
39 Grandad (Columbia 1971) Clive Dunn
40 I Got You Babe (Atlantic 1965) Sonny and Cher
41 Lily The Pink (Parlophone 1968–69) Scaffold
42 Chirpy Chirpy Cheep Cheep (RCA 1971) Middle of the Road
43 Little Children (Parlophone 1964) Billy J. Kramer
44 Wonder Of You (RCA 1970) Elvis Presley
45 Satisfaction (Decca 1965) Rolling Stones
46 Whiter Shade Of Pale (Deram 1967) Procol Harum
47 You're My World (Parlophone 1964) Cilla Black
48 Puppet On A String (Pye 1967) Sandie Shaw
49 Ticket To Ride (Parlophone 1965) Beatles
50 In The Summertime (Dawn 1970) Mungo Jerry
51 Have I The Right (Pye 1964) Honeycombs
52 What A Wonderful World (HMV 1968) Louis Armstrong

53   All You Need Is Love (Parlophone 1967) Beatles
54   Strangers In The Night (Reprise 1966) Frank Sinatra
55   Wonderful Land (Columbia 1962) Shadows
56   Get Back (Apple 1969) Beatles
57   World Without Love (Columbia 1964) Peter and Gordon
58   Wanderin' Star (Paramount 1970) Lee Marvin
59   Yellow Submarine/Eleanor Rigby (Parlophone 1966) Beatles
60   It's Not Unusual (Decca 1965) Tom Jones
61   I Hear You Knocking (MAM 1971) Dave Edmunds
62   It's Over (London 1964) Roy Orbison
63   Oh Pretty Woman (London 1964) Roy Orbison
64   House Of The Rising Sun (Columbia 1964) Animals
65   Maggie May/Reason To Believe (Mercury 1971) Rod Stewart
66   Go Now (Decca 1965) Moody Blues
67   This Is My Song (Pye 1967) Petula Clark
68   These Boots Are Made For Walking (Reprise 1966) Nancy Sinatra
69   Honky Tonk Woman (Decca 1969) Rolling Stones
70   I'm Into Something Good (Columbia 1964) Herman's Hermits
71   Band Of Gold (Invictus 1970) Freda Payne
72   Hot Love (Fly 1971) T. Rex
73   Bridge Over Troubled Water (CBS 1970) Simon and Garfunkel
74   I Can't Stop Loving You (HMV 1962) Ray Charles
75   Love Grows (Bell 1970) Edison Lighthouse
76   Something Stupid (Reprise 1967) Frank and Nancy Sinatra
77   Juliet (Philips 1964) Four Pennies
78   March Of The Siamese Children (Pye 1962) Kenny Ball
79   Knock Three Times (Bell 1971) Dawn
80   Mr Tambourine Man (CBS 1965) Byrds
81   Good Luck Charm (RCA 1962) Elvis Presley
82   Silence Is Golden (CBS 1967) Tremeloes
83   Spirit In The Sky (Reprise 1970) Norman Greenbaum
84   Massachusetts (Polydor 1967) Bee Gees
85   Yellow River (CBS 1970) Christie
86   Yeh Yeh (Columbia 1965) Georgie Fame
87   The Good, The Bad And The Ugly (RCA 1968) Hugo Montenegro
88   Israelites (Pyramid 1969) Desmond Dekker and the Aces
89   Young Girl (CBS 1968) Gary Puckett and the Union Gap
90   Ballad Of Bonnie and Clyde (CBS 1968) Georgie Fame
91   Nineteenth Nervous Breakdown (Decca 1966) Rolling Stones
92   Keep On Running (Fontana 1966) Spencer Davis Group
93   Coz I Luv You (Polydor 1971) Slade
94   Son Of My Father (CBS 1972) Chicory Tip

95 How Do You Do It (Columbia 1963) Gerry and the Pacemakers
96 Albatross (Blue Horizon 1969) Fleetwood Mac
97 Let The Heartaches Begin (Pye 1967) Long John Baldry
98 San Francisco (CBS 1967) Scott McKenzie
99 Paperback Writer (Parlophone 1966) Beatles
100 Crying In The Chapel (RCA 1965) Elvis Presley

For me, this chart is startling for one reason: the lack of T. Rex. Bolan, who claims his records are selling as well as the Beatles were at their height, only comes in this Top 100 at number 72 with 'Hot Love'. This means that 'Get it On' and 'Telegram Sam', the two other number ones that T. Rex had in the period covered by the Top 100, have been outsold by several records from the same period; records such as 'Son of My Father' by Chicory Tip (at 94) and 'Coz I Luv You' by Slade (at 93). Even 'Hot Love', their biggest seller, is nowhere near being the biggest record of the past 18 months. Above it are Rod Stewart's 'Maggie May' (65), Middle of the Road's 'Chirpy Chirpy Cheep Cheep' (42), Benny Hill's 'Ernie' (36), George Harrison's 'My Sweet Lord' (25) and the New Seekers' 'I'd Like to Teach the World to Sing' (18). And T. Rex, remember, concentrates on selling 45s, not LPs. The Beatles, incidentally, take positions 1, 2, 4, 5 and 6.

CLAPPED OUT FACES

That Marc Bolan is the self-made Fabian of his times rather than the Presley, I have no doubt. But evidence for his relative lack of success goes deeper than exposure of a few lies about record sales – it's something of a comment on the way teen culture has split itself up.

In short, it's got something to do with the skinheads, who represent the biggest challenge to T. Rex and the other lesser 'orgiastic exercise' groups. For it's the skins who constitute, at time of writing, by far the biggest single group among this country's teenagers. In the war for the kids' minds raging between Pupil Power, Bolan's Hot Goblinism and the Festival of Light, the skins have slithered in and won hands down. A walk through any provincial town will confirm this picture. It's the Crombies, it's the pocket handkerchiefs, it's the football badges that predominate. For every one little middle-class girl with sequins round her eyes, there must be two dozen in their two-tone mohair suits. It's a walkover.

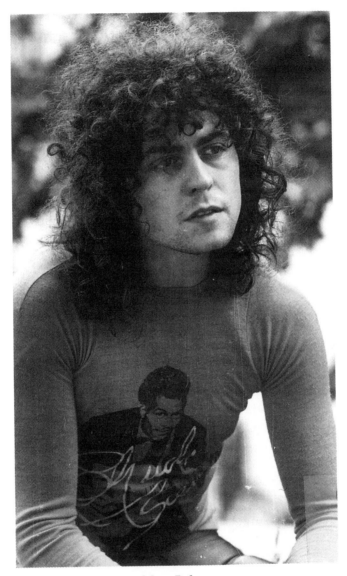

Marc Bolan

There are many similarities between the skinheads of the 1970s and the mods of the 1960s – they tend to come from the same sort of council-house background, they veer towards the same uniformity of dress (the girls' drab two-tone suits of last winter echoing the mod girls below-the-knee skirts of the winter of 1963/1964), and even, in the spring of 1972, the scooter is making something of a comeback. But there are differences: the skinheads were, originally, a reaction against what many of the mods had become.

The mods were dominated by pop music and their lifestyle was dictated by it. They had their own groups: the Yardbirds, the Who, the Stones and the Small Faces. They had their own TV show in *Ready Steady Go*, compered by their own representative in high places, Cathy McGowan. They even had their own drugs, in purple hearts and other amphetamines. But, all of it sprang from rock. Their idols, their trendsetters were all from the pop world. 'Faces' was the word they used to describe them. Eric Clapton, for example: 'Eric', according to the first *Record Mirror* report on the Yardbirds in May 1964, 'is one of the most fashionable dressers in show-biz. In fact, the Yardbirds in general are regarded as the most fashionable group but fashion-leader Eric is often accosted by Mod girls who blandly accuse him of being "one of the top faces".' As the old advert went: 'Everybody knows three feet make a yard, but every moddy knows that ten feet make the Yardbirds.'

If the mods idolised their Faces, the rock stars in return loved the mods – it was this dialectic that was responsible for all the good things that happened in British rock in the mid-1960s. Take the Who, or the High Numbers as they were originally known in the suburbs of London. The *Record Mirror* saw their first record (called, significantly, 'I'm The Face') as 'the first authentic mod record', and noted that 'their clothes are the hallmark of the much criticised, typical Mod. Cycling jackets, tee shirts, turned-up Levi Jeans, long white jackets, boxing boots, black and white brogues.' All those early Who records were taken straight from the mod experience. 'The guy who sings "My Generation"', Pete Townshend said in November 1965, '… well, he's supposed to be blocked … it's reminiscent in a way, because Mods don't get blocked anymore … . Pills was a phase.'

The mod movement was unstoppable – or so it seemed. The kids loved the groups, adored their Faces, and the groups loved the mod experience. It was all very close – and the result of this physical closeness (after all, you could see all the top groups except the Beatles at your local Big Beat Club) was the destruction of the 'star' mentality. Pete Townshend was no more a star than the kids who were dancing, blocked out of their heads, right in front of him and the girl he eventually married was at one time in the audience at the Railway Hotel in Wealdstone, just one of the mod crowd.

Once the star syndrome got smashed, things happened. If Townshend or Jagger could make it, the feeling went, anybody could. This isn't meant to be a slur on their talent in any way – it's much more a compliment. Groups simply sprang up relentlessly. Every week, it seemed, a new group was making it. One week it was the Stones breaking through – the result for us in London was that they left their Sunday afternoon residency at Studio 51 to tour the country. But, not to worry. Their three o'clock to six o'clock spot at the club was taken over by the Yardbirds. A few months later, they made it. Same thing happened – then it was the turn of the Pretty Things. Groups just appeared out of thin air, and the reason for their emergence was the remarkable fluidity of an open scene. The mods were firmly rooted – and so were their stars. Their's was a generation.

And yet, of course, it all ended. It's a sad irony that it was the mod experience that created the springboard for the first significant break-through made by English rockers in the United States, for it was the incredible American successes of most of these groups that wrecked our own pop music. The mods were destroyed not by their 'growing up', as has sometimes been suggested, but rather by their very success.

If the focal point of rock in 1964 and 1965 was Richmond (or any of the London suburbs, for that's where it was all really happening) the focal point shifted in the later 1960s towards the American West Coast. Rock was taken over by the students. San Francisco was primarily dope-centred, and the music became intellectual and hallucinogenic. Looking at individuals is the best way, perhaps, of getting the whole picture in perspective: one minute Eric Burdon was a good old Geordie rocker, the next he was a wet, weak-kneed stargazer ('When I think of all the good times that I've wasted having good times …'), Lennon shifted gear in 'Strawberry Fields Forever', a far cry from 'Eight Days a Week'. And Pete Townshend went from 'My Generation' to the idea of *Tommy*, a rock opera, which eventually emerged in 1969. However much the Sunday papers might latch on to the 'significance' of *Tommy*, Townshend must know deep down that 'My Generation' had far, far more of an impact on the kids than anything he's done this side of 'Substitute'. Similarly, Stevie Winwood's maximum point of impact wasn't with Blind Faith or even Traffic, it was with 'Keep on Running' and 'Gimme Some Lovin'.

1967 was the great divide for rock. The mods lost their Faces to the new Hippie movement. They were absorbed elsewhere. The golden age of 1967–68 was not so golden for everybody. Eddie, a 20-year-old apprentice in Birmingham, remembers 1967 as being something quite different:

I was 15 in '67, and all I remember is what a drag it all was. One minute we had the Spencer Davis Group playing here, and the Stones played here a lot, and the Yardbirds and the Animals. Then suddenly nothing. Nothing at all. I hated fucking *Sergeant Pepper* and that thing the Stones did with 'She's A Rainbow' on it. Me and my mates spent most of the time in the pub after that. I mean, you could hardly dance to the Pink Floyd, could you?

Nik Cohn is the only rock writer I've ever read who came close to the truth of that year. He was afraid of *Sergeant Pepper* and rightly so. Rock became highly regarded by all the 'right' people. Rock columns suddenly appeared in the *Observer* and the posh weeklies. It became (dare I say it?) middle class by default. And, once this absorption took place, rock lost much of its strength and much of its popularity. The old Faces were much richer; they'd made it in the US after all. They had no need to tour round the dingy old clubs any more. Besides, who could afford them anyway? In effect, they became stars – or superstars, as they preferred to be called. They found their level and it was a level divorced from those who had made their success possible in the first instance. Listen to this:

Both in the East and in the West music was separated into two forms. One was court music to entertain the aristocrats. The other was folk songs, sung by the people to express their emotions and their political feelings. But lately, the folk music of the age, Pop Song, is becoming intellectualised and is starting to lose its original meaning and function. Pop is supposed to stimulate people in the audience to think, 'Oh, it's so simple, even I could do that'. It should not alienate the audience with its professionalism but communicate to the audience the fact that they, the audience can be just as creative as those on stage, and encourage them to make their own music with the performers rather than just sit back and applaud.

Sad, really, that that perfect summary of what I've been groping to say should have come from Yoko Ono (in *Rolling Stone*, 17 February 1972). For it was Lennon and the other Beatles who lost contact somewhere back in the late 1960s: they became court musicians.

And, going back to good old Tony Blackburn's Top 100 it's all in writing. 'She Loves You' is at number 1, 'I Want To Hold Your Hand' is at number 2, and 'Can't Buy Me Love' is at number 4. 'All You Need Is Love,' though, is at 53 and 'Eleanor Rigby' at 59. For all those who thought that the Beatles were the saviours of rock, there were at least twice as many who thought John Lennon was going round the twist.

The Emergence of the Skinheads

In 1969, the backlash started. It had to happen sometime: once the star idea was reborn, once the gaps arose between artist and performer, once the focal point of the new culture became rooted in the United States, the time was ripe for change, The skinheads came from the same areas that had witnessed the rise of the mods – the East End of London and the outer ring of suburbs. But whereas the mod had seen his 'enemy' as the rocker, and had rationalised his lifestyle accordingly (Cleanliness vs Grease; Scooter vs Motor Bike; Pills vs Booze), the new skinheads reacted against the hippies. Their hair was short to the point of absurdity, they were tough and went around in their 'bovver boots' for the express purpose of beating hell out of any deviants, and they wore braces. Braces! For God's sake, some sort of weird throw-back to the 1930s.

At Hyde Park in July 1969, they showed their strength. According to Geoffrey Cannon's report on the event, a free concert given by the Stones, it was 'A Nice Day in the Park'. It was things 'nice' that the skins objected to. John Peel and the other beautiful people saw everything as being 'really nice' – the skins wanted others to see them as really horrible.

The concert was odd. Here were the Rolling Stones, the old mod idols, being defended by the Hell's Angels, the descendants of the old rockers, and the whole scene was laughed at by the new skinheads, who were the true descendants of the old mods. After all, it seems likely that most of their elder brothers and sisters had spent their teens down Soho getting blocked on a Saturday night. The wheel had come full circle.

Since that concert, we've learnt to live with the skinheads. They have the same austerity of style as the early mods, and they hunt in packs like the mods tracked down the rockers on the beaches of Margate and Clacton.

Though their style has been determined to a large extent by their opposition to the hippies, other factors have played a crucial role and, in particular, the impact of the West Indian community. Many of the skin gangs have West Indians not only in the group but actually leading them, the short hair style having been, without doubt, lifted from the old bluebeat days in the London clubs.

In Birmingham, a city with a large immigrant community, the pattern is especially evident. The Skins will still profess to hate the niggers, but by 'niggers' they generally mean the Pakistanis. Their hatred of the Pakkis might appear crazily illogical in the light of their friendship with the West Indians, but there is a certain, cruel logic about it. Take the story of Des, a garage worker and a skin of three years standing:

> I'll tell you why I hate the bloody Paks. I'll tell you a story. A week or so ago I was walking down the street with a couple of mates. I wanted a light for my fag, so I walk up to this Pakki git and ask him, 'You got a light, mate?' And what do you think the fucker did? I'll tell you. He walks – no, runs – into this shop and buys me a box of matches! Now, I ask you! What the fuck could I do with a bleeder like that but hit him? And another thing. Have you ever been in their restaurants? Have you seen the way they grovel round you, the way they're always trying to please you? I hate them, that's all.

The next time you go in an Indian restaurant, think of Des's story and look around at the clientele. You'll find an almost straight middle-class content. Des and his mates just go in there for the occasional giggle – all pissed and raring for trouble.

The logic of their hatred is this: the West Indian kids are mixing, and their influence is taking hold. They are beginning to see this country as their home. The Indians and the Pakistanis keep themselves to themselves and in Birmingham interaction between white working class and Asian is non-existent. To put it another way, the Indians and the Pakistanis are aspiring (if they are aspiring towards anything whilst they're living here) towards a middle-class set of values. They dress in carefully tailored suits, they are polite, they are nice. The West Indian kids on the other hand are more 'normal' in the skins' eyes. They get drunk, they like dancing, they like dressing up in skingear. They are willing to join forces.

There's nothing nice about the skins. And likewise there's nothing nice about their taste in music. They completely reject the music of the counter-culture. Nothing is more loathsome to them than the junk of progressive rock. Music is for dancing to. Music is for getting off with birds to. And the best music for that, they have decided, is reggae and Tamla Motown. Their love of this twin spearhead is, of course, a direct legacy of the impact of the West Indians in the late 1960s. But their idolisation of this music should not be mixed up with the mods relationship to their Faces – it's something quite different. For the new relationship is essentially impersonal, whereas the mods related to a set of individual Faces, like Steve Marriott or Rod 'the Mod' Stewart. The skins relate to types of music, like Motown. The Four Tops, to take an example, are not revered for being the Four Tops; they are simply one aspect of the Motown machine. If T. Rex has any appeal with this audience, it's on this same impersonal level, a brand name for formula-produced dance records.

Moreover, there's the question of distancing. A group like the Kinks could be seen 'live' every week somewhere round the country because the central factor of the mod-music scene was the live club appearance. The skins tend more towards discos, mainly because there are so few British groups they like.

The result of this has been important. Music is still important to the skins, but it's not of such overriding importance as it was for the mods. Music, it has been argued, was central to the mod experience. It dictated style. For the skinheads, music has become peripheral: style is in no way determined by it. If the skins do have Faces, they are elsewhere and, usually, they are out there playing on the football field.

JAMES DEAN TURNS UP AGAIN

> Disliked in certain quarters for his virtues as much as his faults, George Best has become a cult for youth, a new folk hero, a living James Dean who has become a rebel with no real cause to rebel.
>
> Geoffrey Green (*The Times*, 22 May 1972)

> Only a few weeks ago, Charlie George scored an important goal at Derby, and then ruined the goal and dragged Arsenal's mighty name through the mud by facing the County crowd and jolting them with a double V-sign... .
> At Ipswich, again just a few weeks ago, he was involved in another unsavoury incident when he refused to retreat the statutory 10 yards from the ball when a Town player took a free kick... .
>   His problems have been likened to those of the other George, Best of Manchester United and Ireland, and his hair is even longer. But there is one essential difference. Best creates headlines almost as much off the field. So far at least Charlie George has confined himself to foolishness only during games.
>
> Iain Mackenzie (the *Observer*, March 1972)

Two views on contemporary soccer idols. Best and George are both relevant to this essay, but for different reasons. George Best is 26 years old, Charlie George 21. They might both be idols (though I doubt whether Best is any more) but they are very different kinds of idols.

George Best's lifestyle was determined in the mod's era. His clothes, his hair, his mode of living were decided by pop. Though he lives in

Manchester, he was, and still remains, a swinging Londoner. Indeed, much of his dilemma vis-à-vis soccer probably stems from this: had he been playing this past five years for Arsenal or Spurs he might have managed all right. But, as he's said so often, Manchester's too small for him. Best sees himself as made for the trendy world of boutiques, nightclubs and dolly birds. He's become, though he might not yet realise it, a living anachronism.

Charlie George, on the other hand, fits into none of these patterns. George is, despite the length of his hair, a skinhead's dream. His focal point, as Iain Mackenzie implies, is on the soccer field. George Best's focal point is in Carnaby Street. The two players are poles apart. Charlie George is a skinhead who's made it: George Best is a Face who's lost his public. This being the case, Charlie George's position in soccer is far more secure than Best's will ever be.

Yoko Ono's observation of a few paragraphs back is relevant. She said that pop 'Should not alienate the audience with its professionalism, but should communicate to the audience the fact that they can be just as creative as those on stage'. When the Skins root for Charlie George at Highbury – they are rooting for themselves. For Charlie is simply one of them who's happened to make it out there on the stage. They hate the opposition, and so does Charlie. They adore him for his V-signs and his tantrums, just as they adore kicking in the teeth of an enemy fan.

Linking this with pop is interesting, for analogies suggest themselves with ease. Watching Charlie George at Highbury is for the skins, much the same experience as watching the Who at the Railway Hotel in Wealdstone was for the mods. Or, to cross the Atlantic, the same experience as watching Johnny Cash at San Quentin was for the prison inmates. They are all watching their equals acting out their fantasies. And they can all hold on to these fantasies because those 'stars' on the stage are just the same as they are.

And this, for the skinheads, is the great difference between them and the mods. Their point of reference is different. The mods were inextricably tied up with pop. The skins are inextricably linked with soccer. Before we ever heard of skinheads, we all knew about football hooligans – but it's only in the last three or four years that the problem has come through with any force. And this is simply because the area of 'play' for deviant teenyboppers has changed.

ROCK AND THE SKINHEADS

The skins have changed a lot since that first major public appearance at Hyde Park in 1969. The braces and the cropped hair gave way to the two-tone Trevira suits, and these in turn have given way to Crombies, and – for the girls – Oxford bags and check jackets. But their attitude to music hasn't changed that much, nor has their attitude to football. On most Crombie jackets there is the obligatory football club badge, as central to the skins' uniform as a pocket handkerchief. But on none of their clothes is there any sign of pop worship.

This, really, is why Marc Bolan isn't as popular as he likes to make out. He's made no positive impression on the skins at all. Bolan is popular and it would be silly to completely write him off – after all, he has had four number ones on the trot – but the basis for his support is very narrowly confined. To be accurate, Marc Bolan is idolised by Grammar School girls between the ages of 11 and 14. (The skins, who might buy T. Rex records to dance to, don't idolise or identify with Bolan at all.)

Other groups win support from this 'teenybopper' area and Slade are the best example. Slade, it might be remembered, were, at one time, a skinhead group though if they ever were really skins I don't know. But it is a fact that they no longer enjoy much support from that area, if they ever did.

Meanwhile, although previous generation groups like the Stones and the Who can still fill a hall wherever they play, their support is not growing. It's a constant factor; those who have stayed with them through their changes over the past five years aren't giving them up, and they could still fill any of their old haunts if they so desired. But they're winning no new fans, and probably haven't for the last three or four years. If this analysis is correct, then the rock perspective that exists is hopelessly out of balance, and has been for some time.

Take, as an example, the pop press. Each of the musical papers have latched on to the wrong equation that Rock = Underground, or, when they are feeling patronisingly liberal, Rock = Underground + Teenyboppers. The last couple of years has witnessed the sad spectacle of most of the pop press trying desperately to halt their fall in sales by becoming fashionable. The Underground, they have decided, is where it's at. So, we have an increasingly one-sided 'too much' 'far out' 'got it together' pop press, ever more channelled into the one area where support certainly isn't getting any stronger.

The same, really, with television. *Top Of The Pops* clings to the teeny-boppers, and the only alternatives are either 'family entertainment' with Lulu or Cilla, or the progressive *Old Grey Whistle Test* (served up, it's true, with a good helping of old rock).

Together, these factors have helped perpetuate the skins alienation from pop.

There have been signs, becoming increasingly evident these past few months, of a change of direction by some of the skinhead girls – two stars in particular have catapulted to superstar/idol status. At the moment of writing, Donny Osmond is at number one in the charts with 'Puppy Love', and David Cassidy at number three (with the Partridge Family) with 'Breaking up is Hard to Do'.

It's appropriate that both of these songs are old 1950s material and that the 'new' treatments given them are in essence no different than the original treatment given in the 1950s by Paul Anka and Neil Sedaka: appropriate because the relationship between the fans and their idols is very close to that of parallel 1950s relationships. When some of the skinhead girls have finally latched on to pop idols, they have done it in such a way as to completely invalidate the British 1960s experience – there is no greater proof of the ephemeral success of the Beatles era than the idolisation of pretty boys like Cassidy and Osmond.

But the boys that these girls go around with – rather than the images they idolise – remain outside the pop experience, and it's this that strikes at the heart of rock. The bovver boys look like becoming the first major sub-cultural group not to produce any major rock stars! They, for rock, are the lost generation.

The survival of rock has depended on its position as the core of male teen culture. But the bovver boys have rejected rock's traditional status which explains the lack of vitality in British rock in the early 1970s.

(1972)

Afterword: The Shadow of Our Night

Pete Fowler

THE HUMBLE OF BIRTH

I was from the North, but lived in London in the 1960s. Drifting through the dream of Swinging London, my love of the new music combined effortlessly and romantically with a political perspective taking its cues from being a student at the London School of Economics. Every now and then I would go back to those northern towns and have a little worry or two.

For in Grimsby, as an example, where my parents lived, there manifestly *wasn't* something in the air. I would spend time there and sit in pubs conscious of the stares. It was all very well my girlfriend putting a flower in the button hole of my dyed purple army jacket; it was easy, too, to light a surreptitious joint and laugh at the primitive jerks sitting there talking about how the Mariners so badly needed a new right winger. It was easy – but its glibness was the very essence of the patronising stench that emanated, day by day, from the environs of Swiss Cottage, the Gate and NW3. The hegemony of the 31 bus route.

My moodset, soporific mainly but occasionally interrupted in this way, was forever broken by that July day in 1969 when the Stones played in Hyde Park in the afternoon; and Chuck Berry and the Who played the Albert Hall the same evening. Geoffrey Cannon wrote a piece on the Stones' concert in *Rolling Stone* which I thought quite stunning in its naivety.

He called it a 'Nice Day in the Park'.

168

On this nice day, the skinheads announced their arrival in Hyde Park by stomping through the masses of spaced-out freaks, spreading their *aggro* and shouting their obscenities at the crowd, at the stage, at the stars, at the world. It was an auspicious debut.

The New Bavarians.

In the evening, at the Albert Hall, their tribal enemies, the teds, their predecessors in the same estates by a generation or two, barracked the Who as they dared to play their set *after* Chuck Berry. They began with a truly frantic version of *Summertime Blues*, as the lads in front of the stage reminded themselves of old nights in the Granadas and the ABCs, hurling bits of seats and bits of abuse at the ex-scooter boys on the stage.

The Old Barbarians.

'Look', said Pete Townshend, 'we thought he was great as well, you know'. Chuck, I would have thought, was more likely to have been haggling over his money backstage rather than witnessing this deeply symbolic (and deeply flawed) triumph.

Those of us who were in the vanguard of the revolution, raring to bring together students and workers in the Common Front, were caught in a classic pincer movement on that July day, trapped in from different sides by the very proletariat we were fighting for.

The Stones' 'Salt of the Earth' rubbing itself into our stoned wounds.

FALSE CONSCIOUSNESS

In the 1970s, I used to teach in FE, General Studies to all kinds of students. I had one party trick that always turned out a treat. With all my groups, I would do what I still remember as the 'Eysenck political test', a set of statements with which the user would agree or disagree. At the end of the 60 questions, it was possible, analysing the answers given, to 'plot' the political perspective of the user. The test was in Eysenck's *Uses and Abuses of Psychology*.

Before they did the test, I used to ask my students what they would vote if there were a General Election on that day. My groups of working-class lads – motor vehicle apprentices, or butchers, or engineers, or the like – would dutifully make my point, after they had completed the test, that they would nearly all vote Labour even though they had opinions, according to Eysenck, slightly to the right of Enoch Powell. They were racist, materialist and wanted nothing more than the instant public execution of any deviant who offended them. I remember getting one Northwich class to define exactly who it was they hated – and the final answer on the blackboard pointed to any unfortunates who did not live down the respondent's street *and* did not support Manchester City.

The middle-class students on the art courses, though, were an almost exact match on the other side of the political divide. They were altogether softer, much more deviant (against national norms) on issues like drugs and religion, and softer on the treatment of criminals. And yet, more often than not they voted either Conservative or Liberal.

I might be exaggerating to make the point, but not by much. There was one occasion, in 1976, when punk was coming through, when I sat with an art teacher in a pub wondering what would happen if someone from the right understood what an enormously rich vein could be struck if the Eysenck 'circle' could be squared. If, instead of feeling embarrassed by the excesses of the working class, the Conservatives simply embraced the crassness of the proletariat right. If they stuck a dagger into the heart of what I was rapidly coming to see as the *real* false consciousness, as opposed to the *wished-for* Marxist false consciousness that I had talked about with such conviction in the late 1960s.

It happened, of course, in 1979.

BLUE BLUE DAYS

The tabloid headlines when the *Belgrano* went down; the 1987 Conservative Party Rally when Kenny Everett asked us to bomb the Russians; the looks on the English supporters at Heysel and hearing a soldier on a train bragging how the Reds had beaten Juventus 39–0, whatever Platini thought he had achieved on that silent, ghostly spring evening; those endless tales from my old friends in Hemel Hempstead about how if they sold their house they could buy an island off Scotland or a village in France – and I would have got the same story in Basildon or Harlow, Ilford or Stevenage, any of those barracks of the soldiers of the *Sun*, spirits shining in their shellsuits; those gifts to the world from Hertfordshire's Tory Parties: Parkinson, the son of a Lancashire railway worker – unbelievably, given a voice that must have been rehearsed in front of a thousand Home Counties mirrors – and Tebbit, on leave from

Mordor, He of the Disfigured Feet; that strange morning when so many of us, ashamed at the directions our minds were taking, found it hard not to mutter a silent curse at the failure of the Republicans in Brighton; 'Rejoice, Rejoice'; Manning, Davidson, Lulu and Lynsey de Paul; Lawson's late-1980s budgets, and the symmetry of the symbolism that it was these that directly led to negative equity for so many of the New Town stormtroopers of Thatcherism; calling cards from the Firm at the Den; ripped seats in the air at Luton; the juxtaposition of thrown banana skins and the elegance of John Barnes, in his glorious Anfield prime in the days before Hillsborough; and that endless, that inane, that eternal emetic, the National Anthem sung as a one-note malignancy by lads on terraces all around the world.

The soundtrack to the decade: sung with one hand, fisted, pointing to the sky, and another holding on to a lager; and sung by the new lumpen, those who, this time round, had nothing to lose but their Rottweilers.

Days I'll remember all my life.

BAD DAY FOR BLACK ROCK

It never occurred to me, at the time I wrote 'Skins Rule', that the alienation I saw in the skins was, in reality, a culture being turned on its head. Their stance, according to conventional wisdom, was seen as some kind of awful aberration; and their affinity with reggae and Motown was seized upon as a portent of better times to come. The paradox of an apparently racist youth group dancing to 'Pressure Drop' and 'Long Shot Kick the Bucket' would surely result in a new synthesis of an entirely benign kind. My optimism coincided with Lennon's when he said, at some free concert or other, 'OK, flower power failed: let's start again.'

But, rapidly, it was *we* who were alienated, hopelessly out of touch with the new brutalism. More and more locked into our houses, going down with Gram Parsons, hitting the escape button with Neil Young, playing the train spotter with Dylan bootlegs.

Digging out the Velvet Underground and hiding the Incredible String Band.

Heading for 'The End' while the 'White Rabbit' gathered dust; and Ray Charles' drug-sodden 'What Would I Do Without You' and 'Hard Times' drifted back into my consciousness, paradoxically seeming – to me – more in tune with the times than the contemporary sounds emerging from black America.

Some of us turned to music from other cultures; some of us hid in the middle of Wales. Some of us began, teasingly and with great hesitation at first, to think of careers. Some of us became mothers and fathers and focused on play groups and standing for the PTA; some of us ended up on committees, taking the matters arising from the minutes, but ignoring the signs arising from the times; some of us turned to the trades, and built extensions, or sold our wares at market stalls.

But our *community* had been shattered.

ROTTEN TO THE CORE

There had been times, of course, when the rock of that community appeared as if it may roll again, and the whistle of Johnny Cash's 'Train of Love' could be heard, somewhere in the distance, heading once more for home.

But it was hard, once it had been understood in the late 1960s, to ignore Marcuse's sections in *One Dimensional Man* on assimilation and absorption. His analysis had been important to me, as a novice lecturer in the late 1960s, and I would hammer his points home to my students: whatever the counter-culture could throw at the brick wall of the establishment, it would be caught, re-shaped and re-worked to fit the needs of those who owned and controlled the state. Any radical idea could thus be neutered. In my youthful innocence, I would bring in copies of an advertisement that was everywhere in 1968 and 1969: 'Watneys *is* the Red Revolution'. Look, I would shout, with a gleeful sense of triumph, the bastards are using *our* ideological message to sell beer! This is Marcusian assimilation and absorption!

If only life had been that simple. What on earth would I have made, in 1969, of a row of Conservative politicians sitting under a banner proclaiming 'Power to the People' and singing a chorus of 'Imagine no possessions' led by the black lead singer from Hot Chocolate?

And what on earth would I have made of punk, a veritable case study for an understanding of *One Dimensional Man*? I cannot, of course, know exactly how I would have reacted because, when punk happened, I was not sitting at the urban heart of the beast, as I had been with the movements in the 1960s – I was sitting in a small northern town; and I was not in my early 20s – I was in my early 30s. I related to punk, therefore, at a crucial *secondhand*, seeing the movement through the eyes of someone who talked incessantly to those to whom it was important, but who could be nothing but the ageing outsider. However, like so many of my generation, I was more than ready for something like punk to happen.

Therein, perhaps, lies the first rub. Punk as a youth culture had been needed *just a little too much*, with all those desiring a re-run of the sub-group highs of the 1960s too desperate by half for the dead-end corner of the 1970s to be turned – and thus hopelessly over-keen to sell what was, in its infancy, a smallish New York-inspired movement pain-stakingly created, fabricated and hyped by a few London-based individuals and marketed by a bizarre combination of radicals and opportunists as The Grand Re-Awakening.

The speed of punk's history – from an esoteric club culture to mass chart success, through the Marcusian assimilation towards extinction – was quite extraordinary. Punk's script had been learned from the generation before; but, in its re-telling, the players gabbled their lines, forgetting the need to inject some meaning into the unfolding story.

McLaren told how the Pistols were from the streets, and how their mission in life was to bury McCartney, Rod Stewart and the Who. The seminal rock 'n' roll moment: the shift in gear, the sudden ridiculousness and sterility of the old generation; the energy, cockiness and sheer fun of the new; the excitement of the overnight fame of a new clutch of groups from previously unknown clubs in often unfashionable cities. The 'classic shot in the arm for pop' as *Billboard* described the effect of the Beatles in those astonishing American weeks in 1964.

But this time the ideologues knew the script word-perfect, even though their perspective was often content-free. And their self-importance was fuelled by a media blitz in which the writers in the pop and rock press didn't just jump on board of the new trend – they steered the bloody boat. It was a long way from those 1950s days when *Melody Maker* and the *'NME'* printed snide articles on the awfulness of rock 'n' roll (remember how one *NME* writer made 'Great Balls of Fire' the worst record of 1957?); or when Jack Payne, on his *Off the Record* 1958 TV show, apologised to his audience after Buddy Holly and the Crickets had just performed a great version of 'Peggy Sue'. 'Well', he said, 'there must be some people out there who like that kind of thing.'

Tellingly, Payne and the pop writers of the late 1950s saw themselves as taking a very clear *principled* stand: the new music was appalling and the quicker the rock 'n' roll bubble burst, the sooner Sinatra, Ella and those classy American acts could again dominate the airwaves. (What they didn't know was that thousands of teenagers – like the young Van Morrison in Belfast, whose 'In the Days Before Rock 'n' Roll' remains a definitive statement on this time of change – were voting with the twiddle of the dial on their transistor radios in searching for Luxembourg.)

Payne's stand was perversely echoed by Bill Grundy in the notorious 1976 TV interview with the Sex Pistols that effectively launched punk as a national phenomenon. 'All great events in history', wrote Marx, 'reappear in one fashion or another: the first time as tragedy, the second as farce'. Grundy took no principled stand at all, only being determined to make *his* name as he relentlessly tried to get the group to swear and curse on national television. Ironically, his instinctive exploitation of the situation was altogether more crass and dangerous than the simple lack of generational understanding that had characterised the 1950s media reactions.

Punk was strangled by a parade of such puppet masters – on every side of the ideological, musical and philosophical divide. Its undoubted creativity did result in real changes, but these did not, ultimately, involve any deep reassessments in the cultural perspectives of the punk audience; the changes centred on, rather, the worlds of those who *marketed* the phenomenon, those who *managed* it and those who *lived off* it. Thus, the record industry had to cope with an explosion in the number of independent labels; and the print media was faced with the rise of the fanzine. The new technologies – in these two cases, developments in recording techniques and the new universality of the photocopier – facilitated a sub-cultural media breakthrough that was potentially very powerful indeed. More, the combination of a new underclass (the urban unemployed) and a new message ('no future') with a cluster of technological breakthroughs that would have been the envy of those in the same game ten years earlier should have led to something very much more substantial.

Instead, punk's story was burnt out before the end of the contents page. It was suffocated by expectation, and directed from within its core (as well as exploited by outsiders like Grundy) in a manner that would have been much appreciated and understood by a man like Larry Parnes. Vicious, Rotten: Wilde, Fury. It was never allowed to find its own *roots* because its *routes* were too quickly mapped out by writers, by fashion trendsetters, by the exploiters, by the managers. It was seized so hard it seized up.

And a great potential was smothered to death. Hiding in the chaos were those who might have taken the culture forward, those who could have transcended the preordained fashion show, the Pageant of the Pogo, those who were discovering the uncharted waters that would lead to a questioning of the old maps of rock 'n' roll. These, too often, ended up either emigrants or dead.

Sometimes I wish all these British stars had been born in Galway or Donegal, giving them the strength of communities still *connecting* and still providing points of view and points of contact; instead of drifting off into a de-contextualised individualist nightmare. But then we wouldn't have had British rock 'n' roll, for an album reflecting the best of British rock might well be called *Rockin' with the Rootless*.

This aborting of the potential life-force of punk and its successors in the late 1970s ultimately confirmed rather than denied the disunity of community in the worlds represented by British rock.

That punk had this potential is, to me, taken for read. Its figureheads and followers, in the classic manner of the best rock moments, came from different worlds, allowing a situation to arise in which a synthesis of views could develop. More, these worlds centred, as in the days before the British rock breakthrough (in 1961 and 1962) on the art schools and council estates environs. But this time the context was different; and the links in the 1970s were altogether more tenuous and fragile.

People from different backgrounds ended up relating to punk for different reasons, as was the case in all the youth sub-cultures since the 1950s: but the social interactions *between* those from the different backgrounds – that characterised, say, the audiences at Eel Pie Island and the Cavern – simply did not take place to an extent sufficient to force a cultural change. The only remaining links were poses and gestures.

Thus, in some of the classes I taught, there were working-class lads who adopted the stance of, say, Sid Vicious, and began to be a bit rude to their teachers; in other educational settings, in the art schools for example, punk was more McLaren than Cook, more *NME* than Sham 69, more De Voto than Gene October. Here, it absorbed a kind of Doors-derived angst, best epitomised towards the end of the 1970s by the first post-punks like Joy Division or the new Liverpool bands.

And, in all settings, it was quickly characterised, very simply, by the way you dressed and the way you walked; the way you stood out from the crowd and the way you smoked your cigarette. Photographed on a London street by the tourists. Absorbed into the freak show; assimilated, castrated, killed.

It seemed entirely apposite that the hit career of the Sex Pistols should have died in an orgy of Eddie Cochran re-treads; for their 1977 anarchy and republicanism had been diluted to such an extent that the whole movement seemed to have reached the point where nineteen-*fifty* seven seemed – just about – a possibility.

PUTTING ON THE AGONY

The punks in my late-1970s classes would have understood perfectly the way Eddie Cochran flicked his head sideways to the camera when he sung with Gene Vincent on Jack Good's *Boy Meets Girl* in 1959. The rock 'n' roll sexual icon.

During this period, I ran classes on fancying: it didn't matter if the students were hairdressers or brickies, illustrators or secretaries, the classes were always a hoot, always revealing and always fun.

After all, it got to the heart of the matter. Why do you fancy her? What makes him attractive? Do you fancy the same kind of person that you did a few years ago?

Ben was 18, a punk with pink hair, safety pins all over his bondage gear. Into the Manchester scene. The King of the Pose. It was 1979.

He was avoiding the questions being put to him. We'd gone round most of the group, and most had talked. But Ben kept his cool and remorselessly smoked his cigarettes. I was egged on by a couple of students to get him to open up.

'Ben', I asked, 'let's imagine you're at a party and there're three girls sitting on the sofa ...'

'And they're all naked', interrupted a girl.

'OK', I agreed, 'they're all naked. One's a bit like Debbie Harry, blonde and sultry ... one's like Charlotte Rampling, willowy and subtle ... and one's like the tall one in Hot Gossip ... you know, because you've just been told, that they all fancy you like mad ... you wander over to the sofa and they're all looking at you ... which one would you go for?'

Ben drew heavily on his cigarette, looking up to the sky and down again. The group, in a circle, waited with baited breath. Ben thought hard about his reply.

'I wouldn't go with any of them', he replied.

'None of them?' I asked, 'none of them? Are you sure?'

'Yep. Sure.'

'But why?'

'Because in the morning when we got up I could find that whoever it was I'd gone with might wear flares.'

THE FREAK AT THE FRONT OF THE ROOM

On that 1979 day, the whole group, me and Ben included, laughed till we nearly cried. I used to get a bit pompous with the stylists sometimes but was always quickly brought down to earth again by the fun and the sharpness of the art students; yes, the easy empathy I had felt with the students in the early and middle 1970s, when I would be given institutional tasks like sorting the druggies out, was less apparent but then I was moving through my 30s; and it hadn't been that long since I had believed that anyone over 30 should not, in any circumstances, be trusted.

I might get cross at what I saw as the lack of a point of view; and I might find the sudden liking for Jim Morrison's lyrics to be a bit bizarre. But at least there were still all kinds of recognitions crossing the generational line. We were, though, in the middle of a sea change; and the tide of my younger days, the hopes of my generation, were profoundly on the turn.

Three years after Ben's group, I was still teaching art foundation courses: it had been ten years by that time. It was 1982. I'd done this same set of lessons for six years or so, ever since I'd read some poems written by Mary Bell, who, at the age of 11, had murdered two little children in Newcastle, in the late 1960s. These poems, written when she was 12 or 13, were beautiful, full of a breathtaking poignancy and sensitivity. I still remember one called 'Stories in the Stars'.

I began the series of lessons with these, reading them aloud, getting the class to read them, to think about them, to talk about them. Getting a picture of the author. Male or female? Old or young? Romantic or practical? Nice? Tender? Warm or cold?

The verdict was usually that the writer was in *his* twenties, male rather than female. He had been hurt in life and was sensitive; very obviously compassionate, and an innocent romantic.

I would end the lesson saying that these poems were written by a young murderer. *She* had killed two children. In cold blood. She had taken them out, looking after them while their mother had gone into town. She'd strangled them.

The next lessons focused on the events and the trial. Straight descriptions of the horror of it all. I realised, as I told the story, I could have heard a pin drop. I used the picture on the book about her, in which she looked every bit the pretty little girl down the street: she could have been a Rose Queen. Beautiful eyes.

And I'd ask the class to think about her: what could have made her do it? We would nudge towards one of the points of the lessons, the nature versus nurture debate.

Then, the lessons on Mary Bell's background, Scotswood Road in Newcastle. The mother who took the four-year-old Mary to the adoption agency and left her there, telling someone in the waiting room if she would mind taking this one in together with her own child; and how the little girl was always swallowing pills and seemingly hell-bent on self-destruction. Being run over; and beginning her murderous activities by killing birds in the playground at school.

And nobody noticed what Mary had been doing. Nobody did anything about this girl who was writing school essays about how she liked strangling things. She was invisible and her increasingly horrendous crimes were answered with a deadly silence.

We always finished the series of lessons with a discussion on what might have made her do these things: was there anything in her background that could explain her behaviour? Was there anything that could have been done to prevent her crimes? And, now that she had done these things, what should society have done with Mary Bell?

In 1982 the discussion was curt and to the point. The uniformity of view symbolised, with a crushing finality, a trend I had detected starting in the late 1970s. Mary Bell should have been hanged. It was her own fault. Lots of kids were in her position. Her mother should have been hanged as well. She should never be let out of jail. It was wrong for society to waste even a penny on scum like this.

The group had a *straightness* I found unnervingly novel in my experience with art students. My teaching was losing its entire point; I was standing there, the *freak at the front of the room*, reinforcing the solidarity of their views with every wrong turn of my desperate argument.

I left the room shaken and spent a few days getting my timetable re-arranged: I moved into Special Education.

SOUTHAMPTON PIER

We'd talk for hours about the changes, sitting in the staff room, drinking in the Red Lion and the Bowling Green. Yes, we agreed, it was unemployment: the students were afraid for the first time in our memories, asking, on interview, about career prospects and even pay levels of jobs that might be achievable at the end of the year. It suddenly seemed a long time since a couple of students had burned their portfolio of work in protest at what they called the Foundation production line, sheep-like students en route for the same old tired combination of 'acceptable' BA courses. Like Fine Art at Manchester, or Graphics at Leeds, 3D at Wolverhampton, and any damned thing at St Martins and Chelsea.

The New Fear had flattened this teenage angst into a state of profound *un*fashion: those in the new art school generation watched from a distance as their contemporaries from another class burned not their portfolios but their own neighbourhoods to the ground.

But it wasn't, as I imagined, these inner-city riots that acted as the catalyst for the transformation of the New Fear; this came from a direction that caught so many of us unawares.

It came from a war: the Falklands War.

When I would show the map of the world, and point out how absurd it was that this country had any right whatsoever to this little dot on the other side of the globe; and when I'd read the history books and come to realise the ambivalence of it all, even when seen from an imperialist perspective; and when I'd rant against that awesome slaughter of 400 boys, sunk in the act of running away: none of this meant anything, because I'd missed the profound symbolism of it all. We were not discussing rational things; we were, rather, being persuaded to immerse ourselves in a myth, a fantasy, a Golden Age.

An age when Britannia ruled and in which the image of the Iron Lady morphed into that of Churchill, or Henry V. And the imagery of some glorious past became all encompassing, taking in not just memories of battlegrounds but the theories of Adam Smith; and pictures of passive, reciting rows of neat children in huge classrooms; or families on their way, Sunday best, to the Methodist Chapels; or Noël, Celia, John and cowardly Richard in *In Which We Serve*; or Akela, sixers and woggles; or the deserving and the undeserving poor.

And, of course, the deeply embedded folklore of the foreigner. We were not fighting the Argentinians at Goose Green: we were fighting the Hun, and not the Hun from the age gone by, but the preposterous cheek of the Germans to build a society that appeared to be richer than ours. Or the Japanese with their silicon chips. Or the French with their ban on our meat. 'If the French won't buy our mutton we won't buy their letters.' Or the Italians who always turned and ran at the sound of gunfire.

We were showing the world. We were still here, still on top. The lads on the terraces caught the mood and began busily reinterpreting past events that became, instead of the defeats they appeared to be on the surface, symbols of glory. Bayern Munich, as an example, had beaten Leeds United 2–0 in a European Cup Final in Paris: but now the T-shirt slogans reversed the score, reminding the nervous German fans in any match we played against them that in the real world they had *lost* 2–0.

Margaret had given us our swagger back. Once those poor kids drowned screaming in the sea near that dot full of sheep, and once the Task Force set sail, the New Patriotism locked forces with the New Fear to create a world fit for Bucks Fizz to shine in.

Arthur Scargill was doomed. 'Ghost Town' had no context any more. In any case, any songs were drowned out by

> that endless, that inane, that eternal emetic, the National Anthem sung as a one-note malignancy by lads on terraces all around the world.
>
> The soundtrack to the decade: sung with one hand, fisted, pointing to the sky, and another holding on to a lager; and sung by the new lumpen, those who, this time round, had nothing to lose but their Rottweilers.

And back in the art school, where sensibilities were way above such things, Charlotte, a deadringer for a star child in 1967, took herself off to Southampton Pier to welcome the boys home. She told me that she had got a warm glow just like she used to do sitting in front of the bonfire on the fifth of November.

Somebody put flags up in the art studio.

TUFTY'S STORY

Tufty was a sad case, a 17-year-old without a chance. He was the perpetual weed, the loser consigned by an awful twist of background and time into a Liverpool-overspill estate during those magical moments of the Mighty Margaret. He wore glasses that were always broken; and he shuffled along as if he wanted not to be seen at all, his gangling tallness cruelly exposing to everyone's view the nervousness of his expression and the weakness of his face.

He came to college on his bike, a sit-up-and-beg that had an apology of a Sturmey Archer three-gear box that dated from the age of my father. He was one of a dozen or so in the class. The Youth Training Scheme.

Most of the others were simply loud. Those who still saw a glimpse of a future somewhere liked Ultravox or Howard Jones. Others were down there with Shakey. It was the time when personal stereos arrived, and I'd teach one or two of them for a full hour before I noticed they'd spent the lesson listening to Duran Duran rather than trying to understand how to read a train timetable.

Then there was Len. His name was a flashback to earlier days but his heart was with the beast of the present. He hated. He snarled his way through my classes, hardly communicating with anyone, just incessantly talking to some imaginary companion who shared his vile perspective.

I walked in to their room to teach them numeracy, July 1983 when the Blue Tide was starting to come in strong. Tufty was on the ground, crying. His bike had been thrown against a wall and the front wheel was buckled. Len was cackling, shouting to his non-existent friend.

'I fucking told you so!'

I sat at my desk maintaining a calm. I asked Tufty to tell me all about it. His crying, a frantic splutter punctuated by words only half formed, was too desperate to allow him to get the story out but I couldn't help but catch, on the periphery of my hearing range, the continuing narrative from Len to his friend.

I called him over and it took about three or four minutes before the truth began to emerge: Tufty had sneaked on them in their woodwork class that morning, he'd told the teacher that he hadn't used the electric sander for four weeks running and he was tired of using his hands to get the desktops clean – Len was always grabbing it from him, he had said, whoever's turn it was.

'He got me into fucking trouble and that spells trouble for him', said Len.

I told him to stop using language like that; he responded by shouting out to his friend.

'Can you fucking believe this?'

I was getting angry and Tufty was still only halfway back to some sense of normality. I tried to point out to Len that his hitting Tufty was no way to respond to any grievance he might have about some bloody sander; and how the fault was the shortage of sanders and not the desire of Tufty to have his turn, to which he was almost certainly entitled.

Len looked unabashed and snarled even louder. He shouted something out about Tufty being a big girl and then he pulled the lapel back on his denim jacket and I noticed the gleaming swastika. Still not looking at me, but again facing his invisible friend, he yelled at the walls.

'You know what would have happened to Tufty in Germany? They'd had had him put down. They'd have gassed him, too bloody right they would. That's all Tufty's good for, a bloody gas oven.'

He was punching the swastika with his index finger as he punched the words into the classroom.

Nothing to lose but his Rottweilers.

For the only time in all those years of teaching, I completely lost control. I pulled Len off his chair and threw him to the ground, kicking him and screaming at him. I ripped off his swastika and chucked it out of the door. The vigour of my punches completely terrified me.

The Walkmans were silenced. Len lay on the ground, his incessant chatter to his friend stopped, stunned in its tracks. Tufty looked terrified, no doubt imagining what would happen to him on the streets of Winsford that night.

I was within weeks of never teaching a class again.

And years away from flowers, aeons apart from the String Band.

> Hey! ... turn to the person next to you, guy or chick ... why don't you smile and say 'hello' ... ('oohs' from audience) ... in the groove! ... (clapping from audience) ... go on, smile on! it's too beautiful and too much! (more clapping) ... far out! ...

> This one's called 'Gently Tender' ...

And, suddenly, my whole generation was 2000 light years away from home; a long, long way from that nice day in Hyde Park, the day when we first saw the shadows piercing those cloudless July skies.

But, on that day, our eyes had been focused mainly on other things. Like those beautiful, flickering, fragile butterflies, freed to the blue skies by Jagger's hand, forever chained to the memory of Brian Jones.

I would really dig it if you were with us in what I'm going to say ... I hope you can just cool it ... I'm going to read out some Shelley ... it's for Brian ...

> Peace, Peace! he is not dead, he doth not sleep –
> He hath awakened from the dream of life –
> 'Tis we, who lost in stormy visions, keep
> With phantoms an unprofitable strife,
> And in mad trance, strike with our spirit's knife
> Invulnerable nothings ...

Dressed up in white; accent sliding into that pouting suburban slur, almost indecipherable, always on the brink of the really ridiculous; 'stretched out on a long white table'.

Preparing for a lifetime watching cricket at Lord's, worrying about his tax position, negotiating with the board at Volkswagen; 'so cold so damp so bare'.

Playing with fire in a block he *owns* in St. John's Wood; *the pond in a children's tale.*

> *We* decay
> Like corpses in a charnel; fear and grief
> Convulse us and consume us day be day,
> And cold hopes swarm like worms within our living clay.
>
> He has outsoared the shadow of our night ...
> He is secure, and now can never mourn
> A heart grown cold, a head grown grey in vain.

And Brian who has outsoared the shadow of our night, knows nothing of the 400 boys; of the sinking of the *Sheffield*; of Basil Fawlty and Basildon; of Sid and Nancy and Nancy and Ron; of cruise missiles and cruising; of Don Revie always losing; of the Liverpool years, in the Anfield, not the Cavern, sense; and the blessed Margaret never sitting on the fence.

Or of Mary Bell and Malcolm McLaren; Tufty and Ben.

Or Rottweilers. And even skinheads.

Or breaking butterflies on steel wheels.

(1995)

Notes on Contributors

Stephen Barnard has been principal copywriter for compilation boxed sets at the *Reader's Digest* since 1976 and is the author of *Rock: An Illustrated History* (1986) and *The Rolling Stones* (1993).

Johnny Copasetic teaches at the University of Pennsylvania and hangs out at Ortlieb's Jazzhaus in Philadelphia. He has been a contributor, under various other nom de plumes, to *New Edinburgh Review*, *Socialist Worker*, *Melody Maker* and *Philosophical Transactions of the Royal Society*.

Tony Cummings is editor of *Cross Rhythms* (contemporary Christian magazine) and former editor of *Black Music*. He is a contributor to *Billboard* and *What Hi-Fi* magazines and is author of *The Sound of Philadelphia* (1975).

Bob Edmands was a freelance contributor to *Ink* and the *New Musical Express* in the 1970s. He now works in broadcasting.

Pete Fowler is Head of Learning Methods Unit, and producer of multi-media learning titles, at Liverpool John Moores University and author of several articles and the book *IT Helps* on new technology in education. He released a single on Oval records in 1975 and is a former compiler of questions for *Pop Quiz* on BBC Radio One.

Simon Frith is Professor of English, and Director of the John Logie Baird Centre, at Strathclyde University, Glasgow. He is chairman of judges for the Mercury Music Prize, and former rock critic for the *Sunday Times* and the *Observer* and currently Britbeat columnist for New York's *Village Voice*. His books include *Music for Pleasure* (1987) and *Performing Rites* (1996).

Carl Gayle, 'undercover agent for Jah', publishes and edits JAHUG, a publication on cultural issues from within the Rastafari faith. He was principal reggae reporter for *Let It Rock* and *Black Music*.

185

Charlie Gillett is a radio presenter and co-director of Oval Records and Music. His programme *Honky Tonk* was broadcast on BBC Radio London from 1972–78 and he presented a weekly show on Capital Radio from 1980–90. He currently hosts *Saturday Night* on BBC GLR. He has been a contributor to *Rolling Stone* and the *New Musical Express* and is the author of *The Sound of the City* (1970, 2nd ed. 1983) and *Making Tracks* (1974).

Dave Laing is Quintin Hogg Research Fellow at Westminster University, London. He is co-editor of *Financial Times Music and Copyright* newsletter and is a member of the editorial group for *Popular Music* journal. He is the author of several books on popular music and co-editor of the *Encyclopedia of Rock* (1974) and (with Phil Hardy) the *Faber Companion to Twentieth Century Popular Music* (1995).

Andrew Weiner is a journalist, novelist and short story writer resident in Toronto, Canada.

Pete Wingfield is a singer, keyboard player and record producer and a founder member of the Olympic Runners. His 'Eighteen With A Bullet' (Island, 1975) was a hit in Britain and the United States and he has played on many recording sessions and toured with stars such as Emmylou Harris, Van Morrison and the Everly Brothers, as well as producing hit records for Dexy's Midnight Runners, Alison Moyet, Mel Brooks, Paul Young and the Proclaimers. He has also worked as a radio presenter and as a reviewer for *Melody Maker*.

Acknowledgements

'Roll Over Lonnie (Tell George Formby the News)', 'Skins Rule' and 'Johnny Cool and the Isle of Sirens' are from *Rock File* (New English Library, 1972); 'Doom Patrol: Black Sabbath at the Rainbow', 'In a Week, Maybe Two, We'll Make You a Star', 'The Philly Groove' and 'Are You Ready for Rude and Rough Reggae' are from *Rock File 2* (Panther, 1974); 'Playing Records' and 'Have Pity for the Rich' are from *Rock File 3* (Panther, 1975); 'The A&R Men' is from *Rock File 4* (Panther, 1976); and 'Youth Culture/Youth Cults: A Decade of Rock Consumption' and 'In Praise of the Professionals' are from *Rock File 5* (Panther, 1978). 'The Northern Discos' by Tony Cummings (included in 'Playing Records') first appeared in *Black Music* and is reproduced by kind permission. 'Johnny Cool and the Isle of Sirens' by Johnny Copasetic first appeared in *New Edinburgh Review* and was originally dedicated to 'Tony the Mod, Rick, Al, Liz, Mod Pete, Rory and all the Rudies. Sorry we had to go so soon'. In addition to the acknowledgements that appeared in the original volumes, the editors would like to make the following acknowledgements.

All the photographs are reproduced from the Charlie Gillett Collection. The photograph of Lindisfarne is by Martin Llewellyn.

Grateful acknowledgement is made to those publishers who gave permission to quote from the following works:

'Paranoid' and 'War Pigs' by Iommi, Ward, Butler and Osbourne, © 1970, Essex Music; 'Children of the Grave' by Iommi, Ward, Butler and Osbourne, © 1971, Essex Music; 'Everybody is a Star' by S. Stewart, © 1969, Daly City Music Ltd; 'Autumn Almanac' by R. Davies, © 1967, Davray/Carlin Music; 'Gypsy Woman' by Curtis Mayfield, © 1961, Curtom Music, BMI/Ivan Mogull Music; 'Isle of Sirens' by Curtis Mayfield, © 1962, Curtom Music, BMI/Ivan Mogull Music; 'Um Um Um Um Um Um' and 'Rhythm' by Curtis Mayfield, © 1964, Curtom Music, BMI/Ivan Mogull Music; 'Sodom and Gomorrah' and 'Madness' by C. Campbell, © 1963, Carib Music, BMI/Melodisc Music; 'Judge Dread (Judge Hundred Years)', 'Ghost Dance' and 'Johnny Cool' by C. Campbell, © 1967, Carib Music, BMI/Melodisc Music; 'Mr Richland's Favourite Song' by

Index

Index by Auriol Griffith-Jones